Pervert in the Pulpit

For my parents,
who brought me up
eighty miles north of Cape Fear,
near Cape Lookout,
which might explain some things

Pervert in the Pulpit

Morality in the Works of David Lynch

JEFF JOHNSON

McFarland & Company, Inc., Publishers
Jefferson, North Carolina, and London

Portions of this book appeared as an essay in the *Journal of Film and Video* (The University of Illinois Press).

All photographs provided by Photofest unless otherwise noted.

LIBRARY OF CONGRESS CATALOGUING-IN-PUBLICATION DATA

Johnson, Jeff, 1954–
 Pervert in the pulpit : morality in the works of David Lynch / by Jeff Johnson
  p.   cm.
 Includes bibliographical references and index.

 ISBN 0-7864-1753-6 (softcover : 50# alkaline paper)

 1. Lynch, David, 1946– —Criticism and interpretation.
I. Title
PN1998.3.L96J64   2004
791.4302'33'092—dc22   2004000955

British Library cataloguing data are available

Cover photograph: Robert Blake as Mystery Man in *Lost Highway* (1997)

Manufactured in the United States of America

McFarland & Company, Inc., Publishers
 Box 611, Jefferson, North Carolina 28640
 www.mcfarlandpub.com

Contents

Acknowledgments

Thanks to Helen Parry, savvy Manchester theater director, for her faith, wit, beauty, and rounds at the pub.

Thanks also to Dr. Mike Kaliszeski and Dr. Rosemary Layne at Brevard Community College for their gracious support on so many projects for so many years, and to Sarah Standing for her comments and confidence.

Special thanks to Carla for everything.

Preface

This book evolved from a paper I delivered at the Screen Studies Conference, Glasgow University, Scotland, 2002. My point at that time was to illustrate how David Lynch, instead of claiming the mantle of a counterculture hipster with an affinity for outlaws and disenfranchisement, more accurately aligned himself with foot soldiers in the contemporary culture wars, carrying a banner for virtuecrats, neo-cons and Reagan conservatives.

I thought the idea would be blasphemous enough to cause—well, a stir, as far as things get stirred in academia. But it was clear from the audience's response—at times downright hostile to Lynch and surprisingly sympathetic to my point of view—that Lynch's reputation as an avant-garde terrorist of middle-class hypocrisy had slipped. My vision of him as a weird sermonizer using subversive imagery to promote a saccharine version of a super-patriotic America circa Norman Rockwell (including a complementary lack of irony) suddenly did not appear to be so far out of the mainstream. This was discouraging, as far as my turning the after-sessions soirée into a snit, but I was glad to realize that the need for an overall reassessment of Lynch's work was gaining popular consensus.

It is in such a context that I consider this book a corrective, fully aware that it is as prescriptive and moralistic as its subject: the Calvinist instinct in David Lynch.

I first reviewed all of Lynch's available films, chronologically, beginning with his experimental art school shorts (just released on DVD). For these I skipped Lynch's autobiographical introductions, going into the material raw, noting recurrent themes and motifs by which Lynch

1

created an innate value system operating throughout his oeuvre. The early films are chock-full of subjects and images Lynch would later develop in his feature films. More curiously, in those later feature films, Lynch employed the same moralistic structural devices that shaped his early work. It was this moral framing that most interested me, not only as an aesthetic phenomenon but as a cosmographical creed through which his work demands to be read.

When I began viewing his features, I found each film the same: one long Manichaean screed delivered by a wacky evangelical. Lynch's zealotry was so pervasive that after my view-a-thon I could not look at any of his work—randomly, in fragments or through entire films—without identifying his moralistic slant toward mythological ideals of goodness, charity and benevolence threatened by forces of evil, calamity and violence. I was convinced that the moral frame in Lynch's work, so archetypically judgmental, condemnatory and culturally monological, would surely cause commentators to qualify Lynch's status (as a cult-film hero of the bizarre) with his "calling" as a puritanical preacher, albeit one with a penchant for pornography.

But when I read the major critical texts available in English, the analysts—sometimes dazzled by Lynch's star power, or myopically centered on their own agenda, or maybe just unconcerned by the implications of Lynch's ethical strictures—consistently dismissed Lynch's reactionary morality. Of the major texts, I concentrated on the most authoritative by both reputation and merit. John Alexander's *The Films of David Lynch*, Michel Chion's *David Lynch*, David Hughes' *The Complete David Lynch*, Kenneth C. Kaleta's *David Lynch*, Chris Rodley's *Lynch on Lynch*, and Martha Nochimson's *The Passion of David Lynch: Wild at Heart in Hollywood* form the core of the section that deals with the critics' responses to Lynch's work.

Taken collectively, aside from some careful exegesis (accompanied, however, by often excruciating minutiae bordering on obsessive-compulsive mania), what I noticed about these major texts was how often the critics self-consciously emerged as apologists for Lynch's Puritanism. Such was not the case when I tried sample searches on Web engines like Google and Yahoo. I even found several websites dedicated to exposing Lynch's right-wing agenda. Nevertheless, many of these on-line critics (in both established electronic journals and freelance websites), while acknowledging Lynch's curious bent for the values of the American political right, tended to dismiss his conservatism. The few who decried his fanaticism seemed shrill, marginalized by their stridence and partisanship,

Ontological peepshow: Jeffrey Beaumont (Kyle MacLachlan) watches Frank (Dennis Hopper) and Dorothy (Isabella Rossellini) in *Blue Velvet* (1986). Lynch, like his Puritan forefathers, understands the attraction of sin. Jeffrey and the audience are situated like motorists rubbernecking at a fatal wreck: fascinated but ashamed for looking. Jeffrey's initiation into the communal necessity of restraint begins with a virtuoso performance in exhibitionism by Dorothy, while Frank denies her the scopophilic pleasure Jeffrey, Frank and the audience share.

silenced by a dedicated cadre of fans and critics that, dismissing the propagandistic lens through which Lynch presents his vision, persists in lauding Lynch for his cinematic mannerisms.

Though I have relied on the intertextual theories of Schopenhauer, Nietzsche and Freud, my purpose is not biographical. I do not intend to prove that these writers influenced Lynch. I do believe, however, that these theorists provide a handy vocabulary within which certain patterns of Lynch's behavior can be both examined and exploited, and I am confident Lynch can appreciate that. As for his spot in the Hollywood-Cannes hierarchy, my objective was not to challenge the hagiography of popular film directors.

Of course, it is no coincidence that when Lynch cast himself in both the television and movie versions of *Twin Peaks*, he played an FBI agent. Lynch identifies with authority.

Like a narc with a weakness for cash and drugs, or a vice squad cop arresting people for doing what he likes to do, Lynch epitomizes the voyeurism inherent in a crusade. The key to Lynch's moral vision, how his strict absolutism shapes his work, lies in his affection for his alter ego, Kyle MacLachlan, whom Hoberman calls an "airbrushed doppelgänger for Lynch himself" (Hoberman, *Vulgar Modernism* 233). The noble Paul Atreides, the remorseful Jeffrey Beaumont, the ethicist Dale Cooper—these are Lynch's archetypes: rationalists plagued by the truth of their dreams. Like Leibniz read through Foucault, Lynch wrings sufficient reason from absurdity. But it is a strict Calvinism that shapes his architectonic moral frame, a puritanical impulse exposing the familiar in the bizarre.

Blue Velvet remains his most significant film, a rare artifact that simultaneously creates and exhausts its own genre. Dorothy's closet becomes the repository for a culmination of Lynch's motifs, images, characters and dyads.

Having viewed dozens of hours of tapes, I was always aware of watching Lynch watch Jeffrey watch Frank deny Dorothy visual pleasure.

I approach Lynch's work the same way: peeking like Jeffrey through the slats of Dorothy's closet, intrigued and repulsed, fascinated and judgmental, cautioning myself that all moralists, as Nietzsche says, are prey to their own morality.

Introduction

Blackbeard, Calvin and the Outer Banks of North Carolina

My first David Lynch film was *Blue Velvet* (1986). I was teaching creative writing and humanities at a technological university in Melbourne, Florida (that itself a Lynchian scenario). I had read about Lynch's earlier film *Eraserhead* (1977) while researching selections for an appreciation of motion pictures seminar I chaired with the local American Association of University Women (more Lynchian weirdness). I remember coming across Tony Schwartz's remark in *Newsweek* that *Eraserhead* was "not for the squeamish" (95). I recommended the film, but the sponsor of the series vetoed me—partly based on Schwartz's remarks—opting, I think, for a "classic" sleeper like Alain Resnais' *Last Year at Marienbad* (1961). As for *Blue Velvet*, J. Hoberman in *The Village Voice* raved about "an American studio film so rich, so formally controlled, so imaginatively cast and wonderfully acted, and so charged with its maker's psychosexual energy" (*Vulgar Modernism* 235). Dependably perspicacious Pauline Kael, in her now famous review in *The New Yorker*, cryptically reported overhearing someone leaving the movie saying, "'I must be sick, but I want to see that again'" (Kael 99).

Needless to say, I was revved to witness *Blue Velvet*.

But because it did not qualify for the multiplex shopping mall circuit in Melbourne (Lynch again), I had to drive to the cultural Mecca of central Florida, Orlando, over an hour away (yet another Lynchian twist). The trip became a vocation, a hajj. Over the next week I cadged rides from students, friends, anyone I could persuade. I became a mad film prophet announcing the arrival of a new cinematic messiah, leading a motley crew of proselytes through a sacred initiation ritual to the altar of the new king of auteurs.

I watched *Blue Velvet* every day for a week. When the video was released, I bought it and soon had the film memorized. After all, I was born and raised eighty miles north of Wilmington, North Carolina. I wrestled and played football against Hanover High, where Sandy and her boyfriend Mike go to school. Surfed the coast from Buxton to Wrightsville Beach. Raced the Michelob Cup in a San Juan 29 overnight across Onslow Bay. A friend taught classical guitar at UNCW. My father used to fly me out to islands off the coast, land on the beach. I knew Lynch country intimately.

By then I had seen *Eraserhead* and waited, almost spasmodic, for *Wild at Heart* (1990). I was fascinated by Lynch's oddball approach to the ordinary. He seemed like a kinky phenomenologist, as appalled at the everydayness of reality as Heidegger, tuned to having been thrown into the world, clueless to the source of our angst yet intrigued by the mysteries of things, what appearances promise and hide. Not quite surreal, not exactly absurd, he seemed to have created a new hybrid of camp vérité. I was seduced—and that is the only word to describe the desire *Blue Velvet* inspired in me. I envied the vitality of Lynch's images, the playfulness of his style, the quirky verisimilitude of the story, the tight continuity of psychology and action.

But after numerous (admittedly, too many) viewings, what I really appreciated most in *Blue Velvet* was Dennis Hopper—now straight after years of substance abuse—reprising his role as Don Barnes in *Out of the Blue* (1980), from which he appropriated, or applied, the idiosyncrasies that became Frank Booth. Directed by Hopper, starring Linda Manz as a punk wannabe and Sharon Farrell as her junkie mother, *Out of the Blue* is an intense study of a radically dysfunctional couple's devastating effect on their daughter. Hopper's performance as an alcoholic former truck driver just released from prison, where he served five years for crashing into a school bus full of children, is a tour de force of restrained intensity, a perfect study to prepare him for his role as Frank Booth.

But for his subsequent films, Hopper has gone to the well more than once too often. In a film released the same year as *Blue Velvet*, Tim Hunter's scathing indictment of disaffected Reagan-era youth, *River's Edge* (1986), Hopper plays Feck like a staged reincarnation of a mellowed

Hopper and Rossellini in *Blue Velvet* (1986). Desire, for Lynch, is a destructive force controlled by the subject internalizing authoritarian restraint. Dorothy insists that she knows the difference between right and wrong, but Frank Booth represents pure id, raw desire untamed by remorse. Dorothy may be salvageable—her debauchery, while violating community mores, satisfies a survival instinct beyond morality—but Frank lacks the interiority required for salvation. In Lynch's eschatology, Frank is the archetypal reprobate, an incorrigible archangel beyond salvation.

Don or Frank. By the time he made *True Romance* (1993), *Speed* (1994), *Ticker* (2001), *et al.*, he had become character-typed. Instead of stretching as an actor, he began to rely on the stereotypical moves that got him from *Out of the Blue* to *Blue Velvet*: the stoical eccentric, soft but tough, or the maniacal bad guy, Frank Booth in any situation (not Don Barnes because *Out of the Blue* was relegated to obscurity by the popular press and film distributors).

Redundancy became Hopper's trademark. The last performance I remember him in was a television commercial selling cars that shamelessly paired him as he is now—a post-abuse neo-conservative, what one critic described as "a walking signifier of harm, self-inflicted and otherwise" (Dieckmann 12) driving, in the commercial, your grandfather's car—with what he was then: Billy the freewheeling biker in the 1969 cult classic *Easy Rider* (also directed by Hopper) who hit the road on a couple

Dennis Hopper as Don, with Sharon Farrell and Linda Manz, in *Out of the Blue* (1980). Don may be a more mundane devil, but his violent narcissim and ruthless self-loathing provided Hopper an archetype for Frank Booth.

of Harley choppers with Wyatt (Peter Fonda) and Hanson (Jack Nicholson) for an unsentimental tour of contemporary America.

The point is that Hopper, since *Blue Velvet*, became only what he was in *Out of the Blue*. The same thing happened to Lynch. After *Blue Velvet*, like Hopper, he became decadent—by which I mean redundant, *Blue Velvet* having become the final repository, the culmination and exhaustion of the motifs and images from all his earlier work. The first few episodes of *Twin Peaks* (1990-1991) were encouraging, but the series quickly spiraled into predictability. *Wild at Heart* (1990) was embarrassing. His most original film, *The Straight Story* (1999), turned out to be his most obtuse, a mawkish, sanctimonious portrait of a grouch. *Lost Highway* (1997) and *Mulholland Dr.* (2001), to some degree, redeemed him, but even in those films Lynch plays it safe, revisiting territory he previously exhausted.

The breakdown of Lynch's aesthetics prompted me to reevaluate his work less from a formal, artistic perspective than in a context of intention. Looking back comprehensively through his oeuvre, I noticed how some of his films that once appeared subversive were, in fact, reassuring. They reinforced a wistful benevolence, projected a vision of a nostalgic America that existed only in a Reaganesque, bright-eyed Eagle Scout's good-deed diary. In hindsight (which is, after all, twenty-twenty), his films, instead of being iconoclastic, read like sermons: the good people, the elect, are beautiful, wholesome, well-balanced, with a penchant for fifties' fashion and family values, while the bad people, ugly and carbuncular, deal drugs, engage in promiscuous sex, produce pornography and mock in blatant acts of blasphemy the virtues of the American hearth and Heartland. *Eraserhead* reads like a save-sex-for-marriage propaganda parable; *Dune* (1984) an anti-gay, anti-drug advertisement for clean living; my beloved *Blue Velvet* nothing but a study in the virtues of restraint and remorse, a celebration of middle-class mediocrity triumphing over excess and extreme individuality; *Wild at Heart* a promotional video espousing the efficacy of neutering to tame wanderlust and make the animal self safe for nesting; *Twin Peaks* yet another anti-promiscuity, anti-drug after-school special; *Lost Highway* testimony that lust leads to debauchery, loss of self, pornography and murder; *The Straight Story* evidence that mythically uncomplicated Midwestern small town values are somehow incorruptible (the complex life, in a strange Socratic perversion, not worth living, period).

Underpinning this doctrinaire vision of moral worth and ethical liabilities is the notion of desire as a destructive force, the root of evil, betraying Lynch's Manichaean certainty in simple, self-evident truths about right and wrong, reward and punishment, salvation and damnation. In the canon of American literature, of course, this is nothing new. It seems that no serious critic, historical or contemporary, can avoid a biblical reading of American fiction, framing critical comments in the context of the writer's attitudes toward guilt, sin and redemption. This moralizing tendency on the part of both American writers and critics can be traced back to the Puritans—John Winthrop, Anne Bradstreet, Cotton Mather and Jonathan Edwards—and their particular (often peculiar) apostolic interpretation of the Bible and its application to everyday life. In the hotbed of zealotry in which the early colonists lived, "every natural phenomenon, every qualm of conscience, was assumed to be emblematic of the great dramatic struggle between good and evil" (Foerster 9).

The Lynch I found, in retrospect, is not the radical groundbreaking filmmaker many make him out to be but a rather straightforward reactionary working within the tradition of typical Calvinist thought in American literature. The revised Lynch I mean to present is a puritanical, hyper-patriotic, idealistic conservative on a reformer's mission, bent, actively through his films, on correcting what he sees as the scourges of American youth culture: drugs, alcohol and hedonism. Lynch promotes a return to the values inherent in a mythological, post–World War II America, embracing wholeheartedly Reagan's reification of the fifties that he, like Tom Brokaw, considers America's greatest generational decade. Lynch told David Edelstein in *The Village Voice*, "There's such a good, clean, beautiful feeling after a war" (20). When asked how he felt about "the Reagan people who would like to see that kind of world again" (20), Lynch replied, "Yeah, I like the direction of pride ... an optimistic feeling" (20).

In this context, Lynch assumes the role of a twenty-first century version of Jonathan Edwards, the stentorian preacher who "turned aside from intellectual argument to preach a demonstration of the absolutely real and meaningful nature of Calvin's tenets [and] vivified the consequence of election, damnation, and God's sovereign will, and pictured the depraved condition of their own unconverted souls in such graphic detail" (Foerster 11).

In Lynch, it is that "graphic detail" that is troubling.

Like Mark Lewis in Michael Powell's *Peeping Tom* (1959), Lynch seems to derive a kind of voyeuristic pleasure from indulging in what he condemns. He asks pretty nasty stuff from some of his actors—portraying characters involved with drug-induced manias, sadomasochistic sex, emotional torture, pornography, self-abasement—stuff the films ultimately condemn. While Lynch's apologists excuse, rationalize or simply ignore his hypocrisy and moral reductionism, other critics, like Hoberman, are quick to point out Lynch's "dreamlike superimposition of the '50s over the '80s [in what he calls a] New Patriotism" ("What's Stranger than Paradise?" 3). Hoberman claims Lynch operates in the same territory as the early Puritans, where "the American landscape is the arena of moral forces. Whatever it may have become, this was once Europe's new Eden, its fabulous Second Chance, its verdant Blank Slate" (4). For baby boomers like Lynch, Hoberman is convinced that "the '50s remain our favorite theme park" (8). He defines this phenomenon of privileging an idealized, simplistic vision of the '50s over the complex pluralism of contemporary society as "Americanarama" (8).

It may seem unfair to attack Lynch for his nostalgia, or even for his politics, but the myth generated around his work tends to conceal an ideological sensibility, a different agenda, less Cocteau than John Milius. Lynch's fascination with *The Wizard of Oz* (1939) has more to do with the man behind the curtain (the gear-operating man in the planet from *Eraserhead*) than with the wish-fulfilling dreams of Dorothy (the desperate, wigged vixen from *Blue Velvet*). Lynch's films masquerade as ironic; but Lynch, as a director, is like a stealth candidate who keeps his value-system camouflaged in slogans, images and sound-bites. Lee Atwater occupies Lynch the way Frank Booth inhabits the Well Dressed Man in *Blue Velvet*, or BOB does Cooper in *Twin Peaks*. Lynch dodges questions about "message" while his films reflect Phyllis Schlafly's paranoid version of America—in images that would offend and disgust Schlafly and that she would lobby to ban. But unlike the compassionate conservatives of the middle right in American politics, Lynch, from the open wounds of his imagery, offers a form of salvation as cynical and Manichaean as that of the British officers who sailed from Norfolk to Okracoke to ambush Blackbeard in 1718.

Reading Lynch through Freud is, of course, irresistible; but more than a method of analysis, Freudian readings of Lynch identify a framing device around which Lynch builds his narratives. Which means, conveniently, that my colonial analogy holds: Blackbeard, the id, is the Frank Booth of Bogue Inlet; the superego, Lt. Maynard, the Dale Cooper of Hampton Roads. Between these two extremes, which in this extended analogy form the ego, are the residents populating Lynch's landscape: the parochial, common-sense folk, righteous in their innocence but targets too of demonic forces: lust, greed, televangelists, politicians, land scammers, drug dealers, double-crossers and pornographers—pirates, essentially, governed by the king's men.

So no matter how grotesque, bizarre, or self-indulgent his images, Lynch sides with Lt. Maynard and the king's men from Norfolk. Blackbeard was bad *a priori*. Maynard's crew had to believe that or they would be no better than any cutthroat cowboy capitalist. Having no restraints, Blackbeard indulged his desire like Lynch's Mr. Reindeer. Maynard was a swashbuckler too, but he knew where to draw the line. He is the archetype of Lynch's salvageable protagonist, the adventurous type who understands the nature of desire but draws back, as Conrad's Marlow did, out of some innate sense of duty, some essential moral quality that identifies good people from bad—unless, as in *Wild at Heart*, you are cool or cute enough to demand, and receive, leniency, even though mitigation from Lynch often involves a painful evangelical justice, where scars are proof of purity.

As for those reprobates who opt to sail on the *Queen Anne's Revenge*, Lynch's sense of justice is as harsh, severe and unassailable as that of Mather's protégé, the infamous Jonathan Corwin, presiding judge at the Salem witch trials.

You dare to dance in Lynch's world, you always pay the piper.

Lynch's short films, for me, are more successful than his features because his ideology in the early work is imagistic. He focuses on process. His features bog down in explication, which is why *Lost Highway* and *Mulholland Dr.* resurrect the best in Lynch, returning him to an open dialog with the audience; even those films, however, become agents for themes that he wore out long ago. His entropic daring relies on a dependable moral spine, an ethical structure that contains—that is, permits—his kinkiness and sustains his perversions by framing the surface action with Old Testament verities.

If not exactly hypocritical, Lynch likes having it both ways. He reminds me of a debauched priest asking for prurient details during confession, or a judge who needs to read a pornographic text a few times too many before he deems the material obscene. In this Lynch resembles St. Augustine who, in his *Confessions* (Russell 391), takes morbid pleasure in recalling explicit memories of his past transgressions while self-righteously condemning his actions and claiming to have since reformed. Bertrand Russell's summary of Augustine could easily be applied to Lynch: "He was obsessed, in his later years, by a sense of sin, which made his life stern and his philosophy inhumane" (345). This is the Augustine who appealed to the Protestants, especially the Calvinists, and forms the context through which Lynch carries on the tradition.

In response to this schizophrenic, sermonic presentation of his material—as I too morbidly indulge in scenes I condemn—the following chapters should be read as a correction as much as a critique, an exposé as much as an explication.

1

The Po-Mo Puritan

As perverse as his films pretend to be, David Lynch actually works within the most traditional canon of American literature. He follows an intrinsically American moralistic obsession with the ideas of innate depravity, a Zoroastrian notion of goodness and evil, and the schizophrenic concept of innocence as both an ideal state and a treacherous, ultimately corrupting vice of the wickedly naïve. Lynch, in this mode, becomes what D.H. Lawrence, describing Melville, calls "*au grande serieux* ... the ethical mystical-transcendentalist sort" (146).

But to sermonize successfully, you have to have something to rail against. The Devil as a material force, a real feature of reality at work in the world—following Zoroaster's belief that evil is a positive principle embodied in matter—has been at the core of American literature since at least 1692 when Cotton Mather, justifying the Salem witch trials, sermonized about a New World in which "the hills were covered with the shadow" (218) of Satan whose "incarnate legions ... persecute us" (218). Mather's devil-in-the flesh, Hawthorne's Chillingsworth, Harriet Beecher Stowe's Simon Legree, Flannery O'Connor's Misfit are all demons no less sinister or "real" than Frank Booth. (Even President George W. Bush, never shy about moral posturing, created an "Axis of Evil" to focus public opinion on a concrete image loaded with religious and historical significance.) Lynch's villains—Mystery Man, Frank Booth, Bobby Peru, et al.—are drawn from the same archetypes that populate American fiction, no different from Melville's whale, Poe's madmen, horror-show monsters, Sci-Fi aliens or the good guys and bad guys in a Hollywood oater. And even if, in contemporary fiction, the forces

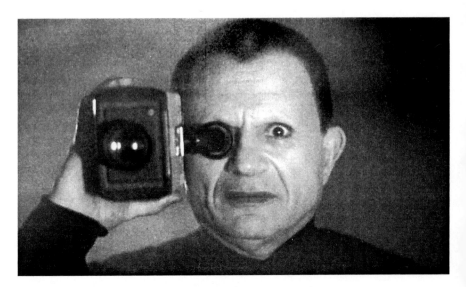

Robert Blake as Mystery Man in *Lost Highway* (1997). Cotton Mather's worst nightmare, Mystery Man joins Frank Booth and BOB in the lineup of Lynch's larger-than-life demons, men of supernatural power who intimidate, possess or otherwise exploit those too weak to resist temptation.

of darkness have taken the form of raging libido in Miller, Roth, and Jong, or purveyors of paranoia in Pynchon, Barthelme, and Wallace, these effigies of anomie, incubi of chaos, are particularly American demons.

The convenience of having an identifiable evil facilitates the curative notion of art, and this positing of dueling corporeal forces contributes to a distinctly American national identity: that of the individual battling not only the wilderness—nature itself—but the sundry demonic and heathen creatures as well, scoring his individualist's mark of survival like a scar across the prairie. As Daniel Bell suggests, paraphrasing Emerson, this "peculiar American inversion of Protestantism, the moralizing style, found its focus in the idea of reform; but it was the reform of the individual, not of institutions" (221). And citing what he terms Bell's neo-conservatism (100), Jurgen Habermas links the privileging of the rebelling individual at the core of American identity to America's rejection of modernism, as "Modernist culture has come to penetrate the values of everyday life; the life-world is infected by modernism" (100), which he defines as "unlimited self-realization, the demand for authentic self-expression and the subjectivism of a hyperstimulated sensitivity" (100–101). Habermas suggests that the "dissolution of the Protestant ethic" (101) created a backlash as "[c]ulture in its modern form stirs up hatred against the conventions and virtues of everyday life" (101). Alfred Kazin describes this cultural estrangement as a "disconnection between the self and the modern world" (20). Kazin writes that, within the tradition of Emerson, Thoreau, Whitman, and Adams, echoed by Carlyle, de Tocqueville and Nietzsche, the American individualist was an "apostle of perfect personal power" (27) who would unleash this "comprehensive power ... by his emancipation from institutions" (30).

Donald Lyons defines this Manichaean spiritual schism in American letters as "a principle of uncertainty ... an existential vertigo, a slippage of self" (4). David Madden concurs: "Since Hawthorne ... [critics have] proclaimed that Puritanistic, Calvinistic concepts of evil and sin poisoned most American Dreams ... so that there was never a natural innocence" (xxix). Madden concludes that "there are two major American Dream myths: the Old Testament idea of a paradise hopelessly lost ... and the New Testament idea of a paradise that a new American Adam will eventually regain" (xxxix). In other words, American writers and critics seem inherently preoccupied with guilt, sin and redemption.

John Alexander, in *The Films of David Lynch*, situates Lynch's moralizing in the ethical ideal of American Gothic:

> Underlying the Romantic Movement is a yearning for the past and a nostalgia for past values. It is a yearning borne of anxieties over the impermanence of things; a deeply rooted mistrust of the present and contempt for the future; ambiguous hallmarks of Lynch's film world [8].

Lynch's image pool teems with icons of the fifties and sixties, when the Cold War demarcations of good and evil were as clear as a Jim Crow proscription at a public water fountain, a Manichaean system of belief permeated instinctual decisions, and the postmodern world was merely a hypothesis. Critics like Alexander hope Lynch's films reveal "cynicism and naïvety" (13). Like other apologists, he tries to explain away Lynch's innate sentimentality, but nostalgia is never ironic for Lynch. Invariably, viewers must return to Lynch's central motif: "games with cliché" (13), what Alexander calls the "artifice of banality" (29). For Alexander, Lynch "creates irony out of horror and transforms cliché into poetry" (29). Whether Lynch transforms cliché into poetry is problematic (as is the question of his creating irony out of horror), but the Neo-Platonic resonance of Alexander's explication indicates the conundrum critics wrestle with while trying to dismiss Lynch's hard-line moralizing. The trouble is, Lynch believes the cliché. His irony, in practice, seems more like self-defense.

Michael Carroll, writing in *Literature Film Quarterly*, locates Lynch in the "most fundamental myths of American culture" (294). In the context of traditional American literature, Carroll reads Lynch through "the Manichaean strain of Christianity" (291), connects Jean Renault to Cotton Mather's "xenophobia" (292), refers to Audrey Horne as "a Puritan at heart" (292), compares Windham Earle to Robert Chillingsworth, cites "the Puritan notion of the evil wilderness" (293) in Hawthorne's "Young Goodman Brown," and finds Special Agent Dale Cooper's counterpart in Rip Van Winkle, Natty Bumppo, and Daniel Boone. He stresses how in Lynch's evolution from *Eraserhead* to *Twin Peaks* "the priorities of imagism have been supplanted (though not without leaving strong traces) by those of mythic narrative, and finally, cultural mythology" (293). But Carroll's vocabulary is evangelical, even in his determination to establish in Lynch's work "a privatized form of American mythology" (294). Cooper is "characterized by his moral superiority" (289), BOB is "the epicenter of evil" (292), Cooper's asceticism is "a symbolic gesture of escape from the corruption of civilization" (289), and "mythic small-town America" (288) mirrors the underbelly of "Hawthorne's Puritan settlement" (288).

The American Revolution unleashed a particularly American version of moral perfection, grown from the seeds of early Puritanism, nurtured by the constitutionalists and refined by the romanticists who equated the growth of the nation with the realization of a virtuous national character. When Ben Franklin decided on the ingredients of moral perfection, he invented a recipe of 13 virtues: humility, silence, order, resolution, temperance, frugality, industry, justice, moderation, cleanliness, sincerity, tranquility and chastity. Franklin, of course, was writing as an unreconstructed rationalist in the tradition of deism and common sense, but his desire, if not his method, was shaped by the moral absolutists railing relentlessly from the pulpits in their Boston churches for self-sacrifice and surrender of the self to the will of God. This secularization of virtue based on biblical precepts spawned a long line of reform-minded writers—satirists, muckrakers, socialists, ironists—all with a view to improving the moral character of the individual, and to reflecting thereby a virtuous nation protected, if not by God, then by sound moral reasoning and self-righteousness.

The key to producing this national reform through the edification of the individual was the creation of a sort of divine dialectic (the same ideal realized in the concept of Manifest Destiny.) Good and evil had to be clearly defined, so the inclusion or exclusion of a person within this moral dyad categorically determined the nature of that individual's character. This was most effectively achieved by establishing a normative value against which a convenient "other" could be constructed, allowing a definitive demarcation between "them" and "us" to promote allegiance within a codified value system identifying the "good" as "not that." Hegel's "absolute" is perhaps the surest model for maintaining the stress between good and evil that, ideally, results in an apocalyptic synthesis: the triumph of righteousness in a perfect union with God. Hegel posited two opposing forces—a thesis and an antithesis—held in opposition, each struggling for dominance. Both eventually destroy the negative aspects of each other and recombine the leftover positive qualities to form a new dialectic that will again resolve into another synthesis and so on. This, according to Hegel, explains historical progress towards an ultimate final absolute synthesis in which all struggle ceases at the point of perfection. The result, in the moral equation, produces a violent clash between value systems that are mutually destructive, but through the necessary struggle the opposing forces drive history toward an eschatological conclusion.

There are, of course, as many variations of moral dualism as there are two sides to coins. Great cultures, it seems, favor diametric powers. The Mesopotamians pitted dueling anthropomorphic earth and sky deities against each other and thought of men as playthings of the gods with no afterlife of punishment or reward to look forward to. More optimistic, the Egyptians proffered immortality, treating death as a mere transition between worlds. In East Asian thought, the earth gods and sky gods were translated into yin and yang, the two complementary forces—male/female, active/receptive, light/dark—that make up all aspects and phenomena of life. The Greeks further refined dualism, as epitomized by Plato's distinction between the material world presented to our senses and the world of ideas accessible only to the rational mind. Christianity in the late Roman Empire incorporated both the soul/body bifurcation and the separation of an earthly existence from the heavenly.

Primitive forms of early Christian dualism were heavily influenced by Zoroaster, the aforementioned seventh-century Persian thinker whose ethical brand of religion valued truthfulness and love and condemned lust, pride and avarice. He believed in a personified Evil and a final judgment day when souls would be sent to heaven or hell depending on their moral conduct during life. Gnosticism also attempted to radicalize dualism within a Christian context. Borrowing from the Greeks, the Gnostics taught that the spirit was good and the flesh evil. The soul, they believed, was trapped within the body, and the only way to liberate the spirit from the flesh was by gaining knowledge through mystical insight. The Roman Church, of course, deemed Gnosticism heretical because, if only the spirit was good, Christ could not have had a body. His Incarnation would then have been merely an appearance.

This controversy over the Incarnation and radical dualism would reappear throughout the Middle Ages. It occurs most powerfully as Manichaeism, in which material forces of good and evil, light and darkness, are locked in an earthly struggle for the souls of men. This Manichaean version played so nicely in the fertile, susceptible, superstitious medieval mind that Saint Augustine was moved to refute it. Augustine, relying on a Christianized Neo-Platonic dualism, claimed that evil was not a feature of reality but a lack of goodness. The more good a thing has, the more real it is. God, being all good, was most real.

But Manichaeism was not so easily explained away by Augustinian subtleties. The idea of a devil incarnate continued to spark the imagination of religious zealots, especially the fire-and-brimstone preachers of the Reformation. Most notable among these reformers was John Calvin, whose concept of Christianity relied on the inherent depravity of man. Preaching an angry God demanding strict ethical behavior, he believed the souls of men were saved or damned by God's predestinating. Calvin also taught that worldly success was a sign of God's approval, poverty a sign of God's disfavor. This brand of Protestant thinking became the favorite of Christian capitalists, and in the form of Puritanism became the quasi-official religion of the New World. James A. Morone, in *Hellfire Nation*, provides a comprehensive analysis of America's obsession with the politics of morality from the Puritans through the Patriot Act, outlining what David J. Garrow, reviewing the book in *The New York Times* and quoting from Marone, describes as "Americans' eagerness to draw distinctions between 'worthy and unworthy, between devout and degenerate' [that] reflects two 'vital urges—redeeming "us" and reforming "them"'" (E7).

It is, in fact, this peculiar brand of Calvinism that informs Lynch's work and places him squarely in the literary lineage of the American Romantics—not the soft Romanticism of Emerson and Thoreau, who tend to mitigate the strict tenets of Puritanism, leaning towards the Utilitarian belief in the innate goodness of man, but the hard-edged Romanticism of Hawthorne, Melville and Poe, who reject the optimism of the Transcendentalists and embrace a darker vision of man's relationship with himself and the world. Their link to the early Calvinists is clear.

"The most vital preparation for such writers as Emerson, Thoreau, Hawthorne, Melville, and Whitman was a religious spirit that goes back to the men and women who settled America" (Foerster 257). Critics inevitably discuss these writers in apocalyptic terms, describing stark visions of men seeking truth in the dark crevices between the material world and the imagination. Warren Staebler notes that Poe "saw human beings as forsaken and moved by dark subliminal forces they were unable to control to the destruction of themselves and others" (52). F.O. Matthiessen praises "Melville's penetration to the primitive forces of experience, to the element of the irrational" (153), and he cites Hawthorne's complaint that *The Scarlet Letter* (1850) was "'positively a hell-fired story, into which I found it almost impossible to throw any cheering light'" (149). Writing in *Literature Film Quarterly*, Scott Pollard compares Special Agent Dale Cooper, who serves, Pollard implies, as a proxy for Lynch's "fundamental American values" (303), to Whitman, "his most luminous predecessor" (297). Pollard notes that "Whitman, like Cooper, lived in a postlapsarian world and used his art as a corrective ..." (298); the difference between Whitman and Lynch, however, is that, according to Pollard, Whitman championed an "open morality" (297) whereas Lynch's motive (via Cooper) is to "protect middle-class hegemony ..." (298).

The American Romantics "boldly unfixed reason from her seat, and declared that the true oracle is intuition—something they knew without reasoning, something that satisfied the instincts of the heart" (Foerster 261–262). The sort of anti-rationalist, prone to hallucinatory revelations, who populates the stories of Hawthorne, Melville, Poe and O'Connor crops up in Lynch's world too. In fact, the issues driving American Romantics—a backlash against Cartesian rationalism, a rejection of industrialization, dismay at the dissolution of the individual in a homogenized society—read like a summary of themes in Lynch's filmography. His characters, too, are forced to rely on their intuition more than their reason, frequently surrendering themselves to inexplicable forces beyond their conscious control. Logical analysis and technical expertise, for instance, are insufficient for Agent Dale Cooper to explain the mysteries of the human predicament in the town of Twin Peaks, just as Paul Atreides must rely on mysticism and predestination for his survival, success and ultimate salvation. Jeffrey Beaumont drops out of college and loses his paternal superego in order to delve deep into his id to discover otherwise inaccessible truths about himself. Fred, the jazz saxophonist who morphs into Pete, finds himself in a predicament beyond rationalization, and his madness results from his need to explain the inexplicable. This inability to intuit meaning, these attempts to reduce instinct to concept, to allow explication to displace sensation, subjugating the primacy of experience to interpretation, represent a moral failing, as if the impulse to synthesize experience were sinful. Especially for the characters in Lynch's early work, guilt results from their imagination acting to remove them from the immediacy of perception. The fundamental ethical dilemma—original sin, as it were—stems from a schism of being, that inevitable spontaneous emergence of the instinctual self into individuation.

Likewise, Lynch's nightmare vision of an industrial wasteland, evident in his earliest work, portrays a landscape of dull noises and mechanical repetition that blunts instinctual life and dehumanizes society. In *Six Figures Getting Sick* (1967), the figures regurgitate blood in an endless loop as a siren wails unceasingly. Mechanized letters in *The Alphabet* (1968) imprison the self in a hostile system of artificial codes. *Eraserhead* chokes with oppressive images and monotonous noises emanating from a dense web of urban machinery. *The Elephant Man* (1980) details the downside of the Industrial Revolution, depicting anonymous automatons toiling in senseless alienation. In *Dune* the profit-driven corporate gangs working for the Harkonnens are either robotic and mechanical or desensitized and sadistic, their sterile environment spoiled by commercialization, a stark contrast to Paul and his family, who thrive on their natural, unpolluted home planet teeming with life, water, and vitality.

Those who escape the insidious, neutering traps of logic and industrialization in their quest for authenticity still must resist assimilation into a callous culture that privileges mediocrity and conformity over spirit and originality. The boy in *The Grandmother* (1970) who grows a grandmother in his attic resists but cannot escape becoming like his parents. Henry, Jeffrey, Sailor, and the good citizens of Twin Peaks or Lumberton are all threatened by normalization. The players in the illogical nightmare surrounding the mysteries off Mulholland Drive do not shape the movie industry: they are interchangeable products of it, puppets whose strings are pulled by unassailable, malevolent forces.

Another concern Lynch shares with his Romantic forefathers is his exploration of the interstitial spaces where dreams and reality conjoin. As Hawthorne explains in "The Custom House" (1850), the concern of the artist lies "'somewhere between the real world and fairyland, where the Actual and the Imaginary may meet, and each imbue itself with the nature of the other'" (qtd. in Hurley 14). Hawthorne is describing exactly Lynch's playground. From his earliest surrealistic collages of film and animation to his more conventionally structured (but not necessarily more accessible) features, Lynch deliberately blurs the binary distinction between dreams and reality, hesitating to separate too distinctly the conscious and unconscious minds. His use of nonlinear narratives, in which he often substitutes strategically juxtaposed images for narrative closure, opens rather than certifies meaning. He subverts expectations, allowing dream logic to leak seamlessly into the surface story. Narrative information— the string of events and images that shape the storyline—often ends up performing the theme instead of representing it. His films, in this sense, do not stand for another meaning but become the meaning: the narrative sequence does not transcend itself. As in a Cubist painting, the result is a portrait not of separate distinct realities but of a simultaneous experiencing of both. This is the same technique employed by Hawthorne and Poe in stories like "Young Goodman Brown" (1835) and "The Tell-Tale Heart" (1843). Seemingly inexplicable events delineate a world more vivid in illusion, where fantasy and reality merge in a miasma of paranoia and guilt, and private meanings take on metaphysical significance. Characters that try to explicate their circumstances using the normal logical and narrative tools of their waking lives are destroyed or go mad. Survival demands that they surrender to an illogical stoicism, as the Cartesian model collapses into itself.

But beyond these common themes, both the American Romantics and Lynch, at the heart of their discourse, display an overriding concern for ethical accountability, and it is mainly in this context that Ahab, Hester Prynne, and Roderick Usher share the same moral universe as Paul Atreides, Jeffery Beaumont, and Diane Selwyn. Pascal Covici writes in *Humor and Revelation in American Literature: The Puritan Connection*, "The Puritan puts more weight in the scales of cosmic mystery and of the soul's dilemma" (1); and like his forerunners, Lynch's puritanical images link the soul to nature, corruption to culture. As Lynch's daughter Jennifer puts it, "'I know that *Blue Velvet* came out of the light and dark extremes that are so much David, his whole world as a child which was very white picket fence and lovely woods'" (Hughes 79).

2

Visionary, Manichee ... or Geek?

Lynch's propensity for moralizing has not gone unnoticed by his contemporary critics, but most tend to minimize his sermonic context, analyzing his films from semiotic or more formal perspectives, concentrating on his technical expertise, his innovative use of cinematic conventions and his stature in the pantheon of influential directors. Others merely allude to Lynch's overt conservatism and his fundamentalist's eschatology, exonerating him because his quirkiness, after all, is literary— his training as a painter more practical than aesthetic. But no critic can discuss Lynch without some allusion, however tangential, to his strict Manichaean context.

Samuel Kimball, writing in *Genders*, immediately brackets *Twin Peaks* in terms of "the failure of a certain cultural tradition, particularly in the transcendental optimism and accompanying moralism of its American incarnation" (19). He casts Lynch's world in its chiaroscuro purity, imagining a titanic struggle between "a daylight world of apparent safety and conventional moral order [and] a nightmare world of shadows and screaming faces" (20). Although the aim of his essay is to explore the gendermandering (Johnson 34) Lynch uses to subvert stereotypes in his narrative, Kimball cannot help transposing Lynch's Neo-Platonism into a Christian moral context, describing, for instance, Leland's confession in *Twin Peaks* in terms of "the self ... guilty beyond all possible atonement" (26). He describes one of BOB's victims as "a person whose consciousness is presented as being completely given over to a bottomless remorse" (26). Kimball correlates Lynch's symbolic reification of guilt and redemption to Emerson's "transcendental imagery" (22), but he describes the Lynch-Emerson connection as ironic, claiming Lynch is "[c]arica- turing the Emersonian discourse" (18). Kimball's tendency to mitigate Lynch's stark Manichaean vision by pleading (on Lynch's behalf) ironic distance is not unusual. Many critics read Lynch sympathetically, but they do so—often willfully, it seems—by overlooking the suicidal impact of irony on a moralist like Lynch. Irony undercuts ethical authority, frees the subject from authentic engagement, so the appeal to irony in Lynch is ideally designed as an "out" for viewers who cannot accept his puritan- ical impulse or his belief in stereotypes, mythical virtues and an idyllic, Reaganesque, top-forty pop version of America.

John Alexander, for instance, argues that Lynch's puritanism is an incidental byproduct, an "over-simplified and clearly labeled division … Lynch justifies as part and parcel of film narrative" (25). By this method, a predetermined ironical reading, Alexander can make the bizarre claim that "Lynch's 'happy endings' are rarely happy" (25). And though he uses phrases like "forces of chaos" (26) and "spirit of evil" (27), he seems more reassured grounding his explication in Jung's mythic psychology, post- modern philosophy and anthropological iconoclasm. This defensiveness leads to some murky conclusions, as when, in one case, Alexander equates BOB's possession of Dale Cooper with Jeffrey Beaumont's process of maturation and assimilation into the adult world of Lumberton. He writes that, "from a psychological perspective, Cooper's conversion from the purely 'righteous' to the purely 'evil' … was inevitable because of his unblemished 'purity'" (27) and that "Jeffrey's 'enantiodromia' takes him from blue-eyed naivity (*sic*) to the pain of knowledge and experience" (27). But to imply parity between the raw, inexplicable and remorse- lessly craven actions of BOB and the comforting, civilizing effects of Jeffrey's inhibitions, created by his deep understanding of remorse, ignores the absolute, uncompromising schema of Lynch's starkly judgmental rough cosmic justice. The subtleties of psychological theories blur the strict demarcations of righteousness and wickedness that define Lynch's moral ideal. Lynch does not recognize degrees of degradation. His char- acters are either damned or saved.

Alexander's desire to read Lynch in psychological terms causes him to understate the moral dimensions, unmitigated by irony, at the struc- tural core of Lynch's work. He sees *The Alphabet* as "a study in creativ- ity and 'abjection'" (31), and quotes an insightful comment by Philip Strick, who "describes the film as 'an urgent message of pity, disgust and shame at the physical process of conception, birth and adolescence'" (32), the key word here being "shame." He cites "[e]strangement, procreation, anxiety, disease [as] the main themes of *The Grandmother*" (36). The theme of *Eraserhead*, for Alexander, is sociological, and he again couches the resolution in psychological terms. "Henry has traversed his psychosis, for on the other side of madness lies redemption. He has regained his identity" (52). Alexander describes John Merrick as "the life-force" (69) and reads *The Elephant Man* as "a social parable" (69), relying on myth for motivations, explaining that Merrick is "driven, not by logos—the word; but by eros—the touch" (72).

Writing about *Dune*, Alexander prefers the psychological conflict of Paul Atreides wrestling with his masculine/feminine dichotomy to the religious strife at the heart of the story. For him, "*Dune* is concerned with male politics, male militarism and male power plays" (76), though he admits, in passing, that on "one level the conflict ... is between good and evil" (76). By foregrounding the sociological and psychological play between gender roles, Alexander diminishes the overriding Manichaean duality essential to the form of the film. He employs a similar method when discussing *Blue Velvet*, suggesting that what "underlies" (105) the film is "a transition of social anxieties" (105) and "an anxiety of the ego" (105). He invokes the playful gods of Greek myth—the "irrational vengefulness" (98) of Aphrodite, for example—instead of the hardcore Old Testament codes of reward and punishment that drive all of Lynch's films, but especially the moral imperatives of Jeffrey's primal journey. He also cites the "lesson in the Aphrodite story" (108) to explain how "chaos and order prevail until Dorothy and her child are united" (108), and he situates Jeffrey's "return to normality" (106) in "the myth of the family unit played out with every new US television network sitcom" (106). He views *Wild at Heart* strictly through the lens of *The Wizard of Oz*, excusing the "'gratuitous' ... number of disparate scenes that intersperse the plot" (123) and that, incidentally, mar the structural integrity of the film, as a "parodic extravagance [and] an ironic commentary on the narrative's singular lack of resolution" (123).

In Alexander's view, finding irony in Lynch creates a catchall excuse for the various aesthetic faults, including what Alexander euphemistically refers to as "loose ends" (123). He continues to link Lynch to Greco-Roman mythology, Hollywood iconology and psychoanalytical evaluations in his reading of *Twin Peaks: Fire Walk with Me* (1992), connecting Laura Palmer's slide into drug abuse and sadomasochistic sex to "Persephone's descent into Hades" (138), citing Otto Preminger's *Laura* (1944) as the prototype for her psychic dilemma, and blaming her loss of "identity' (128) on the community's privileging the "sanctity of the image" (129) over her existential self. This transposition of mythical and ethical systems, shying away from the obvious but less politically correct Judeo-Christian precepts that shape Lynch's material, and embracing the supposedly more humanistic myths of Mycenaean Greece and Enlightenment psychology, reflects an exculpatory trend among many critics who approach Lynch as a disciple might a saint, with a reverence that often befogs critical perspicuity. But in a rare moment of blasphemy, Alexander notes how the film "fails to resolve the dramatic problem of a submissive protagonist and attempts to compensate through sequences of depravity and revulsion" (143). He quotes "a critic who felt 'great discomfort at the end of the film because of ... a sort of puritanical, religious, right-wing attitude'" (144)—exactly what the initiates posing as critics refuse to acknowledge. Alexander does, however, recover a more balanced devotional attitude in his credible and thorough discussion of *Twin Peaks*, which he deems "superior television" (149)—a left-handed compliment at best—while accurately describing the episodes Lynch directed as "the most violent and the most shamelessly sentimental" (159). To his credit he does not appeal to irony as the usual *deus ex machina* designed to save Lynch from his moralistic posturing.

Alexander is not alone among critics who dismiss Lynch's reactionary polemics, what he describes as "conservative in conviction" (180), although, as noted above, he is less quick than others to insist that the absurd Calvinism in Lynch's ethos is ironic. Lynch, at his best, is only incidentally ironic—as when the performers (actors playing characters who act in the film) with a host of costumes and identities, stage anxieties and miscues, object to being looked at. The irony that occurs in Lynch's works exists between the image and the viewer, not between Lynch and his material. Lynch, given his evangelical agenda, must forsake cosmic irony—what Kierkegaard calls "world irony" ("The Concept of Irony" 30). Lynch is too serious. For him, as for Kierkegaard, irony is destructive. Kierkegaard defines it as "infinite absolute negativity" (28). Sartre makes the point in his discussion of self-deception: "In irony a man annihilates what he posits within one and the same act; he leads us to believe in order not to be believed; he affirms to deny and denies to affirm; he creates a positive object but it has no being other than its nothingness" (Sartre, "Self-Deception" 300). This world-historical irony is too nihilistic for a moralist like Lynch. Irony, in Lynch's work, would disrupt and nullify his moral engagement. "In irony, the subject is negatively free, since the actuality that is supposed to give the subject context is not there" (Kierkegaard, "The Concept of Irony" 29). Lynch is engaged, serious, and, like Kafka, often unintentionally funny. Irony, for Lynch, is too subversive. Lynch eschews Kierkegaard's ironist, who "permits the established to remain, but for him it has no validity" (30). Lynch may fake disengagement, and many critics end up as unwitting enablers, infecting his propaganda with postmodern codes, but Lynch actually believes in the duality of things, and irony is anathema to his crusade.

In an article in *Film Comment*, Howard Hampton sees Lynch "[c]onjuring a utopia where the polarity of good and evil holds each person in his or her place" (39). He describes *Twin Peaks: Fire Walk with Me* as "an elaborate pseudo-religious allegory" (48), although it is arguable how "pseudo" the allegory pretends to be. Hampton compares Lynch to that other great American moralistic myth-maker, Ronald Reagan, suggesting both use "coded euphemisms" (38) to promote their shared beliefs in the "myths of small town, cherry-pie America" (38). According to Hampton, Lynch's "gift is for showing how the designations of good and evil are only fronts for a deeper mystery" (49), the same mystery, presumably, that "brought Reagan to power" (38). He argues that Lynch's homespun, enigmatic sensibility makes itself felt as the beatific elaboration of Reagan's mandate: "the dreamscape of motion pictures" (38). But Hampton fails to note how Lynch, instead of correcting Reagan's vision of America, complements it. Lynch's "dreamscape," which Hampton claims has ironically "caught the true radiance of the Reaganite myth" (38), is not necessarily a subversive undermining of Reagan's Morning in America acting as "an agent of compulsion and evisceration underneath the cant of innocence" (40). Reagan was never as cynical as his handlers; he believed his own rhetoric. The same holds for what Lynch believes. The crux of his allegiance to Reagan is that Lynch also believes in "vows of virtue, fidelity, and trust, with their transgression to be the pretext for an eternity of punishment" (49). Lynch does not offer a critique of the never-never values inherent in Reagan's sloganeering as much as he verifies, rationalizes, and justifies them.

Greg Olson, writing in the same issue of *Film Comment*, reads Lynch in a strictly religious context. Olson's language is sermonic. He analyzes Lynch's "exploration of the nature of evil" (44) and notes Lynch's use of "a pure white light of love and goodness" (45) and "radiant angels of saving grace" (45). He describes Ronette Pulaski's desperate pleas for divine mercy, when she "asked for spiritual help and received it" (46) as a crisis of faith resolved in a moment of grace and deliverance. Olson complains

that "hundreds of column inches have been devoted to Lynch's preoccupation with ... every deadly sin. But precious little has been said about
the spiritual nature of his vision, the beatitudes that balance and transcend the universal anxiety and entropy he so viscerally conveys" (44).
Olson (along with others) compares Lynch to William Blake, portraying him as a visionary moralist with the "intuitive ability to flood our
senses" (44), who can "invest a mundane, ramshackle house trailer ... with
an aura of infernal menace" (44). For Olson, Lynch's intense sensibility
allows him a prophet's perspective on the nature of good and evil.

Scott Pollard's essay in *Literature Film Quarterly* is also loaded with
Manichaean phrases such as "goodness can be preserved" (297), "evil may
be expelled" (297), "moral surface" (298), "subterranean evil" (298), "metaphysical purgation" (298) and "universal evil" (298). He describes Lynch's
world as a place "where good and evil are meant to be clearly delineated"
(302), where "a staunch moral order" (303) anchors Lynch's graphic
depictions of "evil and perversity" (303); yet it is a place where Lynch
allows his heroes (Agent Dale Cooper, in Pollard's example) to "delimit
evil" (299) and "restore ... a unifying principle based in a middle-class
nostalgia" (299). But Pollard's thesis is as judgmental and condemnatory
as any exhortation by Lynch. In Pollard's paranoid Marxist vision, Lynch
acts as a nefarious agent of "network television" (303) whose propagandistic purpose is "to promote the middle class" (303) and to secure "separation and exclusivity [as] the standing order of things" (302). When
Pollard contrasts Lynch with Whitman, he allows that the former strives
in his art to "perpetuate the illusion of [the middle class's] totality" (298),
whereas Whitman hoped for "a much more sincere attempt at universality" (298). Pollard accuses Lynch of waging a sort of patriotic guer-
rilla warfare on the "unknown universal powers ... out to get the middle
class" (303). To realize this end, he suggests that Lynch employs "a narrative of redemption" (301) that leads the wayward back to "an ideo-
logue's dream: a binary, black and white world with clear divisions and
all the complexities distilled out of it" (298). For anyone "who may wan-
der from the straight and narrow, the middle class acts as magnetic pole"
(301). The irony of this kind of critical reading inverts the expected moral
dynamic: Lynch's ethos is reversed, so that his conventional vision of
moral order becomes a destructive, subversive factor in the unifying principle of American democracy.

Kenneth C. Kaleta, in his *David Lynch*, while acknowledging Lynch's
Manichaean vision, compares him to Blake too, evoking "a mythic world
of Innocence and Experience ... of spiritualism, dreams and nightmares"

(ix). Yet later he insists that Lynch, as auteur, "shows without editorial-izing, prioritizing, or moralizing" (15). Kaleta also compares Lynch to John Waters (among others, in an eclectic clique that includes Peter Greenaway and Tim Burton), further confusing the distinct Calvinistic absolutism endemic in Lynch's worldview with the camp sensibility of a New Testament satirist like Waters. Waters sides with the meek. Lynch is full of fire and brimstone and Old Testament vengeance.

But Kaleta hesitates to acknowledge the overt moral intention at the core of Lynch's films. He insists that Lynch's focus is aesthetic and concentrates on his "artistic intensity" (15). Nevertheless, "Lynch's world is good and evil" (ix). He traces the roots of Lynch's sermonizing to his time in Philadelphia. Kaleta suggests that the contrast of Lynch's study-ing art at the Pennsylvania Academy of Fine Arts while living in urban rot and squalor across the street from a city morgue led to his Manichaean fervor. "His perception became dual" (6). As he recounts the genesis of each of Lynch's films, foregrounding the "artistic intensity" (6) of the auteur at work, he cannot avoid the stark simplicity of Cotton Mather's puritanical polemics. He quotes Eileen Fisher's description of *Six Fig-ures Getting Sick*: "'one figure looks on disapproving'" (7). In *The Alpha-bet*, he notes the "dual structure of ... the black and white reality" (8). The boy's screams in *The Grandmother* are of "both ecstasy and misery" (9), and the boy's ejaculating on the bed represents "simultaneously his shame and the fertilization of his illusion of salvation" (10).

Eraserhead is "the work of an American visionary" (11). The term, for Kaleta, implies artistic vision, not the sacred revelations of an angry Isaiah. In *The Elephant Man*, Kaleta appreciates the "seething duality of ... the world in black and white" (41), but, ironically, he blames the crit-ical failure of *Dune* on the film's "temptation to preach" (76). Kaleta mis-reads the lack of irony in *Blue Velvet*, suggesting that Lynch's most blatantly moralistic film projects an "economy and restraint" (90) that elevate it to the status of "masterpiece" (90). He claims that "Lynch never comments—he presents" (91). Actually, *Blue Velvet* is perhaps the most pointed, overt piece of moralistic preaching in Lynch's oeuvre. True, it is arguably his most effective film, but its artistic integrity, instead of serv-ing the aesthetic construction, is too often merely a vehicle for the moral message—what Lynch calls "the Western Union school" (20). And instead of developing the central moral structure and engaging the sim-plicity of Lynch's moral vision, Kaleta summarizes it in a cliché that reads like a dismissal: "Life is both good and bad" (91). Likewise, in *Twin Peaks* Lynch "records without comment" (134) even as Kaleta admits

Lynch's "vision is of a dual world encompassing both American Dream and American Disillusionment" (135). But this duality, for Kaleta, is an aesthetic strategy, not didactic bombast. Kaleta's most debilitating blind spot, however, allows him to view *Wild at Heart* as an antidote to a decadent America spoiled by, of all things, neo–Puritanism.

This catalog of excuses, inoculations and mithridates by Kaleta is not intended to undercut the importance of the innovative cinematic techniques for which Lynch is, perhaps, deservedly famous. But to marginalize the moral impetus at the heart of Lynch's work, as Kaleta does, is to misunderstand, if not misrepresent, the quirky perversity of Lynch's vision. When not trumpeting the formal and stylistic elements in Lynch's work, Kaleta finds art in Lynch's metaphysics. He refers to the moral frame as if it were incidental, subordinated to the creative process.

Kaleta attributes some of what he considers Lynch's oblique moral framework to the influence of the Ashcan School painter Robert Henri, whose "artistic philosophy" (5), according to Kaleta, allows him to express the "mundane and the extraordinary … without moralizing" (4). Given the overtly moral context of Lynch's work, this assessment seems disingenuous. But Kaleta remains defensive. Lynch's aesthetic foibles are excused, explained away, mitigated; his sermonic excesses are ignored. Even when Kaleta locates Lynch within the American literary tradition, not implausibly aligning Lynch with Poe, it is the Poe of "Poetic Principle," not Poe posturing as a voyeuristic virtuecrat and railing against the moral failures of a rapidly modernizing America. For Kaleta, Lynch's perceived aesthetic purity immunizes him from the charge of didacticism.

This tendency to underplay the ethical obsessions of a writer to enhance his aesthetic achievement ironically works to underscore the very moralizing tendencies a critic like Kaleta tries to diminish. For instance, while challenging Nathaniel Hawthorne's exceptional reputation in the American literary canon, feminist and cultural critic Jane Tompkins dismisses Melville's positive reviews of Hawthorne as demonstrating not the quality of Hawthorne's work "but rather proof of Melville's own preoccupation with the problem of innate depravity and original sin" (122). She argues that "[w]hat modern critics take as evidence of Melville's critical penetration … testifies rather to their own propensity for projecting onto what is actually a latter-day Calvinist vocabulary, their mid–twentieth-century conviction that a 'tragic vision,' elaborated chiefly in psychological terms, constitutes literary maturity" (122); and that the encomiums with which Hawthorne's contemporaries lauded him "intersect widely held cultural beliefs about the special properties of childhood and the sanctity of the home ... in the nineteenth-century American imagination[,] ... a spiritual force ... and cornerstone of national unity" (123). She cites several critics who commend Hawthorne "for his depiction of 'spiritual laws[,]' ... 'the eternal facts of morality[,]' ... an 'extraordinary understanding of the heart'" (123); his works are praised for being "firmly rooted in Christian precept" (124).

Tompkins, and the critics she cites, could just as easily have been discussing the films of David Lynch. His "literary maturity," like Hawthorne's, has been established by both his style and his themes. Given both artists' thematic obsessions—an acute preoccupation with innocence and evil, the nature of transcendence, the quest for spirituality in the corrupt morass of a materialistic society—and their styles—the reworking of Romance, the use of multivalent, surreal structures to enhance meaning in their tales—Nathaniel Hawthorne and David Lynch are not, after all, such strange bedfellows. Nor are Lynch and Melville. As Lawrence writes, Melville's whale embodies desire and fear, "our deepest blood-nature[,] ... [o]ur blood-self" (160). And no matter what form the demon takes, it is within this distinct dialectic—"discovering" the New World and taming its wilderness while decimating its innocence and appropriating its resources—that the American Dream, allegorical from inception, in the myths of the "founding fathers" to Manifest Destiny, crosses into the nightmare of Lynch's vision.

While Kaleta avoids directly attributing seminal influences to Lynch, he does cite Georges Méliès, Robert Wiene and Luis Buñuel as early forerunners of Lynch's surrealist style (12). He frequently references *Un Chien Andalou* (1928), and insists, "Lynch's films recall the films of Louis Buñuel" (xi). Alexander also locates Lynch squarely in the Surrealists' camp. He dedicates a section of his Introduction to "Surrealism," compares Lynch to Magritte, claims Lynch "cites Jean Cocteau, Man Ray, Hans Richter and other surrealistic filmmakers as his mentors" (6), and quotes Lynch commenting to the BBC, "'I could say I was somewhat surrealistic'" (5). He links Lynch to Breton's manifesto calling for "'the permanent destruction of all other psychic mechanisms and to its substitution for them in the solution of the principal problems of life'" (6), then describes Lynch as "the Hieronymous Bosch of middle America" (6). And while Kaleta notes that Lynch "makes no claim to Buñuel as an influence" (13), Lynch having seen, he says, *Un Chien Andalou* "'a lot later'" (13), a close look at that film may be instructive. It presents the same problems of interpretation that confound Lynch's viewers and critics alike, and may explain why his films appear enigmatic.

On first viewing *Un Chien Andalou*, the temptation of many critics is to "explain" the film by suggesting that, as with Lynch, the narrative brings an understanding of the world inside, using the logic of dreams to express an implied reciprocal dualism between the waking and sleeping worlds of our realities. This explication, however, relies on an allegorical interpretation: each event stands for something else, and the viewer must uncover a message hidden in the image. The process is to project a series of seemingly disconnected events, presented in an apparently meaningful sequence that resists any meaningful context. But the problem with this "reading" of the film is in the inability of Buñuel and Dali—and Lynch, and really anyone—to sustain meaninglessness. The film's technique fails in its intention: the images survive decontextualization by the structure that contains them. Meaninglessness, even in the guise of the apparently meaningful, is implausible: the sequence is the meaning, the alignment the context. Any sequence of images is never truly random. Selection implies arrangement, arrangement denotes meaning. By its nature, all narrative is linear. Any fixed sequence capable of being repeated in exactly the same order is fixed in time—reel time rather than real time, granted, but the arrangement of events, being totally controlled, is artificial anyway, not arbitrary, so in the end the idea of a "nonlinear narrative" is senseless.

But this is where Lynch most resembles his Surrealist predecessors: he reinforces expectations of meaningful sequences and delights in the de-familiarizing of common images.

Following the Surrealists' line, *Un Chien Andalou* would lend itself to dream analysis, relying on Freudian transference and levels of meaning. But the immediate problem with this dream interpretation method is that, whereas dreams are organic, spontaneous, and uncontrollable, art is plastic, contrived, utterly and systematically controlled. Even if an "interpretation" were necessary, the message of the images would be qualified by the prejudice inherent in the judgment of the interpreter: the meaning is confined by the experience of the reader. In *Un Chien Andalou*, the satiric attack on the middle class, explicit in the clustering of images, pretends to be "apparently" meaningful, feigns spontaneity; but in truth, the narrative sustains satire, and satire needs a program.

Another reading might suggest that instead of being closed by the coded messages they contain, the images in *Un Chien Andalou* are open to private meanings; their function is to dismantle public expectations. The mistake here is again to ignore the ostensible target of the satire:

the mediocrity of the middle class, its politics of sex, and its reverence for normalcy. Also, in film, "open-ended" images and sequences of images cannot renew themselves, so they recur in sequence until the sequence is familiar; as soon as the image or the sequence is familiar, it is no longer "open." Both methods, dream interpretation and the privatization of meaning, acknowledge a complexity of networks and coded messages; each triggers the experience-shaping function of consciousness: for one, meaning is latent in the image; for the other, meaning is established by the viewer.

A more straightforward reading would be grounded in craft: the chief irony is in the film's technique. Just as the conventional viewer is disturbed by the indirect presentation of cultural truths underlying acceptable conventions (her confusion a convenient means of protecting herself from criticism), this same viewer objects to any direct representation of the base motives for aggressive sexual behavior, preferring the indirection of what is popularly (and discreetly) referred to as "romance." To protect her veneer of propriety, the viewer begs for indirection; when indirection is used to exploit her conventions (as it is here), the message is so direct that her reaction is to demand the veneer. The film, by its reductive assault, mocks the viewer's process with her own devices: both games are exposed.

What holds Dali and Buñuel's film together structurally is the same for Lynch: tension in the conflict between the rational and the irrational, between restraint and desire, between instinct and dogma. Within these dimensions, *Un Chien Andalou* becomes a morality play that parodies itself, a suicide avatar of the avant-garde. Even the sadistic but comical opening sequence that culminates with slicing the woman's eye is self-referential: a criminal impulse becomes poetic inspiration, as the man in the frame is driven by a cloud slicing across the moon: urged by an image to create an image.

The plot then remains to the end linear and chronologically sequential. A transvestite bicyclist, wearing a nun's habit and a striped box, after a minor crisis (he wrecks) is rescued by a conventional female reader of respectable books. Her first concern is the appearance of the man's clothes (as she sets about restoring order to dishevelment). But even her best efforts cannot keep clothes from disappearing (our director-as-ghost calling attention to himself, to his frame). Then ants crawl out of the man's hand. Obviously, what once seemed certain and expected now is neither. In the street, a woman begins to poke at a severed hand, a look of narcoleptic distance in her eyes. But because of the film's operating parody (mocking moralistic hypocrisy), the "offending" hand is not symbolic but ironic. As Jesus says in Matthew 5:30, "And if thy right hand offend thee, cut it off, and cast it from thee." But in this case the hand, an item of curiosity and pleasure for a woman in the street (as the film is for the viewer), causes the woman to lose herself in her indulgence; in her carelessness, she is run over by a car.

This image of a woman "destroyed" (or "fallen") again incites aberrant behavior; it sparks the lust of the leading man. He advances on the heroine, and although initially she responds, once she considers what she is doing (opening herself to pleasure with a stranger), she suddenly resists. The man is metamorphosed into, literally, a monster of desire, and the woman must flee to preserve her dignity. The man, our hero/villain, realizing the futility of his advances, illustrates the restraints by which society defines itself as "civil" by dragging in all the repressive baggage of responsibility—the heaviest thing he can imagine, which is in this case a piano, two dead donkeys, and two priests roped together by their necks.

As the woman retreats, our hero, who finds himself in the woman's bed, is confronted by another man, presumably his other, more rational self, who chastises him by throwing his ladies' clothing out the window and makes him stand in the corner as punishment. This "other" then offers the hero rectitude in books and drawings; the hero responds by shooting his counterpart, who dies at the feet of a woman posed as a Greek statue of Attic beauty and grace (quite a contrast to the vulgar licentiousness of the hero).

Meanwhile, back in the room, the woman, who is not lacking desire, only demanding that it come wrapped, as it were, in the proper package, transforms a moth (an insect naturally drawn to its death by its attraction to flame, the danger in desire) into a man, but when he wipes off his mouth and grows a beard that resembles a female's pudendum, our femme fatale is reminded of her earlier version of that (unspeakable!) underarm hair, and her desire (seen, so to speak, without its dressing) turns to disgust. In her version, love is suggestive, couched in romance; her passion must be indirect to retain its bourgeois charm. So she walks along the beach, romantically (albeit awkwardly) with her fantasy beau (to whose suggestive fist she defers); the discarded ladies' clothing is found in ruin, suggesting that normalcy prevails when the foul is cast out—which leaves the woman and her new man planted, finally, in the sand, as removed from the vitality of life as the silly censorial game of love our heroine has fought to maintain.

The same surface complexity in Lynch's work masks his core simplicity, and it often confounds even the most earnest critic bent on deciphering the cryptology of his imagery. Martha Nochimson, in *The Passion of David Lynch: Wild at Heart in Hollywood*, is willfully ambiguous about meaning in Lynch's work, suggesting that "cultural forms ... only have the meaning we give them" (4). But she may be a victim of her own methodology. Caught in a typical postmodernist undermining of critical authority, she claims that "[c]riticism is not suited to the heterogeneous work of art" (44). Like Kaleta, she subordinates Lynch's preachifying to his aesthetic exuberance and "blazing originality" (18). Paradoxically for Nochimson, the lessons Lynch imparts through his films ease the postmodern stress of "meaninglessness and fragmentation[,] ... promoting empathy [and] a fundamental connectedness among people and the universe" (13). She sees in Lynch a metaphysical optimism, not dystopic disgust.

In *Six Figures Getting Sick*, the ethical impulse is anthropological. "Vomiting is a brilliant image of the unstoppable narrative compulsion" (149), not the self-reflexive comment of an artist ill at ease with a world in which the black-and-white simplicity of moral clarity has gone gray with global multiplicity. Recognizing the moral context of *The Alphabet*, Nochimson focuses on the metalinguistic movement of the child into the symbolic, linear world of Saussurean significance rather than the biblical parable of the fall from innocence into the troubling postlapsarian world of adult conflict, crises and guilt. In *The Grandmother*, Nochimson's concern is with the child's distress at "social power relations" (165) and the contrast between the "dysfunctional language" (167) of adults and the grandmother's intuitive "touching that is unconstructed by the socialization process" (167). Suggesting that "[t]here is a more simplistic dualistic edge to this film than to Lynch's more mature work" (168), she minimizes the core thematic motifs that inform and structure Lynch's later "mature" work, without which his films would lack the grounding that makes them (like *Un Chien Andalou*) less enigmatic than many critics are willing to acknowledge. She makes the same argument in her critique of *Eraserhead*, claiming that it too is merely a "foundation for ... much more complex ventures" (148).

The case can be made that Lynch never moved beyond the basic spine of his first films. This hesitancy to see the simple basic pattern in Lynch's cinematic strategies may account for the uneven critical response to his full-length "Hollywood" films. Lynch's reliance on a recurring moral certitude as a shaping tool by which he structures his films can be compared to the designs of another American gothic moralist, Flannery O'Connor. Even as the characters, settings, sundry sins and perversities change, her short stories are all cut from the same cloth: self-righteous, hypocritical Christians have a violent encounter that causes them to reevaluate their faith and themselves and to bear witness to God's wrath and mercy. Like having sex and eating food, the general action is always the same, yet the particulars are always different. Lynch alludes to this same-but-different dialectic, and his analogy (not surprisingly) is to sex. "It can be the same tune, but there are many variations" (Lynch 147). His films, like O'Connor's stories, all tend to follow the same logic. Like a Christmas tree whose appearance is changed only by the different decorations hung on it, Lynch's work has a single-minded purity that mirrors his simplistic moral vision. Yet it is exactly this simple structural codification that viewers, and many critics, strive to resist.

Nochimson often slips into the predictable postmodern epistemological speculations about the certainty of meaning, suggesting that one of the keys to unlocking the method in Lynch's art is in understanding his "will to lose his will" (17), what she says Lynch calls "'letting go'" (17). Intent on finding complexity—open-endedness—in the most straightforward narrative devices, she also cites Robert Henri as influential on Lynch's early sensibility, especially regarding Henri's writing on "rational control as a barrier to perception of the real" (21).

But it is rational control that Lynch relies on most. Without his unwavering faith in his own moral framework—the Christmas tree, as it were, on which he hangs his bizarre baubles—his film sense would collapse into trite, flip entertainment. Nochimson doesn't pretend the moral scaffolding isn't there. She merely treats it tangentially. Instead of centering it as Lynch's structural core, she notes it in passing. *The Elephant Man*, for instance, "offers the audience a testament of faith and hope in the failure of the will" (135), yet she insists that "this is not a film about sin" (140). She refers to *Dune* as "anomalous" (123), glossing over the Manichaean struggle at the heart of the film. She reads Jeffrey's quest in *Blue Velvet* as a "desire for the real[,] ... a journey to authenticity" (104) that results in psychological integration but is strangely divorced, in Nochimson's view, from the society in which it plays out. She even dismisses Fredric Jameson's "civic concern" (235) as "a reduced concept of ethics" (235). But that is the point: Lynch is a moral reductionist whose Zoroastrian dualism undermines his complexity, no matter how his clever cinematic pyrotechnics try to elevate the basic context of his films.

The same critical sleight-of-hand occurs in Nochimson's reading of

Twin Peaks, the television series. She sees the show as "the struggle to know the subconscious world [that] means a ceding of the will to a strong mind-body connection" (79). She claims that "the transgressive elements ... do not reflect Lynch at all" (75), attributing "any possession of Cooper by demonic forces" (75) to the work of Mark Frost, Lynch's partner on the series. But this is a distinction without a difference, not seeing the forest for the trees. The whole program is designed around Lynch's moral absolutism: the struggle between good and evil for souls at risk of perdition and bedeviled by temptation.

For Nochimson, the dualism in *Twin Peaks* is Cartesian, not Manichaean. She writes that Lynch is "dedicated to recalling us to what he sees as our natural path to reality through the subconscious" (74). In her view, the conflict is solipsistic, not social, but such a reading is ostensibly at odds with Lynch's preoccupation, in all of his work, with sin and redemption, public punishment and cultural reward. This redirecting of Lynch's focus from the public to the private allows Nochimson to view *Wild at Heart* through the same solipsistic lens "in which the hero transcends his limitations ... and the heroine ... the traditional controls on her" (46). Incongruously, the "larger picture of the culture is of great importance" (47) but only as it serves Lynch's moral affirmation: he "gives people and culture a thumbs-up" (47). Again she locates "the twin Lynchian demons of control and will" (47) in the play between nature and convention. Lynch seems driven to mitigate or restore what Nochimson identifies as a "curative subconscious" (47).

John Caughie, editor of *Screen*, complains that Lynch is so ironic he has a hard time taking him seriously (Caughie, 29 June 2002). But the problem is not that Lynch is flippant but that he is too earnest. And while Caughie may confuse Lynch's corniness with irony, Nochimson's position is just the opposite. In the "Coda" section of her text, her adulation borders on hero-worship. She compares Lynch to Welles and Hitchcock in his ability to "change Hollywood" (199).

But arguing hagiography misses the point. While Nochimson documents Lynch's cinematic strategies, she ignores his fetishistic obsession with fifties-style geekiness and his reordering of the hierarchy of the hip cultural excesses of the sixties. His films often recycle the same hokum— the reification of the fifties—that Reagan hammed up to such dramatic effect. Lynch myopically calls the fifties "a fantastic decade" (Lynch 4) when the "future was bright" (5). It seems pluralism frightens him, evident in his childhood reaction to New York City, which "scared the hell out of me" (7). "'There was a large amount of fear'" (Woods 8). He prefers the white-bread neighborhoods of the Midwest, "elegant Middle America as it's supposed to be" (Lynch 10). He "'didn't take to Europe'" (Woods 10). His "experience as an expatriate fell apart after only 15 days" (Kaleta 2). He famously complained that he was "'7000 miles from the nearest McDonalds'" (Chion 8). His nostalgia is pathologic, his parochialism endemic, and his sense of the present ominous: "that's the way things are right now: people believe the worst" (26). In Lynch's world, men need to be men; women, women. When goodness trumps evil, psychic balance and civil duty are restored. It's a Boy Scout version of the way things ought to be. Moral complexity, in Lynch's films, is as simple as chiaroscuro.

Paul A. Woods, in *Weirdsville USA: The Obsessive Universe of David Lynch*, also subordinates the structural function of Lynch's peculiar moral dualism. He laces his scene-by-scene synopses with biographical sketches and a detailed discussion of technical information surrounding the production of the films. *Six Figures Getting Sick*—Lynch's ticket out of fine art and into cinema—exemplifies the confluence of Lynch's training in art and his emerging interest in mixed media. *The Alphabet*, an "off-kilter" (13) psychological portrait, depicts a child "[a]ssimilating information[,] … a painful, frightening experience" (13). *The Grandmother* "emphasised subconscious themes" (15) and expresses Lynch's "disarming confession of a childhood longing to be orphaned" (15). *Eraserhead* is a transitional work of symbolic naturalism "amplified *ad absurdum*" (28), a "journey into a damaged psyche" (31). The film represents a culmination of Lynch's early thematic concerns while establishing his trademark "askew vision" (38). *The Elephant Man* moved Lynch into "a different league of filmmaking" (46). Woods emphasizes Lynch's use of "dream sequences presented as subjective reality" (50), and argues that the continuity between Lynch's early work and his first studio production satisfied the "cultists" (50). *Dune*, however, was "clearly unfilmable" (58) and, swamped with exposition and heavy-handed special effects, it collapsed.

Woods catalogs the business and biographical contexts within which Lynch developed his films, cross-referencing images and symbols, casts and characters. He de-emphasizes cinematic hermeneutics, but seems blind to Lynch's debilitating moral obsessions. He notes that *Blue Velvet* draws on "the surface memory of Lynch's childhood" (78). He delineates the "psychological sojourn" (87) into the subconscious of Jeffrey/Lynch, having "laid many of his [Lynch's] most precious memories and his darkest daydreams bare" (88). For Woods, Lynch's psyche is a storeroom of bizarre ideas, weird impressions and grotesque images, not the playground of a latter-day Puritan out to repair the torn moral fabric of a post–Edenic America.

Woods, however, is one of very few commentators to distinguish "Lynchian sensibility … [from] what many critics would still only accept as irony" (92). It is an important distinction. When Caughie dismissed Lynch as a charlatan whose ironic distance keeps him from any sense of commitment, he mistook for seeming irony Lynch's defensive use of the macabre to disguise his goofy sentimentality and naïve moral absolutism. Woods' more subtle reading reveals Lynch's penchant for sincerity and sentimentality.

No matter how critics like Kaleta and Nochimson try to elevate Lynch's work, explaining how he strives for some metaphysical ideal, tapping the collective unconscious to express the unifying experience of the creative process, it is finally Lynch's own local concerns that hold him back, lead-footed, firmly rooted in the ethical muck of terra firma. Through the lens of his moralistic viewfinder, sincerity and sentimentality are clearly the primary guides in his films. Lynch's myopia might explain why *Twin Peaks*, the television version, "somehow managed to touch a chord with middle-America" (Woods 111) and garner for the once-heralded deacon of *haute couture* filmmaking the moniker "King of Weird'—the only avant-garde auteur whose obsessive imagery was almost paradoxically accepted by the industry mainstream" (113).

Unable, it seems, to separate the man from the myth, Woods reads *Wild at Heart* as a classic road movie, "the odyssey of two naïve kids through an unnerving but recognizably realistic America" (116), but his analysis bears out Caughie's observation, acknowledging the "detractors who derided … [the] kitsch devices allowing the director to celebrate his own insincerity" (118). What had been obvious, if ignored throughout Lynch's career, was now undeniable: the stuff in his films that so many critics had for so long dismissed as camp, Lynch took seriously.

Unlike the commentators who reject Lynch's sentimental moralizing (Caughie, for instance), Woods disingenuously excuses him as a "Reaganesque nostalgicist for the Eisenhower area (*sic*)" (127). In fact, it is exactly Lynch's reactionary nostalgia that constitutes his moral bottom line. Woods recognizes Lynch's puritanical impulse, but only as a quirky by-product of his craft, not as the organizing principle. He identifies *Lost Highway* as just another Lynchian circle of hell, the funhouse of his characters' perditions: "Lynch and Gifford's irrational narrative traps the main character in a scenario which not only denies self determination or escape, but undermines his whole sense of reality" (173).

In a truly ironic twist, *The Straight Story* becomes the essential Lynch, as if his other films were bilge, purgation—stomach-pumped, as it were. It features "[n]o arty gore, no sex, no physical deformity, no profanity.... [It is] a simple human story ... with an almost total absence of irony" (191)—and a drastic easing of imagistic edginess. Still, Woods and other critics seemed surprised that with *The Straight Story* Lynch gives up the pretense of identifying with his weirdness.

Chris Rodley, in his canonized and definitive *Lynch on Lynch*, launches his analysis with a discussion about "uncanniness" (Lynch ix)—a quality he identifies in Lynch's films that creates something mysterious, unfamiliar, that makes viewers uneasy. He argues that what "lies at the very core of Lynch's work" is "nonspecificity" (ix). He argues that Lynch's "inability to engage in a precise textual analysis" expresses his "extraordinary success" in dispensing with "subtext" (xi). He conjures Heidegger's terms "dread" and "unfamiliarity" to explain what he calls Lynch's "cross-generic confusion" (x).

The term "uncanny," leaked into the lexicon of literary criticism by the Yale Deconstructionist J. Hillis Miller, implies a slippage of meaning in any given textual encounter. Miller differentiates canny and uncanny critics as respectively those that "cling to the possibility of 'a rationalizable activity, with agreed-upon rules of procedure, given facts, and measurable results' and those that have renounced such nostalgia for impossible certainties" (qtd. in Abrams 558–59).

Lynch, of course, feeds this "indeterminable free-play of indeterminable meanings" (559) by his oblique, wink-and-a-nod comments and, less often but more pointedly, his flat refusal to respond, as when Rodley asks about the baby in *Eraserhead* and Lynch curtly cuts him off: "I don't want to talk about it" (Lynch 77). Rodley likens Lynch's process of "defamiliarization" (xi) to that of the Surrealists, although Rodley differentiates between the Surrealists' use of "the absurd or the incongruous" and what he calls Lynch's "'dreamtime[,]' ... the state between dream and awakening" (xi). Lynch, Rodley claims, "has the 'uncanny' ability to empathize with the experience of others" (xii).

Given Lynch's unwillingness "to assign specific words to images or sequences ... for the purpose of explanation" (54), another so-called surrealistic film that may offer an instructive critical context to Lynch's style and reticence is Jean Cocteau's *Blood of a Poet* (1930). Lynch, of course, famously hesitates to acknowledge surrealistic influences, though Alexander quotes Lynch as saying that he sees Cocteau "as 'the heavyweight of the surrealists'" (142). Cocteau claims his film is a "realistic documentary of unreal events" (Cocteau 8), and he takes for its subject the necessarily surrealistic story of a poet "who lives out his own creations" (65). In fact, too often a discussion of Cocteau's film begins with a discussion of surrealism, as if the film can only make sense within this handy critical context; yet Cocteau disavowed any affiliation with Surrealist doctrine (3). Part of the problem is a result of critics who insist that understanding is a process by which a message is decoded, paraphrased by explication, and flaunted as a discovery of meaning. (Recall Wilde's maxim: "All art is at once surface and symbol. Those who go beneath the surface do so at their peril. Those who read the symbol do so at their peril" (69–70).) Instead of elucidating the work, this attempt to discover meaning by decoding messages testifies more to the critic's skill as a cryptographer than to her ability to respond to the operative aesthetics.

Critic Robert Short writes that surrealism "posited a new image of the artist as someone who was characterized by his availability to chance, to the promptings of the unconscious and internal impulses, who welcomed everything that occurred spontaneously" (292). Even though certainly Cocteau would agree with Short's more generic observation that as a result of the Century of Progress, which culminated in World War I, an "over-estimation of reason at the expense of feeling led straight to destructive megalomania" (293), Cocteau's split with the Surrealists has less to do with the intention of art (to revitalize the imagination by defamiliarizing the context) than with Short's assertion that, for the Surrealists, the new image of the artist was as a passive recipient of chance impressions, of impulses, a recorder of spontaneous emotions.

Cocteau, as an artist, would have the same natural aversion Lynch expresses to labels, schools, and genre; to be included in a category allows a sense of grouping, mitigating the chance of being identified as an extreme singularity of genius. Second, Cocteau's interest, by evidence of the film, follows the primary function of art: shaping, controlling and challenging experience. Confronted by a haphazard world of reckless contingency, Cocteau the artist responds by confining the world, so it becomes manageable, explicable, contained by its design against the amorphousness of life. Cocteau offers his vision stamped indelibly with the signature of the poet.

As to whether the action in *Blood of a Poet* is inside or outside the mind of Cocteau's poet-protagonist, it is neither. The poet does not contain the world of the film—it contains him. The poet is of the world, not in it. He is composed as he composes his images around him, and his relevance to what he creates provides meaning in his life: he plays at what it means to be. *Blood of a Poet,* then, for Cocteau, is more an example of lyrical realism than a surreal succession of random images (succession negates randomness once the order is fixed in the print of the film). The poet kills the object as he kills himself, to reconstitute the object as art and himself as artist. So Cocteau, a victim of his own possibility, retreats into a world where even he is transformed by continuity, where his choices are fixed, conjoined from image to image. Heidegger reminds us that the origin of art is art; that art is work. Work is process. Process is method. Method is control. Control is what the artist seeks, a release from contingency. There is no freedom in art. And it is from freedom that Cocteau, like Lynch, flees. But what differentiates Cocteau from Lynch is that where Cocteau is ironically sentimental, Lynch is just sentimental.

The flight from freedom leads the artist back to himself, back to the often distressful murder-suicide of an artist in his object: he destroys the object of his desire as its image becomes both the artist's sentimental tragedy and his ridiculous pose. Romantically, the poet bleeds (as other martyrs have bled before him) so that we may follow him home through the snow to ourselves. Cocteau, while constructing this drama for his poet, displaces himself, and his resurrection is as plastic as the death mask of the poet. His "blood," throughout the film, foregrounds the process of film making, until the process is the meaning, and the blood of the poet spilled is the "cold blood" of an artist who perfects the ability to exploit even himself.

Self-exploitation is the obvious modus operandi of any work entitled *Lynch on Lynch,* and Rodley argues persuasively that Lynch's greatest resource is "an unusual willingness and ability to access his own inner life[,] ... which he brings ... to the screen" (Lynch ix). But what is missing from Rodley's appraisal is Lynch's Abrahamic, apocalyptic judgments passed against the wicked. Lynch has been looking for a cinematic messiah ever since *Six Figures Getting Sick.* And when Lynch the self-righteous director wags his celluloid finger, no matter how bizarre the context, Lynch the man reveals himself as more Cooper than Kyle.

In their *The Pocketbook Essential David Lynch,* Michelle Le Blanc and Colin Odell align Lynch firmly in the Surrealists' camp. They compare his films to "Dali's paintings" (9) and label him as "America's most celebrated celluloid surrealist" (15). Even so, they acknowledge the Manichaean parameters of his moral impulse. They describe Lynch as "a big Hardy Boy at heart [and] the secrets in Lynch's worlds are always dark, fraught with danger, and survived only by those who are pure of spirit"

(9). Le Blanc and Odell also buy into the notion that "the power of Lynch's world lies with the lack of interpretation and simplification" (18). What follows this statement, incidentally, are nearly a hundred pages of interpretation and simplification.

According to Le Blanc and Odell, Lynch's early work establishes themes that have "permeated all of his films[:] ... a perpetually blissful 1950s with dark undercurrents of fear" (15). *Eraserhead* is "a dreamlike indication that he [Henry] should have used a rubber" (28). *Dune* delves into "the nature of dreaming" (37). *Blue Velvet* "perfectly merged the normal with the abnormal" (40). *Twin Peaks* allows Lynch to explore "goodness and sickness" (49). *Wild at Heart* offers "hope ... in a fairy tale" (57). *Twin Peaks: Fire Walk with Me* contrasts "sin and decline with the supernatural and symbolic" (65). *Lost Highway* uncorks, in the persona of Mr. Eddy, "revelations of his depravity" (71). In *The Straight Story*, the moral predicament is reduced to "Alvin's 'straightness' [being] in jeopardy the closer he gets to Wisconsin" (77).

But as reductive and cursory as it is, Le Blanc and Odell's gloss nevertheless reinforces the moral dialectic that frames Lynch's work. The most interesting comment occurs in the "So You Want to Know More?" chapter that lists resources on Lynch's life and works. The annotation describing Michel Chion's *David Lynch* claims his "book feels at times obliged to find things wrong ... because it's cool to be critical" (89). This defensiveness is not unusual among professional Lynch commentators. Rodley, for example, admits that *Wild at Heart* lacks Lynch's "usual perfect synthesis of the extremes between dark and light" (Lynch 192), but as an apologist he explains the poor critical response to that film as due to the "bizarre and often violent encounters" (192), ignoring what other critics see as a failure of artistic integrity.

At least Chion, referring to *The Grandmother* but clearly implying a recurring Lynchian motif, notes "the aggressively Manichaean logic of the script" (21). He cautions that Lynch's films resist reduction to "*a priori* interpretations" (21) and suggests that what accounts for Lynch's "disconcerting world" (21) results from a "far less simplistic treatment which imbues each image with a host of contradictory meanings" (21). While one of the few critics to recognize Lynch's Manichaean roots, Chion too readily buys into the postmodern uncanniness that Rodley celebrates, and which both writers cite as evidence of Lynch's star status among critically acclaimed auteurs.

Rodley finds *The Alphabet* inscrutable, except for a vague allusion to "pedagogical force-feeding" (Lynch 162), as "no particular immediate

connection can be drawn between the film and a particular idea or concept" (13). In apocalyptic terms, all too common in his book, Chion
writes that the film "works according to no logic we have ever encoun-
tered" (14). He calls this general dilemma in Lynch's work "the Lynchian
problematic" (14). In *The Grandmother* this "cosmic lyricism" (23) is manifest in "unusual cause and effect chains defying the first law of ther-
modynamics" (22).

Chion seems less baffled in discussing Lynch's short films than the
features. *Eraserhead*, for example, offers "no reference to a coded, closed,
cinematographic language" (43). He justifiably complains that certain
summaries—one concluding that "Henry Spencer represents the acme
of human misery" (30)—are all too simple. Certainly this is true. But it
is equally disingenuous to suggest, as Chion does, that the film is ultimately indecipherable. Chion goes out of his way to resist a grounded
reading. He recognizes Gnostic virtues in elliptic semiotics, as if Lynch
were a cabalist who speaks in codes understood only by an initiated few.

His approach is not unlike the Renaissance focus on genius, especially in the work of biographers like Vasari, whose cultish historical
record of Michelangelo, written while the painter was still alive, set the
standard for creating artists as men divinely inspired. Likewise, since the
early nineteenth century identifying genius is a tradition in American
belles lettres. John Stafford neatly describes this sensibility as " ... "a familiar 'Romantic' theory of poetry. They shifted the approach to poetry from
the text of the poem to the 'maker' or 'creator' of the poem" (55). Contemporary critics split on this approach. Some, like Foucault, use historicism
to argue for a materialist, Marxist analysis of the power structures that
elevate one style, trend or artist above all others; in the other camp, a
critic like Harold Bloom argues against demystifying the charisma and
anomalous talent of certain extraordinary individuals. Chion—incongruously, given the post-structuralist methodology he himself employs—
clearly identifies with the latter, as if to explicate Lynch discredits him
and somehow diminishes his work.

Many critics accept the idea of Lynch-as-genius, underscoring his
beginnings as a painter, his coming to film through both inspiration and
flukiness, his succeeding with no formal training in film, his disavowing
cinematic influences. But the evidence for Lynch's status as film's idiot
savant is sketchy. Chion, for instance, reiterates how "Lynch always
denied being a film buff" (24), while Kaleta admits that "Lynch knows
his movie history" (13). And whereas Bloom unapologetically argues in
The Anxiety of Influence (1973) that one genius achieves status in an epic

Oedipal struggle against those who precede her, Chion and others—including Lynch himself—are adamant in their dismissal of seminal traces in Lynch's work.

Critics like Chion and Bloom favor appreciation over analysis when accounting for meaning in exceptional work—fair enough. But Chion's method is especially odd. He provides a close textual reading, but avoids definitive critical inferences, preferring to hint at rather than account for possible resolutions of image clusters and narrative sequences, which in Lynch's work are conscientiously disruptive. Chion substitutes mystification for critical insight, obscurantism for value judgments, opened-ended paradigms for psychological analysis. Given this context, it is no surprise that Chion sees the central issue in *The Elephant Man* not as "a conflict between good and bad, but between two men of different social classes" (57). He states flatly that Lynch's "vision does not bespeak any moral condemnation" (57).

Chion is closer to the mark with *Dune*, stressing, in the novel, Frank Herbert's "obsession with ecology" (65), pointing out that in Lynch's treatment the fact that "religion is an invention to manipulate the masses … is passed over in silence" (67). But he fails to acknowledge the obvious inference. Defensive, or naïve, he claims that "we don't know Lynch's opinion" (67) on the fact that the people fighting it out—and winning—on Dune are "fanatics" (67). Then he concludes, as if to dismiss the obvious—and in my opinion the most essential element in Lynch's repertoire—by noting that "Lynch has a religious sensibility" (68). Chion, unlike other critics who willfully or systematically reject or fail to recognize it, acknowledges Lynch's religious framework, but even Chion sees this integral, core structural moral grounding as marginal, subordinate to other cinematic, thematic, or sociological concerns.

Chion laments the "number of holes" (90) in the plot of *Blue Velvet*. This confuses surface plausibility with metaphorical integrity. Chion does recognize the symbolic dualism at the heart of the film, but again he fails to flesh out the distinctive Lynchian moral absolutism that structures both the surface action and the subtext in the film. While detailing the production history of *Twin Peaks* the television series, he denotes the characters by their moral actions but never addresses Lynch's obsession with clearly delineating the battle between good and evil fought out in the ordinary, mediocre front yards of middle-class America. His focus remains on character and the formal qualities of the format, ignoring the evangelical absolutism with which Lynch shapes his episodes, and which, in subsequent productions, guest directors use as a moral guide to their contributions.

Chion's reading of *Twin Peaks: Fire Walk with Me* concentrates on the difference between the television series and the film. He links Lynch to Romanticism, and with typical hyperbole calls him "the romantic film-maker of our times" (158). He likens Lynch, as others do, to Poe, a valid comparison only as it regards the tenor of Lynch's work, not the impetus. In fact, Poe's drug- and booze-addled life and sensibility seem more akin to one of the twisted characters in a Lynch film than to Lynch's Eagle-Scout-from-Missoula ethos. Poe and Lynch certainly connect, however, in their inevitable moral obsession with the corruption of fatally chaste, beautiful young women.

Romanticism is inextricably entwined with Lynch's conservative religiosity, evident as ever in the anodyne saga *Wild at Heart.* But for Chion, the film becomes a paean to Rousseau's idiot savant, "a film of a child who sees everything in large, contrasting terms" (138). He excuses its redundant, often silly nonintegrated sequences, its gratuitous violence and clumsy voyeurism as "a return to the baroque style of his beginning" (123). Relying on terms like "rhapsodic structure" (127) and "rectilinear trajectory" (127), Chion goes out of his way to keep this careening, transcendental mess of a road movie between the ditches, ignoring the fact that without the Manichaean moral map that delivers Lula and Sailor into the good fairy's graces the film would have confirmed even more empirically "an aesthetics of phoniness and fakery" (135).

Chion claims *Wild at Heart* "disconcerted spectators by its mixture of hard-line violence and flowery innocence" (137), but it is not the images of innocence and violence that viewers object to so much as the context in which Lynch presents them. Such subtleties, however, may be lost on critics like Chion who claims, after all, without a trace of cynicism, that *Wild at Heart* "is the most beautiful love ballad which cinema has ever whispered into the night" (140).

3

Shorts

While he may be playful, Lynch is not unreadable. Even uncanny critics relax in the cushioned context of his severe non-consequentialist morality. Most apologists complain that viewing Lynch through such a narrow window of strict morality is fatally reductive. Then they cite Lynch's ambiguity, indecipherability and willful obfuscation as profound, enigmatic virtues. But even dreams have logic, a limited pool of images, a recognizable social application, and a locatable *mise-en-scène*. Intentionally ambiguous art—the very concept is ambidextrous—or true aleatory poetry, for instance, defies consistent interpretation. Given no internal logic, the poems are more free even than nature: the structure is motiveless, essentially non-teleological, so it confabulates beyond will.

But Lynch, for all his crawfishing, is more Calvin than Aquinas, showing little interest in intellectual subtleties. He prefers the straightforward clarity of a literalist, unambiguous in his judgments about obligations and values. In his earliest, instinctual style—in *Six Figures Getting Sick* (1967), *The Alphabet* (1968) and *The Grandmother* (1970)—Lynch is coming to terms with his medium while staking out ontological parameters and psychological quirks; testing, refining his signature. In the full-length films, this visceral aesthetic is replaced by a heavily mannered style that intrudes on the naturalism of the stories. Lynch's thumbprint is so indelible and intrusive that it is the lack of it that gives *The Straight Story* (a pun in this context) a freshness and honesty lacking in other work where his claustrophobic style often stifles by its contrivance. His characters, playing at the other edge of his dialectic, frequently find themselves trapped in one of Lynch's hyper-rational paradigms: find salvation in your intuition or

suffer the wrath of cosmic-logic. Inevitably, in Lynch's tightfisted aesthetic, his characters discover, as Kierkegaard did, that reason can be fatal.
Nietzsche, in his critique of Socrates, complains, "in all productive
men it is instinct that is the creative-affirmative force, and consciousness
acts critically and dissuasively" (Nietzsche, "The Birth of Tragedy" 88).
Lynch, in his early work, expresses this conflict with an acute sense of
immediacy, the honest confessions of an anti-logician reacting to the necessary collision between will and form, recognizing that the nature of the
aesthetic truth of art is to massage the gruesome and terrifying lynch-
pin between instinct and awareness. Ironically, once Lynch exorcises, as
it were, the demons of his own emergence as an artist, from the urge to
the act, from impulse to structuring, he wholly embraces a regulating,
dissuasive consciousness, and devolves into a Socratic type, the kind for
whom, according to Nietzsche, "instinct becomes the critic" (88).

In one reading, then, *Six Figures Getting Sick* is a fairly straightforward observation, as in "it makes me sick," a snide comment on the formal educational process many artists find stifling. A Romantic Idealist like
Lynch naturally rejects authority, projecting—literally, in this case—his
response, in a sophomoric moment, onto himself. (The figures are actual
molds of Lynch's head.) But in Lynch's rendering, getting sick is a form of
transcendental condemnation. The impulse to retch at the sheer physical-
ity of the world, to reject the fall from the ideal into the flesh, echoes Sartre's
Cartesian model in *Nausea* (1938): "Existentialism is a recoil from rationalism" (Carruth vii). Reason stands in opposition to the unconscious "hidden fears within the self" (viii). The object of Lynch's condemnation matters
less than his response: outrage and disgust at the fixity—the stasis—the
sheer plasticness of art. The three sculpted figures express dismay at their
emergence, covering their eyes in shame and disgust, as if guilty of violating the flatness of the 6 × 8 white resin screen. Three more animated
figures are projected onto the screen, adding balance and symmetry. They
join the others in an orgy of vomit that, incidentally, resembles the patented,
cliché streaks of drip painting commonly associated with Abstract Expres-
sionist art. The words "look" and "sick" flash though the repeated series.

Nochimson reads the film semiotically, as a metalinguistic "image
of the unstoppable narrative compulsion" (149). But language—meaning—purchased at the expense of instinct is a theme Lynch works intuitively. *Six Figures Getting Sick* is a violent purgation. What gets puked
up is structural necessity, a rejection of the very continuity he must cod-
ify to illustrate the mysterious madness of being in the world.

The Socratic paradox in *The Alphabet* is even more overt. A young

The mixed-media performance piece *Six Figures Getting Sick* (1967) illustrates Lynch's early commitment to a moral framework. As if purging themselves of guilt for emerging from the instinctual into the symbolic, from the intuitive into the conceptual, the figures reject individuation at the expense of purity and plenitude. They express revulsion at their projection out of what Hegel calls "the unbroken immediacy of naïve psychical life" (qtd. in Fieser and Lilleard 563). (Photograph: Absurda.)

girl is terrorized by the fundamental structural foundation of conceptual knowledge. Her fear is for the loss of her primal, dissolvent desire. In *The Grandmother*, a young boy finds comfort in the primitive, non-verbal, organic presence of his grandmother, retreating from the demands and expectations required for coherent self-presentation. These early films project Lynch's innate anti-intellectualism, that of a crude elitist who pretends to toe the populist, reactionary line. Even Alexander, who otherwise promotes Lynch as a genius (4) and tends to appropriate Lynch's apocalyptic language and biblical references, admits Lynch "avoids self-analysis and intellectualizing" (2). Alexander, seemingly sympathetic to Lynch's point of view, endorses Toynbee's lament for "'the children of a post-Christian world'" (179) and praises Lynch for giving us "traditional moral tales in post-modern apparel" (180).

This is exactly the critical attitude that, instead of a formal anti-intellectualism, allows for a Dionysian rage against the movement from a fluid, undifferentiated world of formlessness and pure will into the representative world of individuation, distinctness and form. In *The Birth of Tragedy*, Nietzsche identifies this movement from the undifferentiated into the symbolic as a process by which "the Apollonian power erupts to restore the almost shattered individual with the healing balm of blissful illusion" (127). The primal self "discharges itself in an Apollonian world of images" (65). The enticing comfort of intoxication—that childish withdrawal—is ultimately dangerous, and because an actual return is impossible, the child (or artist) learns to appropriate an "Apollonian illusion whose influence aims to deliver us from the Dionysian flood and excess" (129).

Controlling this transformation from the dissolute collective-imaginative to the contrived image-of-self is a paradox: emergence both creates and destroys, forcing a synthesis resolved only by representation. The journey into articulation is also a movement into the inauthentic. It is that loss of authenticity that Lynch's early work expresses best. But this emergence into *logos* is also an irreversible entry into a system of prohibition, the superstructure of power relations, reinforced by what Nietzsche calls "linguistic legislation" ("On Truth and Lie" 44) designed to disrupt, limit and control the impulse of pure will. It is this violent eruption of the subject from the formless, inexpressible, primordial experience of plenitude into the counterintuitive world of semiotic and etymological exteriority that Lynch's early work so acutely records.

These early films also reflect Lynch's romantic resistance to the idea that reality is linguistic, and his images seem nothing less than a portrait of the artist's guilt for (dis)locating the self in metaphor. But for an artist, this process is inevitable. Nietzsche is clearly speaking of this phenomenon when he notes that "[t]he intellect, as a means for the preservation of the individual, unfolds its chief powers in simulation" ("On Truth and Lie" 45). Lynch's ontological predicament, however, has less to do with a desire to create art that restores life to its subject than it does with shifting the focus from descriptive to prescriptive aesthetics.

The Alphabet may be the most graphic and artistically successful of Lynch's attempts to satisfy this theme. It opens with two women dreaming, one a pre-pubescent girl, the other a mature young woman. The child has not yet assimilated the easy rhythm of the alphabet. She lies in bed, a white figure against a black background—a clear image of childhood purity and innocence threatened by the scary adult world of shadows and darkness just beyond the safety of her bed. She hears only the merciless chant of children reciting by rote the ABCs. The effect is stifling, a threatening repetition of perfunctory learning that grates like an novice pianist practicing scales. More complex but no less intense, the young woman is confident and stylish in chic sunglasses. In her dream, she animates language into an operatic performance, played out on a stage illuminated by a small orange sun framed in the top left corner. The letters are light and fun. They fall from the sky, or rise in balloons. But even her highly performative language cannot keep her sensual will from driving through in explicit sexual imagery: the woman's sumptuous, hungry red mouth and lascivious tongue, shot from behind a circular grille like a moral coda to her animated dream. Girls grow into women, menstruate, have sex, and give birth. Lynch catalogs this metamorphosis by using images of memory and desire. An egg falls up a fallopian tube. A block-letter A grows a tubular appendage and delivers two lowercase (baby) A's to the sound of an infant crying. A transgendered figure gyrates through a wrenching set of transformations—first penile and masculine, then butchered into a female form—until, in one image, a vaginal heart-like shape metamorphoses into an orifice that spurts blood and lowercase letters into the head of the figure, an action that terrifies the young girl—her fearful visage intercut into the sequence—as the figure suddenly bleeds from the eyes and disintegrates.

Lynch depicts the violence of the young girl's response in images of sex, blood, conception, and motherhood, with a baby's incessant crying in the background. His image of the Madonna is a fragmented, glued-together, nursing psychological wreck. The warning, "Please remember you are dealing with a human form," delivered in a close-up of a distorted face, sounds like Lynch's notes to himself as he incorporates more film into his animation. But the statement also indicates a collision between the instinctual sensual life and the abstract logic-bound conceptual world of self-representation, where culture is no remedy for the demands of femininity and nature terrifies even those for whom the alphabet is easy. After her Lacanian mirror-phase freak-out, the young girl settles into an eerie, rhythmic recitation of the ABCs. She grabs at letters like butterflies just out of reach, but she could just as well be fending off threatening letters swooping in on her like vampire bats, another image of the twin demons haunting Lynch's work: desire and fear, expressing the lure of sexuality and the terror of adulthood. As if resigned to the fact that her move into articulation is a move away from authenticity, she squeezes out her last line, "Tell me what you think of me." It is an existential accusation, and the truth of this, as so often in Lynch, makes her sick. Lynch illustrates her inevitable violation, from innocence into experience, from naïveté to knowledge, by having her spew red on the white sheets of her dreams.

Less mythopoeic than Nietzsche's Apollonian/Dionysian split in the self, Lacan in his essay on the "mirror stage" writes, "the *I* is precip- itated in a primordial form, before it is objectified in the dialectic of identification with the other, and language restores to it, in the univer- sal, its function as subject" (503). Spivak also describes the project of self-construction as being preconditioned by language:

> We know no world that is not organized as a language, we operate with no other consciousness but one structured as a language—languages that we cannot possess, for we are operated by those languages as well. The category of language, then, embraces the categories of world and consciousness even as they determine it [637].

This "dialectic that decisively projects the individual into history" (Lacan 505) thrusts the individual into moral consciousness as well, and it is here that Lynch most acutely illustrates the terrifying recognition of the sub- ject—in this case, the young girl—suddenly confronting not only the traumatic future travails of adulthood but the awesome responsibility of entering the collective social ethos as well. Laura Mulvey addresses this phenomenon in "Visual Pleasure and Narrative Cinema":

> Either she must gracefully give way to the word, the Name of the Father and the Law, or else struggle[,] ... tied to her place as bearer of mean- ing, not maker of meaning[,] ... to fight the unconscious structured like a language ... [747].

In this context, *The Alphabet* exemplifies Lynch's obsession with duty and moral authority. It reveals an essential struggle with the transfor- mational process of art—from impulse to concept, from concept to arti- fact—and a resistance to the critical judgments that follow. This conflict between pre-Oedipal urgency and aesthetic accountability provides a strict Zoroastrian metaphysics that form the metacinematic, overriding structural framework Lynch uses to shape his work.

In *The Alphabet,* and to some degree in *Six Figures Getting Sick,* Lynch illustrates how the constitutive aspect of language imposes a precondi- tioned moral agency on its subject that is incompatible with pure essence. Lynch explores a character's (and the artist's) movement from intuition into logic, graphically depicting how this transition from nature into culture also implies a shift from undifferentiated urges into a moral order, into that legitimatizing system that rewards and punishes, distinguishes good from bad and right from wrong in materialistic terms. Intuition connotes purity, therefore virtue; concepts and formal education are limiting and dispiriting, so represent evil.

In his first two films, Lynch sets up this dialectic as an effective framing device for his imagery, but *The Grandmother* reflects a shift in both his aesthetics and his philosophy. The boy's futility in resisting assimilation into the brutal realities of adulthood from the imaginative carefree world of childhood parallel Lynch's own dilemma as an artist. Having struck, as it were, a bargain with the devil—self-consciously choosing to join the myth-making process of signifying, demarcating and aligning images with value judgments—Lynch reverses his earlier moral position. No longer is the myth-making individuating world of signification the enemy of all that is pure and good. Nature, intuition and plenitude, which in *Six Figures Getting Sick* and *The Alphabet* are depicted as psychic sanctuaries from which separation implies corruption, in *The Grandmother* become the dark inner forces of madness and unchecked desire that drive Baron Harkonnen and Frank Booth. The fear of the animal will—at least the way Lynch portrays it in the actions of BOB and the parents in *The Grandmother*—govern both Lynch's idea of goodness (securely anchored in restraint, balance, guilt and remorse) and his moral attitude towards his subjects. The celebration of Dionysian exuberance is not just transmogrified but suppressed by strict Apollonian objectification. *The Grandmother* is a swan song to innocence, as much for the boy as for Lynch, both having realized the inevitability of positing a semiotic construct in place of the authentic pre-adult self.

The narrative is constructed of animated scenes intercut with film. The animated sequences are safe havens for the boy, where he can pursue his childish fantasies. The filmed sections are ugly and unnerving. The implication is that art is a place of retreat, a sanctuary from the harsh realities of adulthood. For Lynch the artist animation, like painting, is totally within his control, whereas shooting scenes in film is collaborative—working with actors, cinematographers, lights, sets, etc.—and in this sense Lynch is identified with the boy in the film, torn between the private person and the social, collective self.

The film opens with a periscope rising up from the depths of a mysterious subterranean world, bisecting and conjoining the bifurcated landscape and the childish rendition of waves on the surface of a choppy sea. The periscope turns into a phallic extension that ejaculates a white seminal substance into a cavity, which it then waters until a figure of a man emerges and develops like vascular pulp in a tooth, growing upward through a tunnel and connected to his source by an umbilical red tube like an astronaut's oxygen line. The periscopic progenitor repeats its action, producing this time the figure of a woman who also ascends through a tube-like cavity. Lynch is, of course, following the sequence in Genesis, the male being primary and dominant and thus opening further the gap between the brutish father and his sensitive son. The male and female figures embrace like Chagall's angels, but the innocuous child's version of conception is interrupted by film-reality: the parents' actions are cruel, instinctual and crude, their faces scarred, harsh and tortured by guilt.

But back in animation, a red and a white seed combine in yet a third cavity, mixing like blood and milk to produce a child. Unlike his parents, whose animated figures balance themselves with outstretched arms, the child, as he emerges, topples over. His birth sequence, like those of his parents, is initiated in animation, but repeated in highly stylized film sequences. Lynch again invokes an innate fear of the adult world, where decisions have consequences and responsibility boomerangs back to the self; but on another level, less existential but maybe more structural, he is still coming to terms with his emergence as an artist, from art to film, played out in the opening sequence as it will be again in *Eraserhead*. This contrast of the imaginative, animated sequences and the conscience-laden filmic world of Lynch's surrealistic *cinéma vérité* illustrates the child's desire for transcendence—the same sort of escape Henry wants in *Eraserhead*, which is, basically, abnegation.

Instead of the palatable, mitigated world of the boy's imagination—where sperm is as gentle as seed deposited in fallopian flowers, and people grow like plants, mysteriously connect and conceive children—the filmic sequences underscore a savage "real" world in which his parents' desire is reduced to scratching an itch. The dog-like humans growl and yip and root around, frenetic and grotesque. They are slobs, rude and insensitive. Emotionally distraught at the discovery of the unwanted child, the canine father attacks the boy. The child tries to roll away, but only in animation does he manage to rocket above the beating, riding skyward atop a streaming tube, rising beyond his father's blows.

The next shot is of the boy in a state of existential bewilderment, dressed demurely in his schoolboy suit and bowtie, as different from his parents as art is from life. He lives in his sterile bedroom—the only escape, it seems (besides his animated fantasies), from the violence of his uncouth, unloving, narcissistic parents. While the boy savors sporadic peace on the edge of his bed, contemplating his flowers, his parents are crawling around in a clearing, presumably looking for their misplaced newborn.

The narrative cuts to animation again, this time launching the two parental figures out of their dental silos into space outside the frame. But imaginative escape cannot insulate the boy from the filmic reality of life with his abusive parents. Self-absorbed brutes, they drink and preen, his father sloshing down booze, his mother violently tearing curlers from her hair.

Supposedly caused by his shattered emotional state (though psychologically, it is rare for emotional traumas to cause primary nocturnal enuresis), the boy is prone to episodes of bedwetting (or masturbation, a reading that does not alter the meaning of the imagery). Ashamed of his act, the boy transforms the wet spot in his bed into a beautiful sun in a cloudless summer sky. But filmic reality, in the figure of his irate father, again intercedes, and like training a puppy not to piss indoors, the father berates his son, rubbing the boy's face in the spot on the sheet. The terrified boy can only scream in muffled anger and despair. He seeks out his mother for comfort, but she gropes him lecherously. Confused and ashamed, she frenetically scratches her face, assaults the boy, then pushes him away and grovels under a table in self-disgust.

For the boy, sex, guilt and violence are inextricably mixed. Dejected and on the verge of hopelessness, he withdraws to his room, but from out of his solipsistic isolation he hears a birdcall, the soothing, nourishing noise of nature. Following the sound to the attic, he finds a bag of seeds and a new bed as white as redemption, made up with virginal sheets unsullied by his shame. He goes through the seeds until he finds the one emitting the birdcall and, convinced it is the right one, plants it in soil strategically piled up in the new bed exactly where his shame-spot is in the other. This way, just as his animated sun transforms his guilt into happiness, his watering the bed will now create goodness and comfort, not violence and humiliation. Through the power of his imagination, he can turn his shame into abundance. At a structural level, he is attempting to transform his raw filmic existence into an animated transcendent truth that might leave him perpetually in the womb of plenitude. He is literally growing a tree of life.

As the penile stump grows, the boy waters and pets it in an onanistic fantasy. As he waits for his tree to bear fruit, literally tending the entrance of the womb, peering into the mystery of the beginning of life, massaging the vaginal opening at the base of the trunk, the plant exemplifies a confluence of sexes: a phallic stump the boy strokes for pleasure and a fertile feminine birthing hole from which he hopes to create a nourishing presence. He waters the hole, fondles the branches while he

lolls in an autoerotic trance. His animated sun reappears—he is ejaculating into his bed again, but trying to reassure himself with a handy
symbol of vitality, health and goodness. But the filmic reality of the parents intercedes: his mother scratches like a cat in a litter box under the
table where she lewdly came on to the boy, and his father again smears
the boy's nose in the defiled bed. But the extraordinary tree keeps growing, more ominous as the process matures. And soon, sure enough, the
plant delivers, in a gory birth scene, a grandmother, intact, complete with
appropriate granny shoes. The boy tidies his appearance and brings her
flowers. Her love is natural, non-verbal, intuitive and unqualified. The
boy's strategy is to conjoin his organic animated fantasy world with the
cinematic reality of his life.

Yet the boy endures more savagery. The family dinner (that will
later be parodied in *Eraserhead*) is delivered as a straightforward nightmare, a rude, inarticulate feeding ritual during which the parents, obsessed
with cheap, instant gratification—smoking and boozing, gnawing at food
as unwholesome as their life—take pleasure in punishing the boy. He
retreats to the attic, to enjoy strawberries and the easy peaceful sleep of
the grandmother. But one night the parents catch him sneaking upstairs
and, denied his primal pleasure source, he lashes out in gruesome animated fury, guillotining his father, crushing his mother with a heavy
stone, then imagining anti-fertility images that end in the destruction
of his parents. Violence, it seems, breeds violence, and the more the boy
tries to escape the influence of his parents, the more he seems to assimilate their behavior. Distressed, he begins sleeping in the attic, where he
believes the grandmother exudes a genuine kindness beyond language.

But in Lynch's world, as in Genesis, the purity of life is spoiled by
desire. Soon enough, the grandmother starts demanding the boy's presence, whistling him out of his sleep. The roles are reversed: he begins
living for her instead of her living for him. When the boy and the grandmother initiate a game of intimacy, at first merely touching and spoon-
ing, it ends in a kiss of desire that leaves a carbuncular spot on the boy's
cheek. The boy senses feelings of eroticism, which he tries to convert in
the safe haven of his animated imagination to images of penile plants
and vaginal flowers (that in turn morph into the profile of a knight, his
phallic lance doubling as an erection). The plants spawn progeny that
fly away like insects, free and natural. But in the real world, the boy's
Platonic playmate has perverted his transcendental love, and with the
animated sun of his happiness waning like a fading harvest moon, the
grandmother dies in a paroxysm of noise, her tender birdcall amplified

to a shrill wail like a flat-lining EKG. The boy desperately appeals to his father, who responds with violence and stoned indifference, and to his mother, whose response is to mock him. In a graveyard, the boy finds his grandmother like weed in a field of dead grass. Even in her familiar rocking chair, she seems not to recognize him, and the truth of her death overwhelms him. He is alone, isolated and immobile, at the mercy of the world he is doomed to become a part of.

In his guilt, in his sense of imprisonment in a socially alienating world, in his desire for transcendence, and in his desperate search for beauty to assuage the stark reality of a world enmeshed in ugly violence and base obsessions, the boy in *The Grandmother* is a prototype for Henry in *Eraserhead*. In this sense, the film is a seminal work, both artistically—introducing images and sequences that would later define Lynch's signature style—and thematically—illustrating Lynch's fascination with the disturbing eruptions of unconscious urges checked by a stern, absolutist morality.

The Amputee (1973) also figures seminally in Lynch's development, as he moves from mixing animation and film collage to dealing with recognizable characters in a strict, if bizarre, realism. According to his own account, The American Film Institute wanted to try out two different black-and-white video stocks, so Lynch, offhandedly, wrote a script he shot twice to facilitate the testing (*Short Films of David Lynch*). The piece dramatically illustrates Lynch's adaptation of his early moral obsessions to straight narrative.

The action is impossibly static. After all, the subject—or more precisely the object—of the film is a double amputee sitting in an armchair smoking a cigarette and writing a letter she narrates in a disaffected voice-over. She begins in ambiguity—"This isn't what I am telling you"—as if the meaning of what she is reading is somehow outside her expression of it, an easy illustration of Lynch in his early work discounting, or at least distrusting what is, for him, a new medium. But the dramatic tension is maintained in the discrepancy between the woman's situation and her apparent indifference. She delivers her lines like a narrator in a story by Kafka—"The Metamorphosis" (1915), for instance, in which the narrator relates the most bizarre facts with a comically unsettling matter-of-fact voice. This juxtaposition of the mundane and the tragic allows Lynch to play with absurd and disturbing images while subtly satisfying his innate moral impulse. Even when the woman speaks in portentous phrases, hinting at dark motives—"she drank gin with you," "it made me sick" (a common Lynchian conceit)—her superciliousness reduces her

stories to the ludicrously empty patter of young couples stupefied by the
dating game. Yet Lynch's condemnation of her, in the person of the nurse,
is clear. He abandons the job of tending to her no matter how despica-
ble or shallow she is. He denies her subjective self, so repelled by her
disfigured materiality that he is incapable of acknowledging her humanity. He judges her character by assigning values to her preferences. The
story, finally, is cheap revenge aesthetics.

Her letter—the verbal narrative—is an I-told-you-so confession, as
if her injuries somehow proved the petty viciousness of her friends and
the sitcom relationships they share. In this, she becomes a metaphor.
What she is cut off from is a sense of her own reality. She has been horribly injured—the portrait we see may well be a picture of how she represents herself, the slighted party in a jealous lover's quarrel—but no
matter how grotesque and pitiful her wounds, she persists in her superficial life, engrossed in petty relationships. Of course, this withdrawal
into the mundane may be her defense against her disfigurement. In any
case, from her narrative it seems that, no matter how unattractive she is,
she still centers her life in meaningless social engagements.

The male nurse—not coincidentally played by Lynch—first goes
about his task earnestly, carefully unwrapping the woman's stump, clean-
ing and tending to the injury with typical Lynchian hyperbole, rinsing
and swabbing and poking with gothic exaggeration. But as both her narrative and the wound seem insuperable, the nurse's sympathy fails and
he flees in disgust and frustration, unable to stem either the putrid flow
of the suppurating wound or the woman's insufferable narrative. But his
moral disapproval of the woman is clear: she is amputated from any
significance in her life beyond the inane bickering about her friends and
acquaintances. After all, her crisis is that she was accused of being a flirt.
(One of the funniest lines, given her present circumstances, is when she
claims, "I didn't flirt then, and I'm not a flirt now.") She has been reduced
to one of Beckett's immobilized clowns, animated not by cosmic angst
but by kitsch, her existential depth measured by the shallow soap-opera
into which she channels her life.

Her attitude, however, resembles Lynch's: people get what they
deserve. Lynch's judgment is harsh, and reflects more than a touch of the
Puritanism radicalized by Cotton Mather. Like Mather, Lynch's fascination with violence, sex and death did not diminish with age. His *Premonitions Following an Evil Deed* is one of forty contributions made for
a collective film project entitled *Lumiere et Compagnie* (1995). To celebrate the 100-year anniversary of the Lumiere camera, directors were

asked to shoot 52-second film segments, using the original camera, natural light, and no sound, duplicating the conditions in which the Lumiere brothers worked in the late 1890s (*Short Films of David Lynch*). Lynch's contribution is predictably macabre and judgmental.

The film consists of five "episodes" or scenes. First, three policemen in contemporary cop uniforms approach a body of a young man lying in a field. What sounds like gunshots are heard. Next, an older woman sitting on a couch turns in anticipation, as if she hears something off-camera. Then, on a sofa in a leafy bower, several young women in diaphanous gowns suddenly become interested in something in the distance. As if beckoned, one woman leaves the group. A smoky transition clears in a room where three disfigured men march past a naked woman floating in a huge glass tube. One man raps the glass with a cudgel, as if taunting the helpless victim. A fiery transition burns through to the same older woman as before on the couch again, this time sitting with a man in the room, presumably her husband. A policeman interrupts the couple and, judging from their reaction, delivers unsettling news.

Thirty years after making *Six Figures Getting Sick*, Lynch's Manichaean vision is still intact. More poetic than *Twin Peaks*, *Premonitions Following an Evil Deed* nevertheless revisits identical themes—which might, by now, qualify as obsessions. The sexually curious are tempted into vice. The wicked are punished. Wayward children bring grief to their parents. And though the linear narrative is disrupted, the tale is familiar. In the opening and closing scenes, tragedy connects the policemen and the parents—a common occurrence in any community. But the controlling contrast is immediately established between the rational, conscious moral order—the pious parents and the dutiful police—and the irrational excess of desire that leads to suffering and death. The mother's concern is realized in the third scene, where whatever has sparked the sexually provocative girl turns to nightmare in the next scene, the least oblique, most graphic, and arguably the least effective. The image of the woman encased in glass and clearly being abused in some sort of laboratory setting is disturbing, but the devilish figures are merely comical and undercut any uneasiness the scene might otherwise evoke. The operative cliché seems to be "where there's smoke there's fire," but if the scene depicts hell, it also represents the irrational urges beyond explanation that damn the girl to eternal suffering and the parents to a life of grief, remorse and guilt.

The Reverend Arthur Dimmesdale could not have delivered a more effective sermon.

Though *Industrial Symphony No. 1: The Dream of the Brokenhearted* (1990) was conceived as a performance piece by Lynch and Angelo Badalamenti, and staged at the Brooklyn Academy of Music in 1989, it reads like a live performance video after Lynch manipulated the tape with overlapping images and multiple camera angles. The familiarity results not from the faces alone (Laura Dern, Nicolas Cage, Michael J. Anderson and Julee Cruise) or the situation: a lovesick woman expressing a psychological profile after her boyfriend breaks up with her.

But the unmistakable moral structure guarantees a Lynch production.

Oddly, the shape of the piece seems less severe than the hard-core fundamentalism governing Lynch's other films. Structurally, and morally, the film operates not through a puritanical ethos but through Schopenhauer's more refined aesthetics. For Schopenhauer, to perceive—that is, to be aware of consciousness—is to interfere with, or disrupt, the impersonal nature of the will. But music returns us to the unity of the intuitive self.

> Everywhere music expresses only the quintessence of life and of its events, never these themselves.... It is just this universality that belongs uniquely to music[,] ... that gives it that high value as the panacea of all our sorrows [261–262].

In *Industrial Symphony*, Lynch's affinity with Schopenhauer is implicit, and promises a mitigating escape for the woman withdrawing from the phenomenal world.

But the core of Lynch's construction is solidly Calvinistic. The Neo-Platonism he employs, diametrically opposing the mind and soul with the physical and sensual, allows Cruise to represent the universally divine essence of love expressed through music, while the others below her embody the dirt-level, genital, graphic, dangerous itch of desire—images reminiscent of the mechanized depictions of evil in *Eraserhead, The Elephant Man, Premonitions Following an Evil Deed* and *Dune*.

As *Industrial Symphony* takes shape, no matter how extravagant the scene, the frame is familiar. Like the Puritans, Lynch's obsession with sex and guilt, desire and damnation serves as structural necessity. The frame of the piece, finally, relies as much on an unreformed, Calvinistic dyadic moral coding as on the staging, lighting, props and music.

Lynch's moral reductionism demands a certain form for the action: an Augustinian treatment of the two sides to love: the ethereal, uplifting, floating sensation of freedom, bounty and plenitude, and the compulsive, body-bound, instinctual drives of Schopenhauer's blind beast. The dreamself of The Heartbroken Woman tries to maintain a flight of serenity—literally, above it all—while beneath her the vulgar sensual business of the body is exercised by a panoply of peculiar characters: a topless woman, men with searchlights, a midget, an effigy of a tortured animal, other bizarre or banal players and events. Imaging purity, Lynch presents Julee Cruise as The Heartbroken Woman in a white dress, whispering, crooning, her voice a balm of soft sorrow. In stark contrast, Lynch melds shots of Cruise in a virginal aura, singing of possibilities and temptation, with a half-naked woman ranging below her, animal-like, through a maze of bars.

The opening sequence—depicting a phone call during which a man ends a romantic relationship with a woman—provides the exterior context, the motive for the woman's sorrow. That his reason—"It's just us I can't handle"—is so ambiguous only adds to her confusion. The rest of the piece draws the story inside, presenting objective images of the woman's subjective reaction, with no pretense of narrative order. The Heartbroken Woman first appears, ethereal, among the derelict images of her memory, where men tumble free but the topless woman seems trapped as she crawls through the endless tangle of bars. The Heartbroken Woman floats, as in a dream, above her pain, while below her Lynch presents a series of sexual images and raucous scenes expressing raw libido. The topless woman, her naked honesty contrasting with the fully clothed guile of the men in hardhats, balaclavas and flashlights, ends up humping an abandoned car. Then she oozes through the broken-out rear window, her bare legs dangling in the air. A midget sawing wood explicitly replicates sex, methodically thrusting his saw in and out between the splayed brackets holding the log. While The Heartbroken Woman continues to float above the tension, the midget is frightened off by the men with lights, only to return with his own spotlight which he shines on a huge deer-like creature, its antlers like a devil's horns, parading on stilts in a ritualistic fertility dance, a stark image of bestial fecundity and sacrifice. Then, as the topless woman races across the stage in a splash of frenetic lighting, The Heartbroken Woman collapses to the ground, only to be stuffed by the men wearing hardhats into the trunk of the abandoned car. Her mobility arrested, her transcendental aloofness interrupted, she finds herself in the world of pain again, reminded of her plight by the midget who takes the stage to tell the story of "a sad dream … the dream of the brokenhearted." He recites verbatim the opening dialog while a woman in a black dress masturbates in frustration and sensual agony. In a parody of seventies mood music (e.g., the extended prologue by Isaac Hayes in his version of "By the Time I Get to Phoenix") the midget recalls the situation that led the woman to be imprisoned in a performance of her emotional trauma. He ends his recitation with a significantly brutal, blunt and matter-of-fact "click." But it is the finality of that "click" that resurrects The Heartbroken Woman. She emerges from the trunk of the car and launches into another song. This time her image is projected from three television sets rolled onto the stage. Ingénues in white prom dresses sashay around her images. Tranquility is restored— temporarily. After a moment's respite, pregnant with hope, an air-raid siren sounds. Chaos returns as a pair of model airplanes dive-bomb the stage, releasing an army of dolls that descend like paratroopers. The violent industrial nightmare of searchlights and the noise of machine guns resumes, but The Brokenhearted Woman, through music, again rises above the madness, restoring order to the confusion as she whispers her final song, voice fragile as crystal.

4

Features

Lynch's ethical framework is even more apparent in his features than in his short films. The cryptically misogynistic *Eraserhead* (1976), posing as a comically bleak satirical hybrid of surrealism and *cinéma vérité*, is actually a heavy-handed morality play about the dangers of pre-marital sex, unwanted pregnancy, mismatched marriage, and the economic and spiritual squalor of contemporary life in a wasteland of urban America. The tone is bleak, the images barren and mechanical, the universe a sterile, metallic place of suffering and isolation. The film is divided into eight chapter-like units, sandwiched between a prologue and an epilogue, that narrate the marriage-by-necessity of Henry, a printer's assistant, to Mary, his former girlfriend, who gives birth to a chicken-like creature—the product of their "illegitimate" intimacy and an image of their sin, their guilt, their punishment. The film is also the story of Henry's impotent desire for transcendence over his unrelenting hopelessness and harsh poverty.

The prologue resembles the opening of *The Elephant Man* (1980), especially in the blending of a static presence with an active past: the way, for instance, background action determining the fate of a character develops outside the character's consciousness but maintains a subjective point of view—in this case, Henry's. In the opening sequence of *The Elephant Man*, the story of Merrick's mother's mauling by the elephants—the reason for his disfigurement and obsession with conventional beauty—is presented with a photograph as the only visual. In *Eraserhead*, Henry— at least a projected effigy of him—lies horizontal across the screen with a spherical object—less like a planet than a cancerous tumor—superimposed,

as if "in his mind." Henry's entranced supine position implies disorien-
tation, a dream context rich with Freud's ideas on artists and daydreaming. The figure—Henry—floats off, and the camera moves in on
the sphere. Its smooth surface in extreme close-up is pitted and forbid-
ding, more malignant than before. The point of Lynch's frequent micro-
scopic zooming in, of course, is to demonstrate how the most innocuous
object can become weighted, by close scrutiny, with moral significance.
As the camera slips through a portal—another birth hole—The Man in
the Planet gazes out a dark window like an abandoned artist surveying
the field of his creation.

The beginning sequence extends the pre-birth motif as an embry-
onic egg and umbilical cord float out of Henry's mouth, implying the
implanting of conscience—a theme carried over from *The Alphabet* and
The Grandmother. In a fit of inception, The Man in the Planet, the God-
like creator/artist, painfully pulls some levers. The fetus floats away, putting things in motion—the characters *and* the moral test. What appears
to be a ragged gash with a bright light emanating from within reveals
itself, when the fetus plops into it, as a vaginal orifice of muck, spoiling
the image—or, at least, the expectation of light, of passage. The implanting of the image is graphically clear: transcendence for Lynch is not
ethereal. Characters must submerge. No one just flies off into the ether.
The image announces the birth of Henry's physical child as much as the
beginning of Lynch's narrative chain, and as the camera erupts through
another cavity, the first sequence begins: Henry on his way home from
work to begin his vacation.

The shot is close and tight. Henry's face fills the screen with a look
of resigned apprehension. But when he walks away, along the vector of
linear perspective, he is steadily diminished until he disappears in the
vanishing point between two huge sections of blank steel and concrete.
The landscape is dehumanizing, utterly unnatural. The effect is both
haunting and comical as the clown-like figure of Henry is tracked through
a sterile industrial neighborhood, made more pathetic when he plays like
a child on scattered mounds of waste. The pace is frustratingly slow, the
images putrid, the sound gratingly harsh. The anonymous power producers in the underbelly of Victorian prosperity that Lynch introduces
in *The Elephant Man* are not in the building in *Eraserhead*. The dystopia
is not historic. Henry's moral dilemma is contemporary.

Henry crosses in front of bombed-out–looking tenements bathed in
filth, dully animated by oppressive, monotonous industrial sounds. Irri-
tating noises punctuate extended silences. The moonscape is efflorescent

with a visible stench. Then Henry literally "steps in it" when he blunders into a puddle. His goofiness and his angst-ridden humanity immediately evoke viewer sympathy, in spite of his bizarre appearance. But Lynch remains ambivalent. For him, Henry represents more than he lives, and by moving the narrative toward interiority—the same technique he uses in *Blue Velvet*, the camera spiraling in and out of ears— Lynch frees himself from the expectations of naturalism and uses his own brand of surrealistic logic to construct Bible stories no less shocking than a sermon by Jonathon Edwards on a cruel winter Sunday morning in Salem.

The lobby of Henry's apartment building is a prototype for many Lynch interiors, especially The Red Room and Dorothy Vallens' apartment: seedy and kitschy without the metaphysics. Henry's interminable delay in the trashy elevator builds anxiety until, as he is about to enter his room, the beautiful girl across the hall tells him that Mary called and expects him for dinner. Lynch here sets up a typical dyad: the blonde "good" Mary (her name no coincidence) and the dark voluptuous "bad" woman across the hall introduce another prototype: Sandy Williams and Dorothy Vallens, Lula Pace Fortune and Perdita Durango, Diane/Betty and Rita/Camilla. Mary lives at home and has, in her fashion, strong family ties. The brunette is alone, independent and aggressive. She asks Henry the one question he cannot answer. "Are you Henry?"

This bit of dialog also sets up the central conflict: Henry's situation with Mary. Henry is obviously attracted to the brunette, but he is afraid, too, of her overt sexuality. He acts from temptation, in both his instinctual desire and his conditioned aversion, like the child in Kierkegaard's description of dread and freedom.

> If we observe children, we find this dread more definitely indicated as a seeking after adventure, a thirst for the prodigious, the mysterious.... This dread belongs to the child so essentially that it cannot do without it; even though it alarms him, it captivates him nonetheless by its sweet feeling of apprehension ["Dread and Freedom" 102].

Like Camus' Meursault, Henry is both innocent and guilty. In Kierkegaard's view, "he who through dread becomes guilty is innocent, for it was not he himself but dread ... which laid hold of him" (102).

Henry confronts his potential, and shrinks back. Guileless, without affectation, he is disarmed by his own honesty. As ashamed of his desire as he is of his repression, he merely speaks to the woman briefly before he enters his claustrophobic apartment. In the sepulchre of his room, his Beckettian isolation and stasis is complete: he is walled in, more inoculated than withdrawn. The view from his window is filled with bricks. The lights he turns on do not clarify; they create a spooky aura of uncertainty. The scratchy Fats Waller record on his archaic phonograph, which should be reassuring, is disconcerting. But when he lies in bed, staring past his wet sock into the depths of the radiator, he senses something—an imaginary ideal, it turns out, offering, if not salvation, then a respite from the privations of his life. In Lynch's world, salvation must be earned through suffering, and Henry now begins his moral test. The wallet-size photograph of Mary he finds while tossing pennies into a bowl of water in his top drawer is torn—one half her body, the other her head—signifying his rift with her, but also conjuring the Cartesian problems of psychophysical dualism, free will, guilt and determinism— the very existential angst that drives Henry's desire for an "eraser head." He reads the back of the photograph, as if whatever empirical data written there—a date, a location, an epitaph—might provide a clue to his phenomenological predicament.

The next shot transforms the static portrait of Mary from the photograph into the living image now framed in the window of her front door, anxiously peering out for Henry. This devolution from the ideal— the photograph—to the actual—Mary in the flesh—begins the second sequence, a parody of "meeting the folks." Henry traverses more barren terrain—empty lots, desolate railroad tracks, dimly lit alleys that recall Eliot's "Streets that follow like a tedious argument/Of insidious intent" ("Prufrock" 3). He is constantly assaulted by abrasive sounds, dogs barking, pressurized steam emissions. When he arrives at Mary's house, she is back in the window waiting for him. Though she appears meek, she is immediately antagonistic. Neither seems pleased to see the other, but Henry looks more apprehensive than peeved. Mary's "Come on in" sounds ominously resigned.

The family is dissociated; each member seems to occupy a separate reality. Mary's mother is austere, businesslike and inquisitorial. When Mary has a nervous fit, her mother roughly combs her daughter's hair until she recovers. Mary's father introduces himself as a plumber and then launches into a tirade drowned out by ever-increasing noise. Even the cuckoo clock expires in a garbled whine. The grandmother, hidden in the kitchen, is a mere puppet beyond comprehension, but Mary's mother, determined to include the catatonic old woman in the ritual food preparation, holds the salad tongs in her hands and goes through the motions of tossing the salad while the grandmother stares incoherently, smoking a cigarette.

Lynch amplifies the awkward, inevitable first encounter between the boyfriend and his girlfriend's parents with a series of image clusters designed symbolically to highlight Henry's fears—images of birth, lust, and guilt—turning the mundane into an outrageous nightmare. The tension literally pops light bulbs, and the severe images of disease, age, and youthful panic underscore the absurdity of the ordinary. Puppies vociferously suckle their mother. The father tells war stories about his paralyzed arm, complaining that he "can't feel a thing," and asks Henry to carve the man-made chickens he cooked for dinner. On the spot, and understandably self-conscious, Henry asks if he should cut them up the same as "regular chickens," but there is nothing regular about them: they raise their legs, obscenely gesturing and bleeding. Mary's mother builds her disgust into a cry of despair and flees the room. Mary follows, leaving Henry to indulge her father's deafening silence and his weak attempt at platitudinous conversation. When Mary's mother returns, she corners Henry and asks if he and Mary had "sexual intercourse." Henry evades the question. Mary's mother then threatens him and plays out an aching lust, slobbering and rubbing herself on him. When Mary interrupts, her mother tells Henry that Mary has had a premature baby (actually, no one is yet sure if it is a baby) and that Henry has no recourse but to marry her. She says, "You're the father," but his response is again evasive. "That's impossible," he says, his ensuing nosebleed only the beginning of his suffering.

The point of this absurdity, as Henry's understandable discomfort when faced with the unrelentingly bizarre behavior of Mary's family builds toward his humiliating nasal hemorrhage, besides good fun, is to establish sympathy for Henry. Henry may not be the father of Mary's child, yet he accepts responsibility. He gives it, as they say, a good shot. Mary, after all, is the one who abandons the baby. But the moral test is now in place: their alleged illicit sex has produced its punishment, a baby as ugly as the sin itself. The story operates on its surface as a strict puritanical cautionary tale of sin and retribution, berating wayward citizens about the dire consequences of abnegating responsibility; but Lynch's point of view is ambiguous, mainly because he constantly stacks the moral deck in Henry's favor while preparing him for an unspeakable crime. The subtext of the morality tale is critical: Lynch is clearly condemning Henry's weakness for love disguised as lust, but he also mocks the strident rigidity of a self-righteous ethical system that forces two people into such extreme penance for a crime that hardly merits the punishment. Lynch's satirical barbs are directed as much at the judgmental world that persecutes its victims for their indiscretions as they are at Henry, the defeated idealist caught in a vulgar, unforgiving, Darwinian world. Henry's absurdity is merely the state of being human. Given this moral context, their "baby," like Hawthorne's scarlet letter, is a reminder of guilt, the perceived grossness of their transgression—extramarital sex, birth out of wedlock. But the grotesque creature also serves as Lynch's image for the violent inequity of circumstantial retribution. This moral ambiguity, which *Eraserhead* shares with *The Elephant Man*, sets both films off from the rest of Lynch's work.

The third sequence—Lynch's portrait of married life with child—becomes a stern test of the couple's spirit, manifest in their attempts to normalize their meaningless relationship. Mary, more dutifully curious than loving, attempts to feed the baby, but it keeps spitting up the food and whining constantly. Meanwhile, Henry has ordered an IUD, but he is too self-conscious to approach Mary about using it. He comes home to this domestic hell, lies on the bed feigning interest in Mary's struggle with the baby, and spies within the grate of the radiator a potential for an escape to another world. As the unlovable creature taunts them, their shaky marriage degenerates into squabbles, sleeplessness and tension, yet Henry still dreams of transcendence. He also develops a fascination with the IUD, and leaves it where Mary might find it. But when, from out of his pathetic, ragged blankets Henry reaches for his wife, she recoils. Desperate for sleep, she finally leaves him and goes back to her parents. Henry is left to care for the creature that now (after Henry, the paragon of conscientious fatherhood, takes its temperature) is plagued by pustules and congestion. Henry, who plays his expected role with dutiful dignity in a fatuous parody of "the doting father," sets up a vaporizer and nurses the child. "You are sick," he says, but it is a self-referential comment: caring for the unwanted—a demonstrably nonviable abomination—is a task he is morally too weak to endure.

In existential self-defense, Henry lapses into the fourth sequence: a dream of the daydreaming artist wishing for access to the transcendental world between the grates of the radiator. As his need to escape fuels his imagination, he sees a disfigured female, an entertainer. When fetuses drop onto the stage beside her, she merely squashes them and laughs—implying, perhaps, that the easy out for Henry in this situation would have been for Mary to have had an abortion. The singer is a flawed Venus in a carnival world of ready-to-wear innocence. Yet Henry cannot break through.

Instead, in the fifth sequence, he dreams that his wife comes back and, asleep in his bed, bears him fetus after fetus. But this time Henry deals with them the same way his visionary goddess does, by smashing them against the bedroom wall. As if to counter the threat of his fetus-bearing bedmate, he envisions the IUD like an animated worm winding its way promiscuously through a landscape of various holes, finally blooming into a devouring flower.

In the sixth sequence, Henry's reality is now irreversibly entwined with his dreams. After the woman from across the hall seduces Henry into a sexual liaison—they literally sink, in bed, into the mire of their lust—Henry's sins begin to multiply. First he lies. When Mary asks him on his first day home from work if there is any mail, he, self-conscious about the IUD, answers, "No." His desire drives his corruption, as Henry progresses through jealousy, selfishness, and adultery. Still, Henry wishes for expiation as he envisions his angel in the radiator—his pathetic image of redemption—singing of a heaven where "everything's all right ... you've got your good things and I've got mine."

But his guilty imagination proffers another scenario. In a fit of self-recrimination, he is put on trial in the presence of a bleeding tree of life (a larger version of the one by his beside and reminiscent of the tree of life in *The Grandmother*). Henry's head pops off, replaced by that of his child. With his conscience—literally his head—bathed in blood, Henry is flushed into the seventh sequence, his head cracking open as it falls onto a street, exposing the top of his brain. A street urchin takes it to a pencil manufacturer who uses the brain tissue to make erasers. This is Henry's dream of transcendence, to erase from his conscience the black mark of his life, where sin is not indelible and mistakes are not beyond correction.

But Lynch's ethos demands judgment, penitence and punishment. In the eighth sequence, Henry awakens again in his conditional "real-ity," alone with the child. Walled-in, lonely, his wife gone, isolated by his guilt, incapable of attaining the solace of a world he can only imagine, he becomes obsessed with the woman across the hall, spying on her through his keyhole as she returns to her room with a lecherous stranger. Deluded, he senses the mocking laughter of the child, and blaming the baby instead of himself for his misfortune, he murders it—the terror of his deed matching the horror of the imagery—until eraser flakes fly from his hair, the egg cracks, and his sin against humanity—infanticide—delivers him the only transcendence he deserves. A heavenly chorus sings through a blinding white light as Henry embraces the carnival angel of easy answers. Lessons learned, the godlike figure shuts off the machine and the film is over.

Henry is the boy from *The Grandmother* now active in the adult world of responsibility and guilt he could not avoid entering. The contrast between the innocent child's fear of the future and Henry's realization of it is best illustrated in Lynch's approach to sex. In *The Grandmother*, the child's masturbatory fantasy counters the procreative sex of his bestial parents, whose careless indulgence—their coupling ostensibly motivated either by an instinctual drive to propogate the species or a selfish act of carnal gratification—results in his isolated, insufferable existence. Masturbation, of course, is safe—in the sense that onanism does not create another human demanding attention, positive or negative. The grandmother the boy conceives is pure fantasy, and even though in the end he cannot sustain the illusion, by indulging in masturbation the boy's self-loathing at least is contained: his seed, spilled outside the womb, prevents genetic reproduction. Henry's coitus, however, is procreative, and his dreams of birth control—like the child's projected patricide—come too late, so are as ineffective as the child's grandmother in mitigating the truth of the boy's predicament.

Lynch introduces this theme, the fear of procreative sex, as early as *The Alphabet*. The young girl sees motherhood, expressed in her assimilation of the symbolic use of language, as painful, destructive and bloody. *Eraserhead*, as a sequel to *The Grandmother*, amplifies this theme—actualizes it—in Henry's being punished by the unwanted product of his desire. The implication, which runs throughout Lynch's oeuvre, is that desire without restraint leads to misery, moral deprivation and existential suicide. But because he provides no healthy alternative, no opposing normative value—Mary's parents are certainly no model of the happy nuclear family—Lynch's view of marriage, sex, parenthood and family seems acutely misanthropic.

Salvation, too, seems equally antibiotic. Henry's attempts at transcendence are no more effective than the child's conjuring up of a fantasy grandmother. Henry's first impulse is simply to erase his problems. Similarly, the woman in the radiator offers easy, platitudinous redemption. She is more an image of Henry's wishful thinking than a signal on his part of any serious attempt at retribution, reconciliation, or, finally, a necessary, corrective realignment of his skewed value system. The escalation of his sins—from simple fornication, to adultery, to infanticide—also reflects Lynch's belief in the "gateway" effect similar to the idea espoused by anti-drug crusaders who believe marijuana use leads inevitably to heroin addiction. Employing this logic, Lynch too frequently in his films suggests that small sins lead to greater transgressions, and that minor moral failures are sure indicators of more serious crimes to come. Henry's inability to confront, accept, or even seemingly to understand that his downfall is a result of his moral failing is, perhaps, his most fatal flaw. But this context calls into question Lynch's own attitude toward his characters. Henry's situation, for instance, is reminiscent of the characters in Beckett's fiction: they lack both the intellectual capacity to comprehend their situations and the means to affect their plight, so the machinations of their creator-god Beckett—or in Henry's case, Lynch— seem sadistic and punitive, as the characters are left with no recourse but to suffer in ontological doubt.

Henry exists in a sort of spiritual limbo, unable to make the strategic choice, again in Kierkegaard's terms, to move from the aesthetic to the religious life; wanting, it seems, to make the leap into spirituality without first passing through Kierkegaard's all-important ethical stage of existence. Kierkegaard's equally Manichaean vision posits the human predicament as constantly confronting the either/or of actuality. To commit to the ethical is the first step into the religious, and facing this choice is what makes man uniquely human. The one thing a person cannot do is avoid making a decision, so, in Henry's case, his degeneration into existential paralysis is a result of his not being able to commit himself ethically; his frustration is due to his desire for transcendence without the moral fortitude to effect it. But Henry is doubly condemned because even his aesthetic project is failing. His pursuit of pleasure is increasingly solipsistic—as onanistic as that of his prototype, the boy in *The Grandmother*. "A," the narrator in the first part of Kierkegaard's *Either/Or*, cautions against marriage, convinced that it imposes too many limitations on the sensual pleasures in life. But Kierkegaard makes it clear in the second volume, through the narrator Judge William, that the temporal nature of sensual pleasure is ultimately psychologically unsatisfactory for a man to recognize his spirituality and thus to realize the essence of being human.

> My either/or does not ... denote the choice between good and evil, it denotes the choice whereby one chooses good *and* evil or excludes them. Here the question is under what determinants one would contemplate the whole of existence and would himself live. That the man who chooses good and evil chooses the good is indeed true ... for the aesthetical is not the evil but neutrality [Qtd. in Fieser and Lillegard 571].

Henry is paralyzed by his human freedom. He lives in dread of commitment, even as he realizes his potential to make "the leap" (Kierkegaard,

"Dread and Freedom" 105). He is a victim of his own possibilities. "In dread there is the egoistic infinity of possibility, which ... alarms (*aengster*) and fascinates (*Baengstelse*)" (105). But his saving grace is his discomfort at his recognition of his humanity, what separates him from a superficial animal life of mere sensory experience. He is, at least, aware of the truth of Kierkegaard's "objective uncertainty" ("Truth is Subjectivity" 117). Henry's desire for an "eraser," his wish to embrace the woman in the radiator, stem from his subjectivity, and in the end denote a type of affirmation, in spite of Lynch's morbid sadism.

For *The Elephant Man* (1980), Lynch employs the same structural moral dynamics as in *Eraserhead*, but this time his working in black and white (again) allows him a moral surety that escapes his principal characters. The premise of the film questions the neatly drawn borders separating the wicked from the good. The line demarcating the motivations of the earnest if overly ambitious Dr. Treves and those of the repugnant but no less ambitious Mr. Bytes is as ambiguous as the ethical divide between the London bluestockings and the boozing pub-crawling prostitutes the Night Porter sneaks in at night to terrorize the helpless Mr. Merrick. The film is essentially a critique of these two societies: the educated, self-righteous Victorian elite, secure in their benevolence and virtue, who by their very success reflect God's favor; and the Malthusian rabble of social outcasts who, having dispensed with the niceties, operate on a much more intuitive level—closer to the beast, as it were—than the haughty posers of polite society. Between them, The Elephant Man John Merrick becomes a metaethical link, underscoring the class divide while exposing the cruelty and exploitation of both groups. The difference is that the elite seem more culpable than their unfortunate brethren. While the raucous social Darwinists of the brothels and streets expect nothing less than to eat or be eaten, the gentle folk of the literati, who, through education and good upbringing, ought to know better, indulge in a shameful moral sleight-of-hand that can only be described as rank hypocrisy.

The story is straightforward (until *The Straight Story* an anomaly for Lynch). Fredrick Treves, a surgeon at London Hospital, discovers a hideously deformed creature, John Merrick, the star attraction called The Elephant Man, in a freak show off Mile End Road. Ostensibly in the interest of science, he buys access to the creature, and brings him to the hospital where he examines him and displays him to his stunned colleagues in an anatomy lecture hall. But when Treves sends him back to

Tableau from *The Elephant Man* (1980). Dr. Treves (Anthony Hopkins), hunting the Elephant Man, is framed by moralistic images reinforcing his heartfelt Victorian self-righteousness—the temptress, the half-eaten apple, the dead baby, the reference to original sin. Treves' guilt is a natural by-product of his professional curiosity. The beast exposes his weaknesses: pity, fear and duty fed by desire. To conquer it, and therefore to justify himself, he must tame it, appropriate it, and dress it in the latest fashion.

the carnival, Merrick's cruel "owner" Mr. Bytes beats him so badly he must be returned to the hospital for treatment.

This time Treves wants Merrick to stay, but the chairman of the Hospital Committee, Mr. Gomm, concludes that because Merrick is incurable (suffering from a rare malady known as von Recklingshausen's disease) and, in Gomm's view, more animal than man—an insentient being better off in Bedlam—he demands that Treves release him. Meanwhile, Bytes shows up, demanding his "man" be returned. To complicate matters, the Night Porter decides that he too could profit from Merrick and immediately begins to devise a scheme to bring visitors into the hospital for private viewings. Convinced that Merrick is not without human qualities, Treves nevertheless hopes, for Merrick's own sake, that "he is an idiot": for Treves, as for the others in his professional and social milieu, the existential trauma of self-recognition would in John Merrick's case, be too horrible to contemplate. Neither Treves nor the others could imagine how a sentient being could bear the emotional shock of his own image.

But more out of pity than any recognition of Merrick's innate humanity, Treves coaches him to learn a few phrases, hoping that Gomm will then allow the hapless Merrick a decent place to stay. But during his interview with Gomm, Merrick only mumbles a few words, and, believing the man an imbecile, Gomm stands by his order to remove Merrick from the hospital. Then suddenly, unprompted, Merrick begins reciting the 23rd Psalm. Astounded and genuinely moved to discover that this physically obscene monster of a man could demonstrate such individuality, passion and mental agility, Gomm agrees to let Merrick stay. The Hospital Committee, however, is hostile to this idea, one member describing Treves' actions as "competitive freak hunting" and Merrick an "abomination of nature." But thanks to the intervention of Queen Victoria, the committee votes to let Merrick live permanently at the hospital.

What follows is a series of visits to and from the best of London's society. Merrick goes to Treves' house and the latter's wife is moved to tears. While there he looks through their family photos, shares with them a picture of his mother, and explains how elephants trampled her when she was four months pregnant, causing his deformity. One of the "bright lights of the English stage," Mrs. Kendal, meets him. She brings him a book of plays by Shakespeare, reads a scene from *Romeo and Juliet*, and kisses him before she leaves. Other members of the bourgeoisie follow, and soon Merrick is hosting tea parties for the curious, select few. Even the young nurse, who was at first horrified by the sight of him, now visits Merrick with enthusiasm, encouraging him and taking a personal interest in his art.

His newfound status, however, is undercut by a visit from the Night Porter and his drunken mob of gawking punters. Unlike the tender moments spent with Mrs. Kendal, the treatment he receives from the sotted and terrified ladies of the night is violent and abusive. Bytes, who has tagged along with the rowdy throng, escapes with Merrick to the Continent, but treats him so meanly that the other sideshow "freaks" rescue him and send him back to England. Arriving at Liverpool Station, he is accosted by a mob and collapses when the police arrive.

Merrick ends up back at London Hospital under the care of Treves, though it is clear that he doesn't have long to live. Mrs. Kendal arranges for him to be her guest at the Christmas pantomime "Puss in Boots" at the famous Drury Lane Theatre, where he is recognized and applauded by the audience. After the performance, clearly exhausted and suffering, but perhaps more satisfied, serene and happier than ever in his life, he returns to the hospital and lies back in his bed, restricting his breathing so that, in effect, he kills himself.

As usual, Lynch relies on dyadic images to frame the moral issues in the film. The opening sequence establishes the normative value by which all other values are gauged: a lovely face. The shot, a close-up of Merrick's mother, a striking Pre-Raphaelite beauty, tracks her features, lingering on her sensitive eyes, her idealized nose and sensual lips, the composites perfectly proportional, formed into the classical symmetry of grace and desirability. But the camera cuts to another photograph, an older Mrs. Merrick, her face taut, her eyes filled with anxiety, as images of the beasts, the elephants, rampage across the screen. The figure of the woman, so serene in her mantel photographs and ornamental frames, is now in live action, her delicate face reduced to an image of human frailty, a screaming effigy of terror and pain as the brutal animals assault her relentlessly. The contrast between his mother's beauty and the indifferent attack of the elephants creates the moral dilemma in Merrick's value system. The mother and the child are united in violence, and Merrick himself is born as a sort of combination of man and beast. During his visit with Treves and his wife, for instance, Merrick notes that their children have "such noble faces," and when he shows them his mother's photograph, he describes her as having "the face of an angel." His idealized self is shaped by his deformity, as if he, too, conditioned by the vulgar world around him, privileges physical beauty over intelligence and spirituality. He is, after all, inside out, the beast of his will exposed, his civilized self hidden: Frank Booth reversed. This explains the saintly nurse Mothershead's prohibition of "no mirrors" and, conversely, the Night Porter's delight in Merrick's fright at his own image.

The extreme degree of his deformity is essential to the moral structure of the film. When Treves first finds Merrick, he follows a police officer through a Byzantine labyrinth marked "No Entry" into a section of the carnival labeled "Freaks." He passes bits of exotica—a test-tube fetus, a bearded lady, midgets—then proceeds along a corridor where an obviously distraught lady weeps on the arm of a gentleman leading her out of the area. Like Marlow approaching the Central Station, that heart of darkness where Kurtz goes native, Treves approaches the Elephant Man exhibit. But it is too gruesome, and an authority figure is already threatening to close the show. The Elephant Man, it seems, is

beyond freak, actually too repulsive—too "monstrous!"—for the crowd
of virtuous voyeurs crowding around the stage. In fact, the private viewing Treves finally procures is too much even for him, a veteran of bar-
barous nineteenth-century invasive surgeries.

Merrick's conflict between his image and his self is exacerbated by
the dehumanizing hood he wears in public. Even Treves, before he meets
Merrick, identifies himself as "one of the curious" and refers to Merrick
as "it," concluding after the exhibition at the anatomy lecture, "The man's
a complete idiot." But his diagnosis is pure self-protection. Treves *prays*
Merrick is an idiot because when he projects his subjective self into Merrick's, the only way he can handle the ontological predicament is to hope
Merrick is non-cognizant, at least pre–Oedipal. But the Elephant Man
is a philosophical pastiche. He is the animal face of humanity, the Christ
of hypocrisy, a demon of desire, degraded and honest, a Lacanian split-
self personified.

Merrick at first trusts his primal certainties more than his conscience, so when the doctor treats him like a human, Merrick is suspicious. But his transition from the freak shows to the posh apartments of
the West End is nearly seamless; he merely shifts gears. His triumph
over his beastliness is a result of his choosing to enter the human condition, regardless of Treves' requisite tinge of Victorian guilt. The dou-
blings highlight not only the two-tiered class system and Treves'
complicity in it, but also the ironically dovetailing interests of Treves and
Bytes. Like Merrick, they are two sides of the same coin. The only
recourse for Treves (as for Jeffery Beaumont later) is a typically Victorian epiphany: Treves asks his wife, in a maudlin moment of reflexivity,
"Am I a good man? Or am I a bad man?" She reassures him that Merrick is happy and productive and that her husband's motives are intrinsically beyond reproach.

But it is that moment of (re)locating the subject, when Merrick turns,
that reiterates Lynch's earlier concern in *The Alphabet*: the discharging
of the self from the alogical pre-consciousness into the symbolic. As in
Eraserhead, the filthy realism of *The Elephant Man* becomes surreal, and
the factory muck of industrialization is no less dehumanizing. But it is
Merrick's mother's move, from the static photographs where life is
arrested and framed in calm moments of posed beauty into the active
world full of dread and violence, that controls the narrative. This is Merrick's dilemma: a move, like his mother's, from the static will of the beast
to the conceptual world of an affected self-presentation. That means
individuation, articulating a self, and facing the inevitable metaphysical

questions: Is he authentic? A mere curio? Is his retreat from the subjective into the symbolic possible outside of madness?

Once Treves discovers Merrick "can speak," the choice for Merrick as he (re)enters Nietzsche's linguistic legislation plays in the mirrored sequences between the Night Porter's visits to Merrick and Merrick's taking tea with genteel couples. The nurses who were so repulsed by his appearance now fawn over him. He longs to sleep like normal people, but he cannot escape his essence: he is pure other, a grotesque parrot of the clever and dull, a subject unremarkable except for his appearance (for some) and his endurance (for others). His relationship with Bytes is strictly Hegelian. In the master-slave dynamic, Bytes cannot survive without "his treasure," and in a rage of self-loathing, terrified by his absolute and necessary dependence on a *freak* for both his essential *and* economic existence, he tries one last time to cage the spirit, locking Merrick in with the monkeys. This only inflames the humanity in the other freaks, who set Merrick loose again, but not free, as Merrick wades into a failing nineteenth-century British empire not ready to face its own reflection.

For Treves the model is *Frankenstein* (1818). His Merrick, no longer The Elephant Man that defines Mr. Bytes, instead defines Treves as a philanthropist responsible for reclaiming Merrick's humanity. But the doctor's creature performs like a drag queen who has perfected femininity. His attempts at art are competent but amateurish. His perseverance is admirable, but he is ponderous and sentimental, and his stiff (and grossly deformed) upper lip is pure theater when he rhetorically asks Treves, with a faint but proper hint of Victorian self-pity, "Can you cure me?" It is nurse Mothershead who provides the normative value when she tells Treves, after visits by Mrs. Kendal and other members of high society, "He's only being stared at all over again." The visitors care less for Merrick than they do about their own standing. Worse, their kindness toward him is but a testament to their own benevolence and charity. Merrick, seduced by his new role, takes on the airs of a gentleman. But he remains as much an oddity as ever. Seeing his reflection triggers a hallucinatory sequence during which he rages at his disfigurement, his unwarranted, inexplicable suffering, as much as at his corruption: a return to the savage world of the carnival would at least end the hypocrisy and pretense inherent in his new venue.

Yet when Bytes spirits him off to Belgium and tries to resurrect his career as the Elephant Man, the show fails because Merrick refuses to perform. The dialectic collapses. For Merrick, however, the choice seems more like a dispute over a practical career move than an existential crisis.

Spectator as spectacle: John Merrick (John Hurt) at the theater in *The Elephant Man* (1980). Merrick is the metaethical link exposing the hypocrisy of both the carnival louts and the snobbish elite. Perpetually "other," he inhabits a moral twilight zone, always either an animal that people see as human or a human treated like an animal.

In both arenas—London's high society and the carnival sideshows—Merrick (like Frank Booth and Dorothy Vallens) is an actor. The key scene in the film is the visit Mrs. Kendal pays to Merrick. He asks her if the theater is "beautiful." She replies that it is romance. Romance is, of course, the lie civilization uses to divorce itself from its animal roots. Civilized people do not rut like stags in heat: they court. Nor do they mate. After all the wine and dinners, concerts and museum soirees, they make love. Mrs. Kendal tells him, "You're not The Elephant Man at all. You're Romeo." Absurd, but true. Merrick, like Romeo, plays his part in the unfolding drama his sudden privileged status creates for him on the grand stage of Victorian hypocrisy. She kisses him like a saint kissing a leper, as if congratulating herself for her own magnanimity. But the kiss seems to poison him, foreshadowing Dorothy Vallens' classic line, "He put his disease in me." Realizing his essence as spectacle, Merrick is determined to choose his audience. On his return to London, when he is threatened outside Liverpool Station, ill, alone, chased by an angry mob, helplessly slumped in a public toilet, he relies on grandstanding, emoting: "I am not an animal. I am a human being." At the presentation of "Puss in Boots," arranged by Mrs. Kendal, he is mesmerized by the enchantment and mystery, the heightened emotions, the transforming power of art. But when the lights come up, they shine on him. He is again the spectacle, and even the magic of art is powerless to change him. His suicide is a result of both delight and despair.

The central moral concern in the film ostensibly focuses on Treves as he tries to reconcile the competing motivations for his interest in Merrick. To clear his conscience, he must separate distinctly humanistic charity from self-serving pity, scientific curiosity from crass exploitation. When Merrick is returned to the hospital, for instance, Treves embraces him with relief, as much for the fact that his irresponsibility—allowing his patient to be kidnapped in the first place—did not prove fatal as for the return of a friend into his life. Treves' ambiguity acts here as a metaphor for the underlying hypocrisy of Victorian England, with its imperialist pretenses of civilizing the savages abroad in Africa, Asia and the Subcontinent while minimizing its responsibility for and neglect of the needy and afflicted within its own local communities.

Treves first assumes Merrick's imbecility because to see him otherwise threatens his own self-image. As Foucault points out in *Madness and Civilization*, "It has doubtless been essential to Western culture to link, as it has done, its perception of madness to the iconographic forms of the relation of man to beast" (77). Of course, Treves is working within the nineteenth-century rationalist tradition: *monstrum in fronte, monstrum in animo*, convinced that physical deformities betray a depraved soul and "perceiving in madness a fall into determinism where all forms of liberty are gradually suppressed [and a] return to the bleak world of beasts and things, to their fettered freedom" (Foucault 83). For Treves, if Merrick is beastly, his being confined like an animal is natural. "[T]he animal belongs to an anti-nature, to a negativity that threatens order and by its frenzy endangers the positive wisdom of nature" (Foucault 77).

More extreme than Treves' middle-class muddle, however, is Merrick's moral dilemma. His self-presentation is so preconditioned he can never integrate. No group can assimilate him. In the carnival world, he is a person treated like an animal. In London society, he is an animal treated like a person. He is unique, always already Other, and in this sense truly a freak. Ironically, he is at his most human when he chooses death over his indeterminate life, preferring a transcendental escape over inhabiting, as it were, one of Foucault's caesuras, living in that twilight of existence between the rational animal and the intuitive beast.

These moral subtleties may explain the success of the film. But its deserved critical acclaim has less to do with the Lynchian touches—hallucinatory sequences, macabre close-ups, and an unflinching sentimentality—than with the pathos of the original story. Still, Lynch illustrates Merrick's plight with a deftness missing from the films that followed. Where later he was hyperkinetic and overwrought, his subtle conflation of image and theme in *The Elephant Man* distinguishes it as more polished and mature than most of his work.

Lynch's first color feature is more moralistically black and white than either *Eraserhead* or *The Elephant Man*. To accommodate the rigid puritanical clarity in *Dune* (1984), moral subtlety—of Henry's entrapment and his desire for transcendence, or the clash of scientific discovery and the benevolent humanism of Dr. Treves' Victorian England—had to be dispensed with. In *Dune*, the clarity between good and evil is simple, reductive and finally merely cartoonish. The Messianic plot in Herbert's novel yields to Lynch's Manichaean vision, and the film pretends to biblical proportions; but for all its weirdness and sprawling sci-fi excess, *Dune* from its inception was too large a canvas for a director like Lynch, whose best work relies on micro-managing the material, accruing minutiae into a collage of correlative images and creating poetic structures assured of their own logic.

When Rodley asked him what "characterizes David Lynch's *Dune*," Lynch replied: "the character of Paul, the sleeper who must awaken" (Lynch 116). This focus on Paul is not surprising. Herbert's "books revolve around the question of morality" (Kaleta 70–71). And no matter how much Lynch pretends to eschew what he maligns as the Western Union school of art, he stays well on message in Dune, discovering in Herbert's novel that a "new moral order and a new language pervade his world" (Kaleta 71). If it is a new language, for Lynch it is an old context, even if many critics—Kaleta included—discount the Messianic angle.

A goofy fifties-style sci-fi epic, *Dune* does not lend itself to close analysis: hermeneutic scrutiny will not add up, and the critical payoff is not worth the effort. Enhanced with early James Bond movie–type special effects, *Dune* never develops beyond a simple cosmic Christian version of *West Side Story* (1957): a galactic gang fight over turf and spice—the "most precious substance." But in *West Side Story*, the audience is expected to identify with the Jets while understanding that even the Sharks are not all bad. They are human, after all, and sensitive, imbued with a conscience, capable of emotion. The Harkonnens, on the other hand, have no redeeming qualities. They are flat characters cut from the same pattern that prefigures the psychos in Frank Booth's gang, the misfits of *Twin Peaks*, and all the other motley, stereotypical deviants who represent the forces of evil in Lynch's films.

This duality expresses Lynch's deep-seated American puritanical certainty of righteousness. The conflict is set up in a series of Manichaean dialectical categories: Us vs. Them, Our Kind vs. the Other, Good vs. Bad, Beautiful vs. Ugly, and most insidious and subversive of all, Straight vs. Gay. (Sting's appearance as Feyd-Rautha, one of Harkonnen's goons, may seem at first glance to disrupt this neat paradigm, but the charm of his buff, epicene body is contradicted by his brute nastiness, and his madness remains diabolical and monstrous.)

The Atreides family lives on Caladan, a bountiful world blessed with pristine beauty and, most importantly, oceans of water. Paul is a nerdy *ubermensch*. (Paul himself makes reference to a "super-being.") He is angelic, passionate, rational, modest but divinely gifted. He is, after all, the Messiah, the sleeper who must awaken, and as Messiah his mission will be to revive the morally barren planet Arrakis with spiritually rejuvenating rain. He is being groomed to drink "the water of life," though many men have "tried and died." He must learn to "control instinct"— that is, to nurture the fundamental restraint required by civilizations to become productive nations, a quality that separates him from the extremely degenerate denizens in Baron Harkonnen's camp. Paul and his family are sliced white bread, loving, respectful and, most important, heterosexual, childbearing nurturers. Princess Irulan (who, inexplicably, narrates the story), Paul's friend Duncan (whose appearance in the film is as brief as it is irrelevant), Paul's love trophy Chani (whose involvement with Paul is equally incomprehensible), his mother, the faithful concubine Jessica, his father, the erstwhile Duke (who belatedly regrets not having married Jessica)—all the "good" people are clearly Aryan. No coincidence that the Fremen are recognizable by their scintillating blue eyes.

Unlike the Atreides, the Baron's men are loathsome. They are incorrigibly violent spoilers of the natural world, spreading pollution and industrial waste. The Baron himself revels in scarification, his face a cancerous mush of pustulating open sores. His greatest pleasure is terrifying young boys, mounting them and pulling their heart plugs—devices designed to facilitate casual murders—while staring deep into their dying eyes. This mixing of homosexuality with violence, depravation and death operates like a moral code, delineating the reprobates from the redeemed and equating homosexuality with moral depravity. Besides promiscuous torture, mayhem and violence, the Baron's people enjoy self-abasement, crushed-rat cocktails, cruelty to animals, and assorted other abominations far beyond the pale of acceptable human behavior. The men and women of Geidi Prime live in an inverted world where beauty exists only to be scarred. They attend to their sterile duties with their eyes and ears mutilated and sewn shut. The predominant images are of death, decay, and anonymity. The Baron hovers, weightless, unsure of his own empirical existence, reinforcing his worthlessness and unreality, while his minions pursue their own selfish schemes of lust and betrayal.

The contemporary parallel is to the American government's so-called War on Drugs. In the black-and-white moral clarity behind that policy of police and military intervention, illegal drugs, of course, are bad; and the baddies who control the mining and distribution of spice on Arrakis are a disgusting bunch of miscreants. As Princess Irulan explains—if that's the right word—melange—the spice—"extends life." But the rumor circulating among the high rollers and their lackeys who harvest and exploit spice production is that an anti-spice crusader is coming to put a stop to this scourge.

The trouble begins with the arrival of The Navigator at Shaddom's royal court, a cross between *fin de siècle* Vienna and the fascist undertones of the late Weimar Republic, depicting an excessive and libertine fashion Lynch equates with decadence. Meant to be ominous, The Navigator, floating in a pink solution of spice mist, is more comical than scary, a fish-like creature that features a penile shape with a vaginal orifice. His handlers are as ridiculous as the gay-biker narcissists in Kenneth Anger's *Scorpio Rising* (1963). The effect of this opening sequence sets the tone for the rest of the movie, where characters' motives seem inconsequential and detached from the action. Even so, the plot is now in motion. Shaddom is ordered to set a trap for the House of Atreides that will turn power over to Baron Harkonnen, a reliable ally of the spice mining conglomerates.

In contrast to the indulgences and the political intrigue of The Navigator of Shaddom, Paul earnestly prepares for his mission, passing a series of tests in which he proves himself both philosopher and warrior. His dreams too begin to intimate his impending sanctification. Using a navigator and a sort of galactic flatulence—called "folding space"—Paul travels to Dune with his darling puppy, his babe mom, his powerful dad—all, including the dog, seemingly beyond moral reproach. It doesn't take long for Paul to be recognized by the Fremen as the "one who will come ... bringing the holy war." Soon enough he encounters the infamous gargantuan worms—producers of the sacred bile—that protect the spice from harvesters. Intrigued, he tries the spice and hallucinates another prescient vision. He then deals with a deadly assassination attempt, and proves himself preternaturally cool. But during the ensuing battle with the Harkonnen invaders, a traitor, Dr. Yueh, sells out Paul's father. Yeuh wants to use Duke Leto to kill Baron Harkonnen in order to revenge his wife's death at the Baron's hands. Paul's father dies in vain, but Paul and his mother conveniently escape and, equally conveniently, meet the Fremen rebels. (Lynch, unable to condemn Yueh totally, seems incongruously sympathetic, allowing a redemptive tearful scene of remorse—exactly like Jeffrey's in *Blue Velvet*—before he is dispatched by a blade in the back.) The Baron and his men, of course, are not offered, and would perforce reject, any such chance to come clean. In contrast, the one thing the Baron fears most is crying, and ironically it is his fear of this authentic show of emotion in Paul's father that, for the moment, saves his life.

Joining the Fremen, Paul and Jessica begin instructing their counter insurgent troops in "the weirding way." The Fremen have already recognized elements of the prophecy. They are all too eager to accept Paul as their savior, and Chani, the Fremen leader's daughter, wastes no time in claiming Paul. Jessica replaces the Reverend Mother, and miraculously gives birth to a daughter, Alia, who, like a sitcom sorceress, demonstrates remarkable magical powers.

Lynch contrasts this holy birth with images back on Geidi Prime of abortion, disfigurement, and the Baron and Feyd-Rauthal's exquisite torture of Doctor Kynes—he is forced to milk a shaved cat nursing a rat taped to its side every day for the antidote to a poison they have injected into him. Baron Harkonnen, believing Paul and Jessica are dead, sends Rabban—a revolting psychopath—to oversee the spice production on Arrakis.

Meanwhile, in homage to Leni Riefenstahl, Paul is wowing the crowd in a Gothic cathedral with his Messianic message. "He who destroys a thing, controls a thing," he says, in his best Nietzsche, then begins destroying and controlling—well, everything, finally taming even the worms (an image Freud might think a bit juvenile), converting them finally into weapons of terror. For two years Paul and his compatriots wage guerilla warfare against Rabban, until Paul decides to drink the sacred water. No surprise, he survives, and in a spasm of overtly phallic imagery, Lynch has the worms circle-up and praise him. After all, Ahab rode his whale. Paul rides his worm too.

In a politically charged Musketeer speech, he vows to destroy spice forever and is accepted as the sleeper who has awakened. He incites his eschatological followers into an apocalyptic revolution, riding worms roughshod over the enemy, firing "sound" guns. With an Old Testament sense of dramatic tension, Lynch closes out the prophecy. Paul, appropriately, knifes Feyd in the throat, it rains on Arrakis, and we learn that "One cannot go against the word of God."

If *Eraserhead* is a bedtime Bible story for wayward adolescents, *The Elephant Man* an indictment of historical account, and *Dune* a sci-fi Aesop's fable, *Blue Velvet* (1986) is a course in sex education for preteens. Ostensibly a film about growing up and assuming responsibility, of entering the adult world equipped to handle the expectations of maturity, the film also sets a limit on the extremes of aggressive behavior that, when tamed, leads to successful competition, social integration and sexual success. In pursuit of this end, Lynch indulges in primitive images of sado-masochistic degradation, deprivation and discord, offset by images of purity, innocence and wholesomeness. Cleanliness, in Lynch, acts as a corrective, a remedy for cosmic and psychic imbalance between love and strife. Lynch operates within the elemental harmonizing formalized by the Pre-Socratic Empedocles, later refined by Schopenhauer, Freud and Jung, which recognizes the need in humans to strike a balance between the fundamental urges both to create and to destroy.

The film opens with a series of Disney-like scenes portraying an idealized model Hometown, USA: brilliant flowers, deep blue sky, friendly firemen and Sparky their mascot, a crosswalk guard, children with the generic charm of Opie from Mayberry. An older man flush with self-satisfaction waters his garden, an overt image of sexual confidence, experience and maturity. His wife sits in their house intensely watching a detective show on television. (Lynch often crosscuts TV shots into his movie frame as an intertextual device to comment on, foreshadow and foreground action and context in his storylines.) All seems well until suddenly something awful interrupts the sanctimony of suburbia: a pistol intrudes on the television, a classic phallic *film noir* image. In the yard the hose the man holds swells like a sclerotic artery and bursts as he falls in an apoplectic fit. A baby wanders by, contrasting youth and age, the beginning and the end of life. Then a dog attacks the hose, an action which on the surface seems commonplace enough, but when the image is manipulated in slow motion, the dog appears violent, biting at the stream of water which the man, flat on his back and unconscious, continues to hold, the stream spewing skyward from his groin.

In this brief, clever cluster of contrasting images, Lynch introduces the controlling message around which he will structure his narrative: there are two sides to everything, and nothing is ever as it seems. To reinforce this idea, the camera burrows into the ground beneath the manicured lawns, digging into the ugly violent underside of nature, illustrating in imagery exactly what the film proposes to expose: the raw id beneath the carefully constructed egos of the model citizens from the heartland of middle-class America.

Lynch's portrait also suggests his love-hate relationship with the corny plainness of parochial life. His all–American goofy city, the soul of solid "traditional" values where nobody expects anything remotely kinky to happen, is Lumberton, where goodness is represented by simplicity and, conversely, complexity equals evil. Logging, the chief economic resource, acts as an appropriate metaphor for the taming of the wilderness: it signifies in Lynch the belief that to conquer nature represents man's control of primitive drives, his undifferentiated will fenced off from the clear-cut spaces that demarcate civilization. The well-lit small town of frontier America, representing the acceptable, the satisfying image of a civilized community, abuts Longfellow's forest primeval, which harbors the dark, inexplicable urges of the unconscious, secret savage self.

But his portrait of the community is ambivalent, a left-handed compliment that both celebrates and criticizes values he finds both endearing and repulsive. The lives he investigates are both comic and tragic, as their personal dramas play out against a background of small-town absurdities. When Jeffrey visits his father in the hospital, the ludicrous contraption his father is screwed into undercuts the seriousness of his condition. The potentially weepy sentimentality of the scene is checked by the reality facing Jeffrey as he takes his first step into adulthood, forced to confront human frailty and weakness and to assume his father's role in the household. Jeffrey's father's incapacitation is a convenient and necessary device to remove the father from his patriarchal authority in the nuclear family unit, allowing Jeffrey the opportunity to explore his own unfettered desires without the prohibition imposed by his father.

This removal of the father/superego barrier is an opening for Jeffrey, free now to develop his adult self on his own terms.

Jeffrey is also home from college, and in Lynch this represents Jeffrey's liberation from another institution of authority, regulation and stricture. Lynch's anti-intellectualism is noted in more detail elsewhere, but suspicion of institutional learning, evident in much of his work but explicit in his early films like *The Alphabet*, is acute in *Blue Velvet*. Jeffrey's being out of school is essential to his self-exploration after his father's hospitalization. What Jeffrey needs to learn before he can matriculate into the "real" world, Lynch believes he cannot find in books, theories, classroom lectures or fraternity parties. College taught Jeffrey nothing but posturing. His preference for imported beer, his choice of sunglasses, his style of clothes are all coded campus fashions fostering a sophomoric idea of "being cool." Jeffrey's self-serving, condescending attitude towards Sandy and Mike, combined with his posing, smacks of the pretenses of adulthood. The idyllic life at the state university, like a campsite at the edge of a deep woods, offers nothing more than another shelter from the harsh truths just beyond the campus gates, its superficial façade as thin as the undisturbed surface of a reflecting pool. Jeffrey's true education begins when he stops wading through the shallows of his college career and plunges into the Deep River apartments.

On his way back from the hospital, Jeffrey spies a severed ear, and with a child's delight in mystery finds not only the first piece of the puzzle which drives the action of the story but also the essential first clue in his quest for self-knowledge. Not surprisingly, his first instinct is to take the ear to a surrogate father figure of authority: the police. The ear is an anomaly, upsetting the normal narrative of events in Jeffrey's ordinary day, so to restore his sense of normalcy, he seeks out the force entrusted to preserve order in the community. But when he first brings the ear to Detective Williams, the police are bureaucratic, formal and dismissive. The police, like Jeffrey's father, cannot provide satisfactory answers to Jeffrey's inquisitiveness because his quest is no longer an inductive investigation into the facts of a crime: it is ontological. Jeffrey is more than just a psychological type: he is a mythic counter-force of goodness sent, as it were (like Paul Atreides and Agent Cooper) to check both civic and personal corruption in the community, manifest at its most dangerous levels within the very police department charged with maintaining stability.

The next shot is a total blackout, suddenly violated by Jeffrey emerging from a brightly lit upstairs room and descending a dark staircase. The imagery indicates a movement from the cerebral to the intuitive, reinforced by his grandmother's warning: "You're not going down by Lincoln, are you?" Jeffrey replies, "No," but of course that's exactly where he goes, drawn to that mythical wrong side of town harboring the temptations every decent family fears but knows instinctively will, in the end, claim their children and deliver them, like the witch in her seductive Gingerbread House, from innocence into adulthood.

What follows is a sequence of openings, Jeffrey entering one portal after another, delving deeper into the complications of his journey, like Ulysses touring the underworld to learn from the dead how to appreciate living. His passage though the ear leads him to the door that opens into Detective Williams' house, though the focus is on the framed high school photograph of Sandy (as Laura Palmer will be represented later in *Twin Peaks*). Sandy's father reinforces the central theme, the duality of experience, as he agrees that his work is "great" but adds that it is "horrible too." He admits that he felt "the same when I was your age" but warns Jeffrey to leave the detective work to the police. He sends Jeffrey away dissatisfied and still too curious to let the matter rest.

When Jeffrey first meets Sandy, she, like Jeffrey, is still an ingénue. A study in contrasts, she is goofy and voluptuous, sexual but innocent, with one foot in her prom dress, the other in a negligee. As he and Sandy stroll the neighborhood, a carload of locals cruises by shouting sexual epithets. Their uninhibited expressions of sexuality directed at Sandy— "Hey, babe!"—contrast and coincide with Jeffrey's first encounter with the Deep River apartments. He is not ready for his initiation, and as if intuiting what awaits him inside Dorothy Vallens' apartment, he willfully regresses, resisting his loss of innocence, trying to impress Sandy with his version of a "chicken walk."

But his desire is too strong. No matter how he tries to maintain his sophomoric pose, he is drawn to the mysteries "down by Lincoln." The central metaphor, throughout these sequences, is that of the Manichaean double-vision controlling the film, constantly reinforced by double-imaging: the village idiot, a man-child, obese himself, casts a knife-thin poster-like shadow; a huge man walks a tiny dog; "Double Ed," the two black store clerks, one sighted, one blind, sell a double-edged ax. Jeffrey's doubling—his innocence coupled with his desire for experience—is also implied by his banter with Double Ed. Jeffrey holds up four fingers, the blind one of the pair identifies them correctly (as his sighted partner taps his shoulder), and Jeffrey, amazed at the trick, says, "I still don't know how you do that." Meanwhile, he is preparing his disguise to infiltrate the mysteries of Dorothy Vallens' apartment, a locale that symbolizes for Jeffrey a visit to interiority, a descent into the subconscious, where Jeffrey thinks he "could learn a lot." Of course, what he will learn is all about himself.

Sandy and Jeffrey's relationship drives the surface action of the film—discovering the mystery behind the ear and the characters associated with it: the Yellow Man, Frank Booth, Dorothy Vallens; but the real mystery is their discovering, beneath the veneer of social restraint, habit, expectation and repression, their desire for each other. Jeffrey, by now infatuated with Dorothy, concocts a ludicrous plan to break into her apartment. Masquerading as an exterminator, "the bug man," he steals a spare key to her door. He takes Sandy to the Slow Club where she sits uncomfortably while Jeffrey watches, with obvious sexual interest, Dorothy Vallens, the pathetically sentimental torch singer, as she oozes through Bobby Vinton's "Blue Velvet." In a sophomoric attempt to impress Sandy, Jeffrey orders a Heineken. (Sandy's father drinks Budweiser.) Jeffrey relies on his college pose to create an image of sophistication while merely proving that he remains, at this point in the story, all style without substance. (Significantly, it is the Heineken—his college prop—that causes him to use the bathroom once he is inside Dorothy's apartment. "Heineken," he says, relieving himself, as the untimely flush of the toilet covers the sound of Sandy's warning blasts of the car horn signaling Dorothy's arrival.) Before leaving him at Dorothy's apartment, Sandy wonders if Jeffrey is a "detective or a pervert." He tells her, "That's for me to know and you to find out."

In the first apartment sequence, Jeffrey watches from within the closet as Dorothy takes a break. She is, after all, an actress, changing from one gig to another, going from torch singer at the Slow Club to a grieving mother and Don's wife. She is caught sidelining, an entertainer swapping costumes between shows. Ironically, even as she tries to live out her private life, she is still performing: both for the audience and, as his subjective perspective is identified with that of the audience, for Jeffrey. On the ordinary stage of her living room floor, unaware of her constant objectification by the camera, by the audience, by Jeffrey's gaze, Dorothy is barely able to snatch back her performing self when Frank calls. Now she is the "Mommy" to Frank's alternating "Baby" and "Daddy"—the two personas of his peculiar obsessions. She strips out of her glamorous gown, wig, and heels—briefly real, naked, vulnerable, and desperately honest, until she catches Jeffrey in the closet and starts performing again. Only this time she reverses roles with him. When he confesses that he "wanted to see her," she says she wants to see him, too, and tells him to "get undressed." An archetypal castrating woman, she appropriates the proper phallic image—a huge kitchen knife—and forces Jeffrey to perform for her. She is the director now. But she prefers an active role, taking charge the only way she knows how: through sex and violence, drawing first blood by cutting Jeffrey's cheek, then threatening to kill him while fellating him, knife against his throat.

While Dorothy performs sexually for Jeffrey (in yet another role), she shouts, "Don't look at me." It is the same command Frank gives her, later, during his assault. This metacinematic moment validates, but also reverses, Laura Mulvey's reading of films in the Freudian context of scopophilia; that is, "taking other people as objects, subjecting them to a controlling and curious gaze" (Mulvey 748). For her, "the erotic basis for pleasure in looking at another person as object" (748) accounts for the essence of cinema. Frank and Dorothy, instead of recognizing "scopophilia in its narcissistic aspect" (749), exhibit a fear of being seen. (When Frank shows up, Dorothy is so rattled she forgets her lines. She greets Frank with "Hello, Baby." He responds, "Shut up. It's Daddy, you shit head." She plays the confused actress, he the frustrated director.) Mulvey establishes the female figure in film as both provoking pleasure and "implying a threat of castration and hence unpleasure" (753). She offers "[t]he male unconscious ... two avenues to escape from this castration anxiety: ... reenactment of the original trauma [or] substitution of a fetish object" (753). In this context, Dorothy provides a mythical synthesis for Frank. She is "Mommy" when Frank, like the boy in *The Grandmother* fingering his tree, kneels between Dorothy's legs, ordering her like a sadistic OB/GYN to spread "wider" while she stuffs a blue velvet cloth into his mouth, which he then crams into her vagina, shouting "Baby's coming home!" But she is a different "Mommy" when Frank needs to be "Daddy." She becomes a passive sexual object existing solely to satisfy Frank's fragile male desire. As "Daddy" he calls her "tits" and humps her in a wild fit of frottage. In his postorgasmic self-loathing and shame, he again reverses roles by threatening her with scissors, an instrument of castration. Her husband's severed ear, in this context, serves as an image of castration—or impotency—haunting Frank. After all, he can only simulate sex, his essential connection to nature, the womb and the mysteries of life embodied in that umbilical strip of blue velvet.

Frank and Dorothy have worked out a complex moral scheme to protect their subjective selves at the most instinctual animal level. Of course, in the master/slave dynamic, Frank is doomed. Dorothy perseveres. She is Apollonian, plowing stoically through each scene, while Frank is lost in his existential pantomime, fiddling with the lights, getting high, correcting the other actors while putting on a lousy performance himself. "Now it's dark," he says, setting the mood for his big scene, again, umbilically attached, like the father in *The Grandmother*, to his tube, canister and mask. Dorothy could shatter him with her Medusa's gaze, what Sartre describes as "the battle to the death of consciousness" (*Essays in Existentialism* 176). Like the characters in Sartre's *No Exit* (*Huis Clos* 1945) who cannot close their eyes (and conclude Hell is other people), Frank cannot maintain, in bad faith, his self-presentation under Dorothy's intrusive gaze. The triangle she forms—herself at the apex, Jeffrey and Frank the respective sides—allows Jeffrey to watch unimpeded while Frank denies Dorothy any visual pleasure. But she has become ironic: it is a disappearing act she performs for Jeffrey, demonstrating how she escapes the horror of her situation by objectifying herself for Frank. Frank in turn plays her nightmare super-ego, beating her only when she looks at him, when she asserts her subjectivity. His only recourse is to prevent her gaze from reaffirming his impotency and latent homosexuality. Her watching him ruins his projection of himself upon her, just as, for Sartre, being looked at implies a loss of control. This is what Frank fears. But for an actor like Dorothy, the gaze of another delivers escape. "A person frees himself from himself by the very act by which he makes himself an object for himself" (*Essays in Existentialism* 177). Linda Williams, keying off Mulvey's essay on scopophilia, finds a subject's panic at being perceived (like Frank's) rooted in "the power and potency of a non-phallic sexuality ... so threatening to male power, it is violently punished" (570). Williams, citing Mary Ann Doane's essay "The Woman's Film: Possession and Address," describes a situation that neatly sums up Frank's predicament: "'the woman's exercise of an active investigating gaze can only be simultaneous with her own victimization.' The woman's gaze is punished, in other words, by narrative processes that transform curiosity and desire into masochistic fantasy" (563).

Whereas Frank is too evil, Jeffrey is too innocent: in effect, neither can perform sexually, but for opposite reasons. What is required is a blend, a reconciliation of opposites (to borrow a phrase from Coleridge), a tempering of evil and innocence into a unified whole. Frank, because he can't "fuck," is obsessed with the idea: he calls everyone "Fuck." He reduces all motives to "fucking" and expresses his frustration in perversity, the only release available to his dysfunctional longing. Significantly, his perversion is fetishized in blue velvet, the actual fabric, just as "Blue Velvet" the song represents the smarmy world that Dorothy so desperately craves. Frank's flaw is that he lacks restraint, discretion, and remorse, so he can't integrate into any acceptable social or sexual norms. He represents the potential Jeffrey must recognize within himself yet still conquer and control. When Frank finishes savaging Dorothy, he tells her to stay alive. "Do it for Van Gogh," he says, meaningfully. Besides the cynical, macho humor, the line connects Frank (and Don, his victim) to self-sacrifice: he is a performance artist, crazed and suffering for love, however perverted. And while Jeffrey is no psycho-maniacal Frank (or Van Gogh), he is incapable of satisfying Dorothy. This mutual incapacity links them through the same object—Dorothy—and sets up the moral scrum: a primal, male-domination ritual between Jeffrey and Frank for possession of Dorothy. But again, in the master/slave dynamic, Dorothy controls them both, a central irony often overlooked in the scene when Frank rapes her. After all, Frank (and Jeffrey) can only simulate sex. Frank's command—"Don't you fuckin' look at me"—is a plea. Her look penetrates his self-deception. She is his temptation and his punishment. With Dorothy, Frank can act out his existential fears, but only if Dorothy alternately plays the appropriate primal bitch/goddess/earth mother role, depending on Frank's need at he moment. He is weak and ashamed, but only in front of her.

Knowing Frank's secret self, and being the object of his desire, Dorothy lords it over him: her submissiveness dominates him. With Jeffrey, her role is more actively seductive as she coaches him through the subtle limits of sexual aggression, fear and self-abandonment. This initial encounter with Dorothy begins Jeffrey's initiation. He is both intrigued and repulsed by what he has witnessed (as is, supposedly, the audience). Alone with Jeffrey after Frank leaves, she prompts him through a series of caresses, sensually inviting him to explore her body. He touches her breast, and she asks, "Do you like how I feel?" This is an especially ambiguous statement, given the layering in the scene: real people acting as actors self-consciously performing. But Jeffrey, fascinated and aroused, cannot keep Dorothy in her role. He is too green, too hesitant, having not discovered yet what he is capable of. Then she asks him to hit her. When he denies her this final, ultimate control, she reacts like a director who cannot get a performance out of an actor. Her sexual frustration is ontological. As if to deal with the trauma of losing her family, Dorothy has parked her existential subject and has allowed herself to be driven— that is, defined—by others. She sings at The Slow Club, submits to Frank, and educates Jeffrey, emceeing a three-ring circus she orchestrates to excuse herself from the role she failed at most: mother and wife.

But true to the film's Calvinist core, both Jeffrey and Dorothy, though ultimately salvageable, must first suffer for their transgressions. Before he leaves, dismissed by Dorothy, Jeffrey discovers she is married, but he continues the liaison anyway. This, in Lynch's world, is a moral lapse that must not go unpunished. Dorothy is equally culpable—not for what she endures from Frank, but because, while her husband has been kidnapped and tortured, she is sleeping with Jeffrey. Her penitence is painfully documented by her episode with Frank (her transgression with Jeffrey after the fact, but no less self-sacrificial, with a promise of more to come). As for Jeffrey, Lynch intercuts his moral corruption—"the dis-ease"—in stark, if surreal, ethical imagery, repeating the phrases "Now it's dark" and "Hit me" until Jeffrey awakens from his nightmare and sees the screaming face of an animal carved into a coconut, a reminder of both the joy and pain of experience.

Now Jeffrey begins a duplicitous life (sexuality, in Lynch, implies corruption; education, hypocrisy). Jeffrey nonchalantly tells Sandy, when she asks, "How'd it go last night?" that his extraordinary adventure into violent sexual promiscuity and torture "went okay." Significantly, while Jeffrey graduates from the chicken walk to walking the dog, Sandy becomes more entrenched in her naïveté. In her fantasy, everyone will be safe and happy when the robins come. A typical Lynch Aryan, she believes in a Reaganesque, fictional America. In front of a church, accom-panied by pious organ music, she tells Jeffrey about the robins bringing unconditional love to "a strange world" where Frank Booth can steal lives, but also where Jeffrey, like a remora, can enjoy the immoral scraps Frank leaves behind. Sandy, however, sees Jeffrey as her savior. Her dream of the robins is a hopeful sign that Jeffrey will transform her mundane exis-tence, but only up to a point. And that point is what Jeffrey must dis-cover, that critical confluence where curiosity becomes criminal. But when Jeffrey revisits Dorothy, intrigued, curious, testing himself, Dorothy coddles his innocence like a vampire, telling him, "I looked for you in the closet tonight." When she asks, "What do you want?" he answers, "I don't know." This, at least, is more honest than his response to the same question during his first visit, when Dorothy asked him what he wanted and he answered, "Nothing." Clearly, now he wants what Frank has, but within limits. And that is the difference. Until he can answer the ques-tion, "What do you want?" he will remain an *ingénu* in existential limbo.

Jeffrey's willingness to explore the temptations Dorothy offers him, as an ontological odyssey, reflects Kierkegaard's view that "In the state of innocence man is not merely an animal, for if at any time of his life he was merely an animal, he never would become a man" ("Dread and Freedom" 103). Jeffrey must awaken, by desire and dread, the "Spirit … dreaming in man" (101). Otherwise, he will remain bestial like Frank, "not qualified by spirit" (101). For Kierkegaard, what separates man from beast is spirit, "a synthesis of the soulish and the bodily" (103). If, as Kierkegaard insists, "prohibition awakens the desire" (103), Dorothy acts as the catalytic agent for Jeffrey's move into the symbolic, his so-called coming of age. Only when he realizes his freedom—"possibility anterior to possibility" (101)—will he be able to move beyond the animal aesthetic and enter the ethical world of choice, responsibility and consequence. But for the moment, he is content to enjoy Dorothy within the safety of his limited imagination.

After sleeping with Dorothy the first time, Jeffrey drops by The Slow Club to catch her show. He still postures with Heinekens, but this time his sophomoric aloofness has been replaced by a newfound authenticity, a solid street credibility: after all, he is having sex with the object of desire of every other man in the bar. When Jeffrey spots Frank Booth and his gang, Frank is fingering a piece of blue velvet he cut off Dorothy's robe in his last attack, the cloth now an image of both the sweetness and violence of sex. Yet even Frank, surrounded by the desperate trappings of ritual male-bonding—a gang of tough-talking rednecks in leather jackets with a burnt-out hot rod—appears malevolently remorseful. He kneads his piece of robe like prayer beads, watching Dorothy pour on the syrup. Jeffrey follows Frank and his gang, at this point still hoping that solving the mystery of the surface action will explain the deeper, mythic, psychological and religious ramifications of his metamorphosis. He is still faithful to logic, trusting his inductive reasoning, hoping his "detective work" will lead to some analytically sound empirical evidence. But reason alone cannot help Jeffrey explain the images he snaps with his homemade dashboard spy camera, especially the archetypal Well-Dressed Man—dressed, of course, in an outlandish plaid suit, ridiculous wig and fake mustache. But the implication is that inside every well-dressed man is the potential for evil. Jeffrey's attempts to understand this process—to come to terms with the duality of his own nature and reconcile the impulse to emulate his domesticated dad while dabbling in craven passions—parallels Schopenhauer's image of the human situation: a sighted but lame man riding, precariously, on the back of a blind beast in perpetual heat.

Lynch's parody of melodramatic detective mystery film becomes a 1980s version of *The Catcher in the Rye* (1951), a postmodern saga of the

American innocent learning the ugly truth, or as Jeffrey puts it, "seeing something that was always hidden." Jeffrey confesses to Sandy that he is "in the middle of something." He is, actually, along with the audience, in the middle of the movie. And he is gaining confidence, enough to kiss Sandy, who is by now more than willing, having all but called it off with her boyfriend Mike (whom she had earlier claimed to love). When Mike, decked out in his football gear, first sees Sandy and Jeffrey together— the fake knight out to fight for his princess—his pathetic "Sandy?" underscores the stark contrast between him and Jeffrey: how they think, what they know, what they are capable of. Mike still lives in the illusory world of homespun Lumberton, where time is marked on the local radio by the sound of a falling tree. He believes in his image—stud jock—and the stereotypical loyalties so essential in high school. But the more Jeffrey learns from Dorothy, the more Sandy is attracted to him, and, given Jeffrey's training with Dorothy, in the realm of psychosexual politics Mike has no chance. At first, Sandy kisses Jeffrey demurely, starts to let herself go, then breaks it off, her caution more conditioned than authentic. Her high school loyalty cuts both ways. But with their kiss all the various plot lines, themes and images conjoin. Jeffrey is halfway though the movie, halfway through his personal quest to understand himself, halfway to solving the mystery of the ear, and halfway into his fledgling romance with Sandy.

But he has yet to experience his limits. When he next visits Dorothy—who is by now obsessed with the reversal in her life: corrupt herself, corrupting others—she asks him, "Are you a bad boy?" Filled with self-loathing—powerless to help her husband and child, ashamed of enjoying Frank's abuse—she begs Jeffrey to hit her. Instead, Jeffrey wants to call the police, appealing to the force of community values—the collective super-ego—as an antidote to what he considers Dorothy's runaway libido. She panics because she knows, to paraphrase the Rolling Stones, that the cops are criminals and the sinners are saints. The police, for Dorothy, are as indictable as Frank. But Lynch often casts the police symbolically, as a super-ego: the sirens in *Six Figures Getting Sick*, Dale Cooper in *Twin Peaks*, the detectives in *Lost Highway* and *Mulholland Dr.* who haunt the guilty, hounding them into self-destruction. Frank is a natural fugitive, the antithesis of both society's normative values and institutional corruption. Dorothy, while her husband and child are hostages, lives in ethical abeyance, having relinquished her existential self and abandoned the principle of guilt in an instinctual strategy of survival. She wants no part of restraint, limitations or prohibition, which is all the police represent for her. Given her circumstances, she finds comfort in excess, losing herself in an act, a disguise, escaping the self-loathing born from her powerlessness.

Whereas Dorothy resists the police—because of her innate distrust and her lack, for the moment, of restraint—Jeffrey and Sandy rely on and defer to the authorities. Sandy's father is an archetypal heavy, a patriarchal figure forever warning and threatening, suspect himself, suspicious of others, setting parameters, enforcing moral codes and boundaries of acceptable behavior. But just as the characters are corrupted by desire, so is the community itself plagued by corruption in the police force, that mythical-psychological agent of stability and security. Jeffrey represents a counterforce of righteousness charged with restoring faith in community values like fairness, decency, family cohesion and respect for tradition and authority.

Yet Jeffrey must take that step beyond, into the flame, in defiance of boundaries and authority, into the essence of desire. He must go too far, must let the animal loose. And when he does—he hits Dorothy—it is her moment of triumph. She has seduced him beyond his will. "I have your disease in me now," she says: his corruption. But slapping her is a triumph for Jeffrey too, the impact transformational. By satisfying her, he satisfies himself. In an earlier episode with her, he felt a sense of disappointment, frustration and incompleteness. This time, after he hits her, successfully performing the role she expected of him, he feels a sense of closure, of cool assurance.

"I'll call you," he says, before sauntering out of her apartment.

But he is too cool, too indifferent, and in the hands of the Calvinist Lynch, another moral lesson begins. Leaving Dorothy's apartment, Jeffrey meets Frank in the hallway. Frank is Lynch's leveling agent, a corrective to Jeffrey's cocksure pose. Dorothy appeals to Frank's "passive" persona, saying, "Hello, Baby" (instead of "Hello, Daddy"), but Frank, calling Jeffrey "neighbor," transforms the word into an insult, an invitation for revenge. Dorothy, bizarrely, continues to appeal to Frank's sense of decency and civility. "He's a good kid, Frank," she says, an observation that infuriates Frank, reminding him of his own inadequacies, his innate deprivation. So Frank switches to the evil sophist, the paradoxical agent of Calvinist justice tempered by the possibility of salvation through sacrifice. Jeffrey's purgatorial initiation involves a "joyride" to Ben's, a Platonic cave of illusions, fueled with sex, drugs and rock 'n' roll, another theater where Frank plays out his hard-core routine. The "joyride," an overt threat of rape, is a reminder to Jeffrey of his contingency, his need for humility. In the car, the others tease him and call him a "pussy." (Frank reminds them, "But he's our pussy.") They feminize him, objectify him, but he resists, and this resistance is his moral coup. One of the gang asks Jeffrey if he has ever been to "pussy heaven." Jeffrey says, "No," the only answer he can give, honestly. But his induction into the position of patriarchal figurehead of Lynch's idealized middle-class mythology, which Dorothy perversely began, is still incomplete. Jeffrey has yet to realize the bloodlust that will, like Nietzsche's pre–Socratic Hellenes, transform his potential into self-actualization, securing him a dominant position in the family hierarchy he is ineluctably destined and anxious to enter—with at least enough innate restraint to succeed in a small business, ascend the parochial social ladder, and not be overly indebted to the local Chamber of Commerce.

Like a Freudian Dante descending through his subconscious into the nether stages of a redneck hell, Jeffrey's next performance is at Ben's, a cheap facsimile of the idealized world promised in Roy Orbison's dreams, peopled, in Lynch's eyes, with reckless, unattractive, dangerous degenerates (who are, as subjects in the lens of a sadistic director, still a ton of fun). In a theater where anything goes, emceed by Ben, avatar of raw impotence, Frank is the primal director of absurdity. When he asks Jeffrey what kind of beer he wants, Jeffrey answers, "Heineken." Frank's response is as honest as it is contemptuously jingoistic. "Heineken!" he shouts. "Fuck that shit." Frank drinks the all–American cliché of a workingman's beer, Pabst Blue Ribbon. This privileging of American iconographic labels over European products is another example of Lynch's "America first" patriotism. (Heineken, remember, meant trouble for Jeffrey ever since he tried to impress Sandy at The Slow Club.)

So Frank, playing the sadistic director, takes on his understudy, forcing a reluctant Jeffrey to act and punching him if his performance slips (as when Jeffrey's toast to Ben is unconvincing). Frank gives him director's notes like "Be polite!" He tells Ben, "I can make him do anything I want." Ben, too, joins in beating Jeffrey, if only to satisfy his part in Frank's histrionics. Ben and Frank, when they have no roles to play—the Well-Dressed Man, the Candy Colored Clown, the high school stoner playing air guitar—lose their essences. They are phantoms, necessary demons playing with stilettos and muscle cars, living by the strict codes of masculine signifiers. Frank's primary signifier is "fuck," the one act he can not perform. For instance, Raymond, his sidekick, asks him if he wants him to pour the beer. Frank says, "No. I want you to fuck it." Then Frank toasts "fucking." He shouts, before they leave on their joyride,

"Let's fuck!" Frank likes to think he comes in dreams like the "candy colored clown they call the sandman." While Ben does his cameo, Frank feels a merging with the persona in the Orbison song. This masquerading connects him to Dorothy, except that where Dorothy seems aware of her playacting, Franks believes in his roles—there is nothing else for him; he shifts, ontologically, like a chameleon, as comfortable dealing contraband with Ben as leading his gang of deviant boy scouts through a series of violent crimes. But when he feels he is being upstaged by Ben, he interrupts the show, recovers himself by drawing back the action, quickly resolves differences, gathers his boys, recruits the stripper for Raymond, and reorganizes the chaos into the car. Lynch demonizes Frank's exit, leaving his maniacal laugh to linger. He disappears, shouting "I'll fuck anything that moves!" in a squeal of burning rubber, careening his Dodge Charger down the highway, a close-up of the yellow median line shifting back and forth at speed from lane to lane, Frank in a rage, Dorothy trying desperately to resist and satisfy Frank at the same time— the joyride merely a pretext for Frank to manipulate the next scene, to control the situation, to keep the play onstage, his ontological theater active.

What Jeffrey begins to understand is the true nature of theater— the difference between posing with superficial props and phenomenological presentation. At this point in his Oedipal drama, Jeffrey's existential pursuit will eventually lead him safely into the bourgeois theater of middle-class mediocrity. He craves more authenticity than a mimed, cassette karaoke show at Ben's, front-lit by a mechanic's droplight. To establish his ethical self, he must resist Frank's attempts to possess him, to corrupt him beyond redemption. But he is cowed by Frank's glare. During the joyride, Dorothy infuriates Frank by revealing her concern for Jeffrey. He nearly wrecks the car pulling off the road. He slides the car to a stop and turns to Jeffrey. His "Don't you fuckin' look at me" routine with Jeffrey does not work this time. Frank is center stage, but he is ready to be challenged. When he begins torturing Dorothy, savagely pinching her nipples, Jeffrey yells at him to leave her alone. Frank tells Jeffrey, "You're like me." Which is true: Frank loves and loathes Jeffrey's innocence—his "neighborliness"—as Jeffrey loves and loathes Frank's depravity. But as if to refute Frank's assessment of his final performance, in an audacious show of free will and commitment, and without any sane concern for himself (while ritualistically being prepared for rape in a car full of knife-wielding strangers and a stripper dancing on the roof of the car), Jeffrey punches Frank. Here, like Paul Atreides, he becomes a crusader, matching the violence of the enemy, but justified by a righteous cause.

But his heroism is still contingent on his exiting Frank's Grand Guignole with all his physical and psychological parts intact. After punching Frank, Jeffrey is hustled out of the car at knifepoint. In a macabre episode of male bonding, Frank and his gang merge in the aesthetics of torture, effecting the final breakdown of Jeffrey's pretense to purity. But after this initiation, Jeffrey, as Dorothy taught him, will make no more appeals to the police. He enters indeterminacy, where only choice can save you and prove your authenticity. He learns that to survive Frank is to become Frank. With the girl from Ben's grinding on top of the car, the gang holds Jeffrey for Frank's final sermon. In a significant reversal, he tells Jeffrey to "look at me." He is in costume, but his role is ethereal, cosmic and absolute. He is the devil of Meadow Lane who will send Jeffrey "straight to Hell." He recites the scripture according to Roy Orbison, confessing to Jeffrey that he is indeed the dark force of Manichaean evil itself, the candy-colored clown. Frank transforms himself and Jeffrey, joined at the hip through Dorothy, into lipstick effigies of each other, until the union is complete: Frank kisses him, an image more violent than the beating Frank gives him. The last punch sends Jeffrey through the flame, but he survives.

And by surviving, Jeffrey realizes the Frank inside him, the demon of desire, understanding suddenly that he too is as capable as Frank of irrational violence. But unlike Frank, Jeffrey feels remorse. It is Jeffrey's sense of restraint, of atonement, that differentiates him from Frank. True to his puritanical belief in good deeds, Jeffrey's salvation lies in his sense of guilt. Temptation is normal, but so is self-control. He learns that the trick to an integrated personality is to assimilate cultural values without losing touch with his primal self, to exploit his potential for action *and* restraint. When he thinks back on the night's events, he cries cathartic tears, filled with self-pity, terror and compassion. Crying humanizes him. He recognizes his guilt, as well as the guilt of others. In Lynch's moral context, this is healthy, allowing Jeffrey to channel his violence into positive aggression tempered by his superego (the same process Freud defines as aim-inhibited love). Given his cultural context, of course, he expresses his new assertiveness by telling his aunt "you're gonna get it" when she inquires about his black eye, or when watering the yard with his cool sunglasses on, he assumes his father's socially and sexually dominant position in the family. He can also, now, having survived the training from Frank and Dorothy, claim Sandy, his reward for having successfully completed his initiation into the rites of adulthood.

Jeffrey assumes the role of a Southern gentleman (after all, he took acting lessons from Frank and Dorothy). His euphemistic phrasing—e.g., "Things got a little out of hand"—sounds, perhaps, to progressive women, like a condescending paternal benevolence, but to women like Sandy, who find security in deferring to male authority, Jeffrey's evasive nonchalance embodies the reassuring voice of control. Jeffrey is learning to rely on himself, to trust his family and his instincts more than the government. He tells Detective Williams, "Frank Booth is a very sick and dangerous man," and Sandy's father replies, "Behave yourself. Don't blow it." Sandy, on their first date, asks what the two men were talking about, and Jeffrey is again evasive, answering, "Fatherly advice." By assimilating the patriarchal values of the small-town South, he reinforces established social mores, and his induction into the community is all but guaranteed.

At the party, Sandy's being with Jeffrey enhances her status. He is a nascent adult, one step away from authenticity, and her kiss, this time deep and hungry, draws strength from Jeffrey's control. His authority allows her the freedom to let go, to pursue her desire. As Jeffrey provides Sandy the comfort to explore her sexuality, their kiss this time is sustained through the Julee Cruise pap. They pledge their love to one another, but the lessons are not over. On the way home from the party, a crazed driver assaults them. Sandy asks Jeffrey, "What's wrong?" He replies, "Frank." For Jeffrey, Frank has become a rarified devil; but Jeffrey's surprise that Sandy's ex-boyfriend Mike, out for some petty high school ritualistic face-saving revenge, could perpetrate the assault reveals his need for further education. He must realize that, in Lynch's world, Frank indicates the universality of an evil that can possess anybody, anytime, a well-dressed man as easily as a teenager.

Desperate for safety, Jeffrey heads for his house. Mike cuts him off and threatens to "kick your ass"—of course, nothing Mike could dole out (in this context) could be worse than Frank's joyride, so Jeffrey is immune to Mike's idle posing. But the point of the confrontation is to prove that a potential Frank lives inside everyone: Mike yells at Sandy the way Frank yells at Dorothy: "Shut up. Just shut up. Nobody's talking to you." Mike, the all–American boy, has assimilated Frank's violence, but not Jeffrey's control. When a totally naked Dorothy Vallens—the primordial image of lust—appears on Jeffrey's porch, her castrating presence immediately disarms Mike's gang. And aside from the hilarious, if atrocious, classic first-date parody—a beaten and naked Dorothy Vallens screaming in front of Sandy and her mother, "He put his disease in me!"—Sandy, at first repulsed and shocked out of her hunky-dory childish dream of the robins, after some reflection, is more impressed with Jeffrey than ever. Clearly she is a product of the dominant phallocentric discourse of her socio-economic class, in which women "surrender" to the firm guiding hand of patriarchal authority. But the authority Jeffrey needs ultimately to seal the romantic bond between the passive damsel and the gallant knight is established only after his final act, killing Frank.

Yet Jeffrey's killing Frank implies also that he replaces him. Jeffrey's evolution from an innocent college kid, to a depraved pervert, to a "normal" citizen is complete. By sharing in all of Frank's deeds—including murder, no matter how justified—Jeffrey has completely appropriated and sublimated Frank's character, and Sandy rewards him with a deep long kiss. As the camera draws back from within his ear, Jeffrey resurfaces from his subconscious. In all his middle-class glory, he awakes in a lawn chair, his and Sandy's parents breaking bread together, his neatly pressed open-collar shirt making him look suddenly older than his years … but he is more than ready to claim the mantle of middle-class legitimacy. And in Lynch's view, violence, sanctified by the machinations of restraint, has its rewards. Jeffrey's father recovers, Jeffrey and Sandy become "a pair," Frank and his gang are punished, and Dorothy is reunited with her child—yet there is always a fly in the soup—or in this case, a beetle in the robin's mouth: people are not pure, and if they pretend to be they are handicapped by their pretensions. But Jeffrey has graduated, having learned that his violent impulses, as long as they are tempered with restraint and social codification, pay off in the rugged wilderness of American social Darwinism.

Whereas *Eraserhead* proves Lynch's ability to handle a surreal narrative rooted in the grit of naturalistic realism, blurring the line between avant-garde and documentary, and *Blue Velvet* manages to combine the best of postmodern pastiche, combining a comic-book detective story with a dystopic *Bildungsroman*, *Wild at Heart* (1990) and the equally pretentious *Twin Peaks: Fire Walk with Me* (1992) are good examples of, in Lynch's case, a virtue becoming a vice. When his allegories work best, the action is grounded in logical circumstance, in a plausibility that manages to create a weird sense of cause and effect, framed by the bizarre imagery that became his trademark. But in *Wild at Heart* and *Twin Peaks: Fire Walk with Me*, Lynch foregrounds allegory at the expense of the odd verisimilitude that prevented his earlier work from devolving into self-indulgence.

Addressing this issue in *The Art of Fiction*, John Gardner writes that the key to allegory is to "treat the surface story with full respect[,] … at the same time to work in signals of the deeper meaning" (146). He cautions that if "we begin to suspect that the basis of profluence is nothing but mad whimsy, we begin to be distracted" (168). It is this lack of convincing flow that causes the structural failure in *Wild at Heart* and *Twin Peaks: Fire Walk with Me*. In *Eraserhead* and *Blue Velvet*, Lynch engages the viewer by, according to Gardner, "translating ideas into appropriate characters[,] … each event expressing in mysterious but concrete terms the active relationship between the central ideas" (168). The complaint of mishandled allegory could be of course made of Nathaniel Hawthorne at his heavy-handed worst, and of Melville when he is less than subtle in, say, "Bartleby the Scrivener" (1853). The flaw seems egregious when the artist allows the moral imperative to interfere with the story at hand, or, as Gardner puts it, "the artist murders actuality" (133) by using allegory as "a means of expressing what the writer already knows" (84).

Incongruously, for a film that bears so little resemblance to the book on which it is based, the problems with the film version of *Wild at Heart* are also inherent in Barry Gifford's original novel. The story unfolds in a series of anecdotal vignettes with, ironically for a road novel, no strong narrative drive, so the plot stalls before it even gets started. The first third of the novel describes Lula's reunion with Sailor after his release from prison for a manslaughter conviction. The vignettes, composed around static action, are little more than blocks of exposition. Lula and Sailor relate past events—their abusive childhoods, their first sexual experiences, Lula's abortion, Sailor's experiences in prison—but the tales they depict are irrelevant to the plot. Also revealed, in a minimalist style that self-effaces nearly into oblivion, is the scheme involving Lula's mother Marietta, her rage against Sailor, and her hiring Johnny Farragut to track down her daughter—the chapters peppered with passing references to a panoply of tangential characters.

The road trip in Gifford's novel amounts to nothing more than an excuse for idle conversation, pseudometaphysical chitchat made comical by an overly stylized dialect and exaggerated idiomatic phrasing, detailing the couple's romp through a decadent strip-mall of Southern stereotypes. In a self-referential moment that neatly summarizes the novel, Sailor confesses: "'We didn't do nothin' special I can remember. Just talked, is all'" (Gifford 64). Lula responds, "I'm a big believer in talkin', case you ain't noticed'" (64). Chion suggests that the stasis in the novel is exactly what "may have seduced Lynch" (125). He describes the book as a "destructured ballad" (125) and Lynch's adaptation a "rhapsodic structure" (127), but the stories Sailor and Lula tell each other, for all their quirkiness, do not advance the narrative. Instead of creating Chion's "poetic quality" (126), they impede both the psychological impetus toward profluence and the resolution of the action. The surface story—the westward drive—provides no linkage to events, so it becomes merely a pretext for conversation. The action picks up when the couple arrives in Big Tuna: Lula discovers she is pregnant, and Sailor meets Bobby Peru. But by then the trip is over. After the botched robbery, Sailor is sent to prison again, his final separation from Lula all but inevitable.

Lynch's enthusiasm for Gifford's novel—"barely off the printing presses before Lynch had written his adaptation" (Alexander 108)—is as mysterious and inexplicable as his reverence for Sheryl Lee's acting talent—"'an unbelievable actress'" (qtd. in Alexander 144). And despite what some describe as Lynch's being "benignly faithful to the plot structure" (Alexander 19), his version of the story *Wild at Heart* deviates so far from Gifford's that any appreciation for the book does not survive comparisons to the film. Using the skeleton of the novel—the bare bones, essentially—Lynch constructs an allegory that seems, compared to the same approach in *Blue Velvet*, more like self-referential doodling than an artist discovering the possibilities inherent in new material.

The typical road movie is a well-worn convention perfectly suited for a parable, especially one that follows the proverbial yellow brick road that, according to film critic Caryn James in *The New York Times*, leads "through danger and disillusionment to healthy self-knowledge and back to the safety of home" (1). *Wild at Heart* certainly fits this pattern, embodying what James describes as "a violent story of romance on the run" (1). The difference, however, is that this movie swerves, as James maintains many contemporary road movies do, into "forced happy endings, which suggest a nostalgic longing for the road to Oz even while the film's surface depicts a broken-down society" (24). The immediate archetype is *Route 66* (1960–64), the television hit about two young drifters in a Corvette tooling along U.S. Highway 66, encountering in each episode an assorted mix of losers, loners, dreamers and outcasts. But a more accurate model for Lynch's vision of Gifford's novel is Terrence Malick's *Badlands* (1973), the Martin Sheen and Sissy Spacek vehicle about a 25-year-old trash man, Kit, who meets a cute, innocent 15-year-old, Holly, whose father will not allow them to continue their relationship. Holly's father's unwavering resistance sends Kit and Holly on a murder spree across the Midwest. As shocking as his cold-blooded killings is Kit's nonchalance.

His narcissism, tempered by his style and fatalistic humor, makes him a sympathetic character even while he's killing innocent strangers.

While acknowledging the road-movie formula, Lynch may have opted to drive *Wild at Heart* into that wreck of a happy ending to satisfy his wistfulness, reinforcing his vision of an all–American longing for a return to Edenic purity. Even as the imagery and situations strain to be different, the theme of *Wild at Heart* is overly familiar: learning to control passion, to channel sexual energy into constructive behavior, even in a world that, as Lula learns, is "wild at heart and weird on top." The characters split starkly into black-and-white Manichaean camps of goodness and evil, where child molesters, greedy con-men, the naysayers to loyalty, love, fidelity and compassion are set against the children of fun, prophets of style, who follow their idealistic dreams, true to themselves and each other. Not surprisingly, given the strictures of Lynch's allegorical frame, the heroes and villains never develop beyond stock, two-dimensional functionary pawns in an overly contrived parable peppered with overt allusions to *The Wizard of Oz*. Lula, an honest and charming ingénue, is caught between her mother's vindictive jealousy and her lover's murderous impetuousness, both victims of their single-minded passions. Marietta, the "wicked witch" of a mother, and her ilk, including Santos and Bobby Peru, represent adult corruption, but they are no match for the "dangerously cute" dynamic duo of youth and innocence, Sailor and Lula, children whose hearts are in the right place even if their sense of responsibility is woefully skewed. But Sailor and Lula are not morally lost. In Lynch's evangelical ethos, they are salvageable reprobates, cursed with a wild lust but blessed, too, with Kierkegaard's "sweet anxiety" ("Dread and Freedom," 105). All they lack is the taming social whip of restraint, and once they assimilate proper normative values and curb their appetites they can join the Epicurean community as honest productive citizens. What others might see as caging wild horses, cutting the rebellious individual down to size by reining in her excess self, Lynch sees as a necessary virtue, an imperative.

The story, such as it is, opens with a typically Lynchian fire of passion and purification, of desire and destruction. In this instance, it is also the fire of perdition (as in Perdita Durango)—making *Wild at Heart* one of Lynch's most Catholic films. Sailor and Lula are not, after all, bad, if not conventionally good. But given the choice of living in the adult, loveless world of Cape Fear or fleeing the trappings of madness, corruption and displaced allegiances, Lula and Sailor (predictably) hit the "yellow brick road" for California, the preferred Promised Land for interstate expatriates. Their road trip becomes a purgatorial journey through excess to purity, as if Lynch took literally Blake's metaphysical musings about the road of excess leading to the palace of wisdom.

In the aesthetic world of sensation, on the road from one context to another, Sailor and Lula maintain a purely superficial essence. This keeps them disconnected, disavowing links to the world outside their kicks and avoiding commitments—except to their tenuous, ephemeral ties to each other. (Lula does, fatally, send a postcard to her mother.) They burn their youth like so many cigarettes, fueling high-octane sex with booze and music and imitations of Elvis, tuning out whenever the radio switches from music to what passes for news: the sordid atrocities, misfortunes and natural catastrophes that plague the landscape this side of the rainbow. They stick to their instinctual archetype like Meursault: the innocent criminal. Lynch's less Calvinist, more Lutheran brother Kierkegaard identifies this dissolute existence as the aesthetic stage of life, the first in his hierarchy (granted that, for Kierkegaard, aesthetic is too often synonymous with "prosthetic"). Sailor lives in a world of simulation, imitating Elvis, always in costume, posing and playing roles, ever on stage. H.J. Blackham, in a comment on Kierkegaard's *Concluding Unscientific Postscript*, explains: "If one goes to history for one's life without having first a life of one's own, one has nothing to go by, no means of discrimination between the authentic and the inauthentic; it is to abdicate the responsibility of living and resort to helpless imitation" (20). To transcend their immediate situation, to move into Kierkegaard's ethical stage and at the same time escape their perdition, Sailor and Lula, lost among spirits eternally corrupted by their craven desires, must accept the world not through images of a reconstructed past or a prefabricated future, but in all its harsh immediacy, staking out commitments stronger than kicks. True to their anti-intellectual instincts, Lynch and Kierkegaard—whom Kaufmann describes as "anti-philosophical and individualistic" (18)—both reject the trappings of rational thinking.

Despite its Catholic overtones and pretensions to Kierkegaard's Lutheranism, the film is anti–Thomas Aquinas, espousing Lynch's strict Calvinist doctrine whereby Sailor and Lula, obviously among the elect, must prove their worth. But because they are among the elect, their participation in their own salvation is existentially problematic: for Kierkegaard, as for Sailor, there is "no rational choice between the two alternatives" (Scruton 237), the aesthetic or the ethical. "The aesthete ... falls in love with himself like Narcissus. Even the ethical life is unchosen by the one who pursues it, since he receives it as a command" (237). In the end, Sailor receives his platitudinous command from Glinda, the Good Witch, who tells him, "Don't turn your back on love." Paradoxically, the aesthetic failure of the movie may hinge on the inability of Sailor to finally move from the dutiful to the irrational. His life is never "truly chosen" (Scruton 237), therefore never actually authentic.

The fire in the opening shot dissolves to the present crisis. Marietta hires Bob Ray Lemon to knife Sailor (ostensibly because he would not have sex with Marietta in the toilet, but also because she thinks Sailor is a witness to her complicity in the murder of her husband). Sailor, lacking restraint, retaliates beyond what might be considered by law to be necessary violence. Maniacal, he literally beats Lemon's brains out. While Sailor is cracking open Lemon's head on the concrete, spraying blood and brain matter across the screen, Glenn Miller's "In the Mood" plays in the background. The incongruity of the airy, upbeat big-band sound and the savage visual violence echoes Leland Palmer's murderous passion for show tunes in *Twin Peaks* as well as the stylized jitterbug sequence that opens *Mulholland Dr.* But for Leland, popular music is a narcotic, the innocuous songs a place of refuge from the heinous reality of his being possessed by a demon, and for Diane, the happy-go-lucky dance hit represents a sugar-coated counter-balanced idealized life she uses as a psychic self-defense against the sordid world that destroys her in Hollywood. In contrast, the opening scene of *Wild at Heart*, juxtaposing Miller's swinging hit with Lemon's brutal murder, without the moral context or psychological grounding that in *Twin Peaks* creates the striking pathos of Leland's suffering, seems flippant, more of a mocking gesture than a serious attempt to draw any metaphorical companion between the coziness of the imaginary life and the harsh reality of the lived one.

Sailor's imprisonment at Pee Dee Correctional Institution is viewed through a crystal ball, the first imagistic sign of a parallel narrative indicating Lynch's initial moral intrusion. This simplistic attempt to infuse *Wild at Heart* with moral seriousness by imposing an allegory of intercessional love loosely borrowed from *The Wizard of Oz* fails to elevate *Wild at Heart* beyond a soft-core comic piece of fluff, the kind Sherilyn Fenn made a career in before *Twin Peaks*. As a distancing device, framing the story through *The Wizard of Oz*—interposing yet another perspective layer between the viewer and the image—does not allow Lynch the moral seriousness or the license for ambiguity he seems to have assumed. The psychology so instinctive in *Blue Velvet* seems contrived in *Wild at Heart*, conditioned by the medieval miracle play Lynch forces into the material.

The allusions to Oz are as disruptive as the gratuitous flashbacks, not in any Brechtian theoretical or constructivist sense, but in self-indulgent ineptitude. Lynch borrows the moral recipe from *Blue Velvet*, but Jeffrey Beaumont needed to push himself, to try to go too far. Only then could he know when to draw back and assume his role as an adult in the community, defending its mores and speaking from experience while free to satisfy himself and Sandy in a world removed from any normative social values. Sailor, on the other hand, is already out there. He needs to pull back. Sailor is anarchic, Jeffrey repressed. Whereas Jeffrey defers too quickly to authority—to his parents, to Detective Williams, to Dorothy and Frank—Sailor bows to no one, until the end, when he receives his divine walking papers from the good witch Glinda. Nevertheless, Sailor fits the archetypal pattern of a typical Lynchian hero: another one of Kierkegaard's aesthetic beasts, whose entry into the ethical—that is, whose salvation is contingent on accepting limitations—requires him to endure a series of brutal tests of the will so that he might emerge with an acute, almost transcendental understanding of moderation and psychosexual balance. The trouble, in Sailor's case, is that he doesn't understand his own motives (nor is the viewer given much of a clue beyond Sailor's self-pitying complaint that he lacked "parental guidance"), so his seething rage seems conditioned: he is incapable of choosing to correct his situation, because his actions are outside any innate moral framework through which he might assess his behavior.

Sailor and Lula begin their journey in the East, near Cape Fear, North Carolina, and drive themselves and the narrative westward. Moving west implies traveling the metaphorical road of life: from the sunrise of youth, into the midday of maturity, arriving eventually at the sunset of death. But while Lula flees death—of her father, her mother's love, her abortion—she simultaneously powers, like the revelers in Poe's "The Masque of Red Death" (1842), straight towards it: Farragut, the girl in the accident, Bobby Peru (among others) all die during the trip. Sailor too, hoping to escape the restraints of parole and the penal system, heads straight back into it. Their journey, without the ethical framework, would be circular, but their moral progress can be graphed as a learning curve leading them to their separate epiphanies about restraint and responsibility, duty, faith and family. The paradox of their quest is that most people move to California for its "youth culture," but Sailor and Lula, who, significantly, do not make it, are chasing the sun to its demise. California will not, for them, be a place of new beginnings and second chances. Their life-lessons must be learned now while they are, like Dante, midway through life—Big Tuna being halfway between the Carolinas and California—and in order for them to move into the ethical family nexus so critical to Lynch's vision of the American ethos, they cannot continue life's journey until they learn that their actions have consequences, and that they must accept responsibility for them. The world, according to Lynch, was not created to accommodate their insatiable desire for kicks, and until they understand that, they will remain stalled in the purgatorial wasteland of Big Tuna.

Even as they steer west, the disruptive flashbacks act as a countercurrent, flowing in reverse and connecting Sailor and Lula to their past in the east, preventing the couple from escaping the consequences of their immediate behavior. The flashbacks upset and interfere with Sailor and Lula's flow into the future, just as, aesthetically, the flashbacks are the least integrated of the narrative elements. They merely provide a background, the reasons why Sailor and Lula hit the road. As a result of her violent sexual abuse at the hands of Uncle Pooch (who later died in a suspicious fiery crash), Lula's trauma was aggravated by her subsequent pregnancy and abortion (another instance of Lynch's anti-abortion politics, as he equates Lula's trauma of being raped with her distress about the operation). The flashbacks also establish Marietta's complicity with Marcello Santos (another cartoon villain, for whom Sailor was once a driver) in the death (again, by fire) of Lula's father. Marietta's suspicion about whether Sailor knows of her involvement—a fire, she tells Sailor, he was "too close to"—explains her lethal determination to keep Lula away from him and, perversely, fuels her hatred of him after he refuses her grubby attempt to seduce him in the toilet. Marietta told Lula her father's death was a suicide, and Lula remembers running through the smoking house calling for her father. A pair of irrelevant flashbacks recall an earlier episode in Sailor's plump sexual history, and another describes Lula's Cousin Dell's eccentricities. These last two sequences, even in a road movie, which by its nature relies on a loosely connected series of adventures that fray plausibility, betray the worst of Lynch's gratuitous use of imagery and perhaps best illustrate the aspects of the film that frustrate many critics. (Although some diehard apologists nevertheless tried—with overheated logic—to defend Lynch's self-indulgence as, for instance, a reflection of a cultural epistemology dominated by "fragmented narratives of rock videos and television advertising" (Alexander 124) or, in another instance, illustrating "a return to the baroque style of his beginnings" (Chion 123), these excuses seem disingenuous at best, if not evidence of willful critical misreading.)

Meanwhile, Sailor and Lula begin their lesson: no matter how idealized and rarefied their lovemaking, the road is no escape, and past every
temporary oasis lies another stretch across the polluted morass of contemporary American society. As reality continues to intrude on their
idyllic romp, Sailor concedes that "we all got a secret side," and soon
enough, when they happen upon the portentous wreck (juxtaposed with
the murder of Farragut), they realize that their idealized love alone is
not enough to transcend the physical world where people suffer and die
and where, too often, there is nothing you can do about it. In Lynch's
moral scheme, these kinds of discoveries are the keys to the doors leading to adulthood. As the allegory veers along, incessantly contrasting the
selfish, immoral machinations of the unredeemable adults with the
romantic antics of their children, the collage of bizarre tableaux, loose
plot lines and oddball characters that mechanically popup like cardboard
cutouts continues to confuse more than clarify the central moral context. As a result, the story bogs down from its own dead weight long
before Lula and Sailor reach the literal end of their road in Big Tuna.

Only Johnnie Farragut, sent by Marietta to track down the lovers,
displays any potential for complexity, but in the world he inhabits, good
intentions are not enough to save him, and he is conveniently killed off
before he develops any psychological depth. In his murder all the stories collide, exposing and resolving the relationships involving Farragut
and Marietta, Santos and Marietta, Mr. Reindeer and his gang (including Juana, Perdita, and Bobby Peru), and finally Lula and Sailor, the target of his pursuit and the reason for his predicament. Dramatically
conflating sex and death—the central concern of the story—Farragut's
execution (along with the seduction scene with Bobby Peru and Lula),
is one of the most successful scenes in the film, illustrating the moral rot
in Marietta's soul while highlighting the vicious and debased inhumanity of Mr. Reindeer's criminal associates—including Santos, Marietta's
replacement lover and, in the end, Lula's new surrogate father figure.

The Farragut sequence begins with Marietta persuading him to go
after her daughter, threatening, if he balks at her request, to call on Santos, who, Marietta reminds Farragut, is still "sweet on me"—reinforcing
the implication that her main transgression, in Lynch's eyes, is not acting her age. When Farragut fails to find Sailor and Lula, Marietta con-
tacts Santos and asks him to kill Sailor. Santos agrees, but also plans to
kill Farragut, afraid he "will find out what we're up to with Mr. Reindeer."
Mr. Reindeer lives like J.K. Huysmans' Des Esseintes in *A Rebours* (1884),
surrounded by all the trappings of a decadent aesthete: a refined, eclectic

taste for topless strumpets and ritual assassins. He is typical of Lynch's omnipotent manipulators, miraculously orchestrating grand schemes of evil—usually involving drugs and prostitution—and threatening community standards of decency.

After Marietta unleashes Santos, she has second thoughts and tries to stop him, but Santos rebukes her, saying he is "in a killing mood." Overcome by guilt, selfish and self-loathing, she symbolically cuts her wrist with a tube of lipstick. Life for her, after all, is makeup, costumes and acting. By the time she telephones to warn Farragut, she has painted her face red, having become the image—the caricature, actually—of the devil (as comical as the demons in Dante's *bolgia* of the Malebranche), right down to the wicked-witch slippers she wears and her spectral ride on a broom. But she becomes literally ill over what she has done, the paradox being that, surrounded by sadists, Marietta's innate moral awareness is acute. She lacks the ethical fortitude to trust the people that, by nature, she should. Childish and impulsive, having made a misery of her life, she suffers for casting her lot with vicious nihilists like Santos instead of keeping the faith with Farragut.

While Farragut watches wild animals on his hotel television shred their fresh kill, Marietta phones to tell him she has done something "real bad." She flies to New Orleans to try to detour Farragut from the destiny she has set in motion for him, and in a cheesy downtown restaurant she tries to persuade him to change tactics and take her along. After Farragut is kidnapped and prepared for slaughter, in a scene later echoed in *Twin Peaks*, the aged concierge apologizes to Marietta, telling her "I'm so sorry" while handing her a message. He is, it turns out, sorry for more than he knows, but he also introduces one of the few clever, self-reflexive moments in the film. The note, which Marietta says aloud, reads: "I've gone buffalo hunting." Irritated, she asks, "Who the fuck goes buffalo hunting?" Lynch's intention with this repartee seems to be to poke fun at the critics, decipherers and crypto-logicians who (as, perhaps, in the present instance) tend to explain rather than experience Lynch's work. Like many of Lynch's detractors, Marietta misunderstands the meaning of the situation until Santos delivers the news and tells her, "Cut the crybaby stuff. You're my girl now." As expected from a comic-book creep, Santos denies harming Farragut while scenes of Farragut's ritual torture and murder by accomplices of Santos are intercut with scenes of Sailor and Lula discovering the realistic carnage littering the yellow brick road.

Though desperate about Farragut's well-being, Marietta, like Dorothy Vallens, wants nothing to do with the police. They represent a

Bobby Peru (Willem Dafoe) spoils Lula's trip (Laura Dern) in *Wild at Heart*
(1990). She is about to discover that Big Tuna is not Kansas, and Bobby Peru is
not the Wizard of Oz. Big Tuna is, in fact, a place of perdition, and Bobby Peru
the ugly face of desire that Lula cannot resist. Once she and Sailor have both been
morally compromised, they must suffer a purgatorial period of purification until
they give up their childish detachment and join the community of good citizens.
In her desire to be domesticated she plays Penelope to Sailor's Ulysses.

community conscience antithetical to Marietta's instinct, licensed as they
are to enforce logical restrictions on her irrational perversions. In this
sense, Lula is her mother's daughter, the fruit, as it were, not falling far
from the tree. Both share burning passions and acute aversions to authority. But Marietta calculates, and that is the source of her corruption. Lula's
cupidity is genuine. She gives herself up with honest abandon. She is pure
instinct, going with what feels good—until she feels good with Bobby
Peru, and, like Meursault recognizing the *fact* of his action—shooting
the Arab several more times—Lula learns how far raw undiluted desire
can compromise not fidelity, but self. She flirts with primal will, her body
dissolving in intense, unfiltered sensations. Her identity, bounded by
conscience, is threatened as she essentially becomes ethereal. This is the
ultimate climax, complete abandonment of identity. Bobby Peru is a
mind-fuck. He assaults Lula's identity, her will, initiating the same loss

of self-control that the early Christian elders like Paul, Jerome and Augustine feared most.

The encounter frightens Lula too. After the events in Big Tuna, she retreats from the instinctual into the safety of the conceptual self, ducking into the collective conscience of the conventional world—specifically into the role of mother, not of course like that narcissistic wreck of a martini Marietta becomes, but as an intuitive mother, relying in the end on her character, forged by the same restraint, denial and self-gratification posturing as moral fortitude that Lynch preaches in *Twin Peaks*. A neorealist, Lula stoically accepts her trophy (her son) as Lynch dutifully fetishizes the boy in a cornball scenario that, in all its smarminess, nevertheless marks a seismic shift from the situation faced by Henry and Mary in *Eraserhead*. A perfect white-bread kid grinning out of what could be a J. Crew photo shoot has replaced the grotesque chicken-baby. Lula, unlike Henry and Mary, loves her child. He is, after all, photogenic. Jeffrey Beaumont channeled his guilt to check his spirit; Henry had no spirit, only desire and remorse; but Lula is different. She may have given up her illusions, but she thrives on hope now more than desire. When Sailor betrays her by breaking his promise not to "let things get no worse," confessing, face down in the dirt while being arrested, "I really let you down this time," Lula is forgiving because she has betrayed Sailor too, with Bobby Peru. But her salvation lies in the fact that she has learned clicking her red heels together will not deliver her from shame. Through this revelation, she is spiritually salvaged, crying guiltily in a scene morally synonymous with Jeffrey Beaumont's redemption in *Blue Velvet*.

After all, it is Sailor who experiences the vision of Glinda's command, the final ethical epiphany, and this reversal—Lula losing faith in magic and Sailor suddenly believing in miracles—expresses a value transference as natural as passing a virus. Sailor's singing "Love Me Tender"—the one song Lula wanted all along—broadcasts his inability to escape the symbolic: he is still simulating, annealed by the fire of the film into a transparent cliché. But his inability to move beyond simulation and into the authentic illustrates a moral failing that spoils the reunion of Sailor and Lula as an idealized, actualizing synthesis linking the parents through their child. After being violently beaten by a gang, and having his gummy vision of Glinda, Sailor reverts to his former posturing, going into "Love Me Tender." The only difference between his performance on the hood of Lula's car (his little boy beaming in the bucket seat), and his earlier Elvis impression is that, in the first, Sailor humiliates a punk who comes on to Lula; in the second, his tough-guy act has almost gotten him killed. He apologizes like the punk before him, and, defeated, retreats to Lula. Sailor's authentic self remains hidden—for instance, we never see him living in prison: he does his time, as it were, offstage.

The difference between the road trip proper—as Sailor and Lula blow from town to town, bar to bar, dancing and jiving, carefree, existentially disconnected—and their stagnant layover in Big Tuna, where lies replace dreams, promises are merely pathetic gestures of fidelity, and the cuddly munchkins of Oz turn out to be dangerous deviants, is essential for effecting the moral superstructure that, however tenuously, holds the film together. The raucous sex—invariably dissolving into a fiery red haze—starts as soon as Lula picks Sailor up from prison, and on the road their relationship burns with a sexual fever that purifies their hedonism.

Sex is the basis for their relationship. Everything they do is an excuse for, or a prelude to, sex, and achieving a climax is the expected return on every investment. But just as their spontaneity, however refreshing, offers no reward other than itself, their sex is honest in its abandonment, but it takes them no further than the next party. Even the mother-daughter rivalry is sex-based, part of Marietta's revenge for being sexually scorned by Sailor. The only difference—and it is a significant one—is that Marietta uses sex as a manipulative tool, whereas Lula enjoys sex for pleasure. But in Lynch's moral playbook, sex for its own sake is not enough: its anarchy is too open-ended for a teleological virtuecrat like him.

The first part of Sailor and Lula's journey is punctuated by hot sex and steady context, but by the time they reach Big Tuna, their passion is smoldering, the kindling of their ardor reduced to ashes. The fire of their sex, now linking the deaths of Uncle Pooch, Farragut, and Lula's father, creates a sex-death matrix that breeds disillusionment. Along with the image of Marietta as the Wicked Witch hounding them like the Furies chasing Orestes, three intrusive episodes foreshadow Sailor and Lula's ultimate disenchantment on the road: they escape the radio news by tuning in mindless music (leading to another sexual embrace), witness the aftermath of the wreck where the girl dies in front of them, and meet Bobby Peru. These events are sexually stifling, not stimulating, and signal a distinct change in the mood of the film. Death is, after all, what youth must come to terms with, living, as many do, with personal death deferred as an abstraction to some distant, incoherent future. As Kierkegaard explains, death is what gives life value, and those who take life for granted do not truly appreciate life in all its precarious intensity. "This need for values and decisiveness in the face of the uncertainty of all things provokes ... a kind of dizziness that reveals the true human condition as one of anguish and despair" (Palmer 248). This ontological dizziness, anguish and despair strand Sailor and Lula in Big Tuna, but they are not hopeless: in true Lynchian fashion, once they have reached the bottom there is nowhere to go but up.

As childish dreams go, this one too quickly turns sour. Instead of the Emerald City (or California, for that matter), they end up "broke down on the yellow brick road" with Lula pregnant and forty dollars between them. Stuck in Big Tuna, the last outpost of lost chances, they are beyond easy salvation. It is a mean-spirited, moral wasteland where, at the end of the road, dreams remain "over the rainbow." Sailor and Lula begin to experience all the drawbacks in relationships that personal hardship exaggerates: jealousy, domestic squabbling, alcoholic rage, money problems, and infidelity. Ironically, Lula discovers her pregnancy in this sterile sty of piss and vomit and "shit, shit, shit," and where the couple's early flaming desire is reduced to Sailor's kissing Lula on the forehead before passing out curled up away from her in bed, Lula crying in her pillow. The corollary flashback implies that Lula is keeping the baby to make up for the one she aborted from Uncle Pooch. Lynch seems to consider this quid pro quo pregnancy a moral correction while never addressing the truth of Sailor and Lula's reality: he is a violent criminal who has spent eight of their years together in prison; she is an aimless, unemployed twenty-year-old engaged in an active sex life without, it seems, the sense to use responsible birth control. In a desperate act of economic determinism, Sailor (like Lula in the motel room) succumbs to the "dark angel" Bobby Peru and agrees to armed robbery. It all goes terribly, violently wrong, but *Wild at Heart* is, after all, a fairy tale, and Lynch must provide a happy ending. Sailor will pay his dues, as even in fairy tales there are no free passes.

When Sailor is released from jail some five years later, the world is no less scary, vicious, or frighteningly contingent—violent accidents still happen—but Lula's triumph is complete. She has matured into a beautiful, confident young woman with an equally beautiful and well-adjusted child, while her mother, having tortured herself into a hideous alcoholic ghoul, is reduced to crawling around her floor. In Lynch's vision, of course, convention is the only defense against the vagaries of a crazy world where self-doubt can destroy the nuclear family's American dream. Sailor, after his near-death experience, is given a second chance. Vowing to change his ways, and having cleansed himself of his transgressions through the power of love and faith, he reunites with his wife and child. The corny circle is closed. The transition is complete. Sailor is finally, fatally, domesticated.

Some critics connect early American Calvinism to "the relatively uncomplicated theology of St. Augustine" (Foerster 4)—not the anti–Manichaean Augustine but the Augustine of God's elect, stressing the importance of good deeds and, most important for Lynch's moral paradigm, suppressing disordered desire. Byron, trying to explain *his* wickedness, makes the same connection, describing himself as "'Methodist, Calvinist, Augustinian'" (qtd. in Russell 749). According to St. Augustine:

> All wicked people, just like good people, desire to live without fear. The difference is that the good, in desiring this, turn their love away from things that cannot be possessed without the fear of losing them. The wicked ... try to get rid of anything that prevents them from enjoying such things securely. Thus they lead a wicked and criminal life, which would better be called death [qtd. in Fieser and Lillegard 184].

Lynch's Calvinism, not surprisingly, fits nicely with his belief in the prosperous, Reaganesque "happy days" of the fifties. After all, as Bertrand Russell points out, "when Protestantism arose, its support—especially the support of Calvinism—came chiefly from the rich middle class" (623). Lynch's obsession with disordered desire and fatalism in *Twin Peaks: Fire Walk with Me* (1992), combined with a nostalgia for purity and patriotism, drives him to stretch the allegorical frame he foregrounded in *Wild at Heart* while returning to his signature theme in its most facile, childlike form: the fall into corruption from prelapsarian innocence. Again, Lynch's theme is that maturation—emergence into the world, thus into the symbolic—comes with a price. Recognizing the potential for evil within, man must remain on constant vigil. As the Jungian shadow-side of the self is revealed, the inevitable temptations of adulthood must be tempered by prudence, and those who lack the self-awareness to control their raw sexual impulses, to channel them (as Jeffrey and Sailor do) into constructive, civilized (aim-inhibited) behavior are doomed to self-destruction.

The self-reflexive opening sequence—an assault on a television—establishes a cross-textual reference to *Twin Peaks* the television series, rife with inside allusions, double-entendres and self-conscious image clusters. Destroying television in and by the film, then opening the action with himself, the director, playing an actor playing a deaf character shouting into a telephone in front of a Hollywood façade, Lynch may have misjudged how difficult it would be to shrink the successful television serial style into a two-hour cinematic package. The formula proved irreducible, especially given all the exposition Lynch considered essential. The entire first section of the film is filled with gratuitous, inconsequential events: the dance and subsequent interpretation of the Lady in Red signifies nothing but an inside metacinematic joke; Agent Stanley's examination of Teresa Banks' corpse and his discovering the letter T under her fingernail are not followed up as clues to any crime; the conflict between the federal agents and the local sheriff's department contributes nothing to Laura's moral dilemma. Desmond and Stanley's encounter at the diner, the significance of the blue rose, Carl Rod's trailer park, a child in a bird mask made to look like a ludicrous Halloween sprite flitting in and out of scenes—all are supercilious, disconnected images serving no contextual purpose, as empty as Cooper's amateur gee-whiz fascination with technology as he fiddles with a closed-circuit television, trying to trace the "reality" of Agent Phillip Jeffries. The narratives are as inane and irrelevant as Cooper's visits to the Red Room, the flimsy scenes mere isolated vignettes, more perfunctory and less seamless than in the television series. The sequence ends with Chet Desmond's mysterious, inexplicable disappearance: an unintentional, perhaps metacinematic, metaphor illustrating the irrelevance of the first twenty minutes of the film.

Lynch's sophomoric giddiness with po-mo puzzles is best illustrated when, after watching a series of gestures performed by the "dancing girl," Agent Stanley asks Special Agent Chet Desmond, "What did it mean?" This is the question Lynch must have anticipated the critics would be asking after he released *Fire Walk with Me*. Lynch's response to his detractors is a parody of critical cryptography: Agent Desmond's explanation relies on an invented personal code of significance, relayed to Agent Stanley as if it were public language. Ostensibly, this rudimentary lesson in semantics promises a film that will explore the murky surface of human understanding, of the codification of signs and the vagaries of meaning, the arbitrariness of language. But instead the film degenerates into its own ambiguity. Cause-and-effect is not deconstructed; it is abandoned. The film tries to link several disparate chains of events, but as the episodic story lines develop, instead of dovetailing into a coherent whole they spiral into a mobile of coincidental events governed solely by the whim of the director, suggesting only the most tenuous sense of linear or spatial integrity. This incoherence may well be explained in terms of the movie being a prequel to the television series *Twin Peaks*. Strategic marketing demands aside, some of the surreal sections are very effective, especially when grounded in concrete details, as in the roadhouse bar scenes. Otherwise, the inexplicable dreamlike narratives seem contrived, superficially imposed, treacly with tedious, overly mannered acting. The story is designed to defy paraphrase, but, as Agent Cooper says, the clues lead only to a "dead end." Still, the moralistic dichotomy in Lynch's *modus operandi* remains intact: pitting innocence and virtue against evil and corruption in an attempt to recover an Edenic America that even in nostalgia never existed.

In *Fire Walk with Me*, as in *Wild at Heart*, Lynch continues to privilege fifties iconography. Just as Sailor telegraphed his appropriated life through his Brando snakeskin jacket and Elvis karaoke moves, James evokes James Dean, a Harley-riding, tough-on-the-outside lamb of a stud, a typical fifties macho gay closeted in self-preserving denial. Bobby Briggs, too, affects a *West Side Story*–hood look. But Bobby is a hothead, never comfortable with his persona, while James is the epitome of calm understanding and control. Donna, like James, represents down-home, Donna Reed values, but in a kinky twist Lynch uses her innocent curiosity to increase her value, when she is eventually naked and submissive, as an erotic image. But it is exactly the pure intense innocence and honesty of James and Donna that Laura craves as much, at least, as her drugs. Even Chet Desmond—played by the fifties-style rockabilly artist Chris Isaak—represents Lynch's faith in personas, casting the icon of authorial benevolence as the sort of faithful, true-blue public servant of the law that truly exists only in the collective fictive imagination of the Fox Network show *Cops*. And though he is more of an intrusive force invading a reluctant local authority than that emissary of goodwill, Dale Cooper in *Twin Peaks*, Desmond (as a moral mouthpiece for Lynch) reveals an odd, Hamiltonian affinity for federal power. Lynch portrays the county police as corrupt petty tyrants, compromised by philandering and complicity in criminal schemes, but he presents the federal agents as serious professionals, not above a cheap good-natured prank or sardonic joke, but dedicated to work and clean living. When Carl Rod asks the agents if they want a cup of Good Morning, America—coffee, of course—the phrase resonates with Reagan's ditzy Morning in America campaign slogan. The coincidence is not ironic. Agents Desmond and Stanley hear it too, and appreciate it: it normalizes an otherwise aberrational trailer-park psycho. Lynch's identity with the fifties, Reagan's America-first propaganda, and the sanctity of cultural myths are evidence of his sympathy with the feds. After all, he casts himself as an agent operating alongside his iconographic comrades Desmond and Cooper, his deafness a tool for clarity and cutting through endemic bureaucratic legalese.

Except in this case it seems that Lynch the director, not Bureau Chief Gordon Cole, failed to hear the discord in his film. *Fire Walk with Me* is such a loose knot of irrelevant threads that its moral coding unravels in the first sequence. When Gordon shouts, "What's going on here?" he speaks for the audience. Often the problem is that a viewer must be familiar with the television series to appreciate many of the implied connections that otherwise seem gratuitous—the phrase "Let's Rock," for instance, scrawled on Desmond's windshield (referring to the Man from Another Place and his invocation to Cooper in the original Red Room). But even for viewers familiar with the series, the aesthetic integrity of the narrative in *Fire Walk with Me* is seriously flawed. Lynch (like The Man in the Planet in *Eraserhead*) operates three main narrative streams that cross but never merge, as if he spliced three films together with no regard for coherence, in dream-logic or otherwise. The forced imagery that results from such a weak narrative necessitates an essential, teleological moral structure, often more integral and significant than the characters, to drive the film forward and provide motive and context for otherwise meaningless action.

In the television version of *Twin Peaks*, Lynch is not sidetracked by the ur-passions of the soul (*Eraserhead*), the psychokinetic Freudian forces of sex and violence (*Blue Velvet*), or the perversities of an Electra conflict (*Wild at Heart*). His focus in *Fire Walk with Me* is much more pedestrian. With the subtlety of a jingoistic Reagan-era superpatriot, he creates a propaganda extravaganza detailing the dangers of that trinity of predictable American scourges: sex, drugs and rock 'n' roll. The film is less an aesthetic project than an essay against the pernicious effects of drugs on youth, society, and community values, a Calvinistic sermon about the temptations of the soul, carnal corruption, the desecration of innocence, and the purifying principles of guilt and remorse as the only antidotes for the craven impulse of desire. Laura represents Lynch's image of spoiled youthful vigor, innocence and potential. She is smart, pretty, popular, and fast becoming a common coke-whore. When Special Agent Dale Cooper describes her as "in high school ... sexually active ... using drugs ... crying out for help," Albert responds, "You're talking about half the high school girls in America."

The action picks up when, walking to school, Laura, the perfect face of innocence corrupted, meets Donna, the perfect face of innocence. As archetypes, the two girls represent a moral reversal for Lynch. His blondes are usually honest ingénues like Sandy Williams in *Blue Velvet* or Diane as her idealized self in *Mulholland Dr.* Lynch's brunettes are vixens and femmes fatales like Camilla in *Mulholland Dr.*, Dorothy Vallens in *Blue Velvet*, and Woman Across the Hall in *Eraserhead*. Donna, the brunette in *Fire Walk with Me*, exudes a heartland wholesomeness that, for Lynch, becomes a gauge by which to measure (and, in Lynch's view, approve of) her moral character. While Donna socially interacts with others, and successfully integrates her life with school, Laura gets through her schizophrenic day on lines of cocaine, seesawing between caustic bitch and submissive Barbie. An intuitive manipulator, she carefully gives herself to James, then later that same day uses her raunchy sexuality to switch Bobby Briggs on and off like a lava lamp. Concerned about Laura but also intrigued by her freedom and recklessness, Donna appeals to their friendship to try to get Laura both to confide in her and to include her in her debauchery. Donna still romanticizes clubs, sex and boys—especially James. She calls Bobby a "goon" and thinks James is the one who offers Laura "true love." Bored with Donna's romantics, but envious of her nostalgic simplicity, Laura wishes she "wouldn't feel anything" and wants to "burst into fire, forever." A fatalist, she tells Bobby, "I'm gone. Long gone."

Laura is the token reprobate, a lost soul, her nihilism and violent, drug-induced mood swings a result of having been sexually abused by her father, Leland. Possessed by the demon BOB, Leland is the murderous Jekyll and Hyde, an avatar of evil, as real in Lynch's world as the serpent in Eden. Laura confesses that BOB/Leland "has been having me since I was 12," and her struggle with her desire for forbidden knowledge, embodied in a mysterious ring, leads her through a series of moral compromises—lies, betrayal, criminal enterprise, promiscuity—and finally to complicity in murder (again, shades of Jeffrey in *Blue Velvet*). Laura herself is on the verge of possession. When she visits Harold and asks him to find her lost diary pages, her eyes and mouth turn a demonic red in a maniacal (and comic) moment of violent lust. She sees apparitions—the boy in the bird mask and a grandmotherly figure, for instance—who deliver cryptic messages to her and beckon her into strange circumstances. She soon suspects that her father and BOB are one and the same, and Leland, in a clear allusion to his own guilt, accuses Laura of having "filthy" hands. Tortured as much by the knowledge of his transgression as by his impotence to stop it, Leland terrorizes Laura with psycho-patriarchal abuse. She, in turn, inherits her father's schizophrenia, and soon begins to experience hallucinations brought on when she replaces a painting of angels in her room with an image of an open door, symbolically trading the selfless temperance of devotion for the existential excess of possibility.

When Donna visits Laura before one of Laura's nocturnal orgiastic debaucheries, she finds her well versed in the vices of adulthood, smoking, drinking, vamping in a cocktail dress. Donna supplies a simple contrast, dressed like a modest, straight–A student who might find the Glee Club racy. Mortified, she is still curious enough to ask where Laura is going. Laura answers nonchalantly, "Nowhere fast." Running into Laura at the roadhouse bar, The Log Lady tells her, "When this kind of fire starts, it is very hard to put out[;] ... the tender bowls of innocence burn first[,] ... all goodness is in jeopardy." She is referring to the fire of Buddha and St. Augustine, the passion that corrupts and purifies, inspires faith and prevents regeneration (cf. Eliot's "the Fire Sermon" in *The Waste Land* 42–46). But Laura is beyond redemption, having switched the painting of the angels on her wall with that of the door open to experience. So while The Log Lady ineptly tries to protect her, Julee Cruise coos of doomed innocence. Laura cries, it seems, for her loss of self-will, her willing submission to predestination, accepting her fate by prostituting herself as if she has no alternatives, her choice conditioned by her history of abuse. When Donna ambushes her and wants to join in, Laura tests her, giving herself up to the pleasure of a stranger. Unlike Jeffrey and Sailor, who are redeemed by restraint, Laura is consumed by desire. Even though she acknowledges her seductive clout (she appeals to older men who long "to fuck the homecoming queen"), Lynch allows her only a smidgen of hope for salvation: she feels guilty about the corrupting influence she has on Donna. But Donna matches her move for move, offering herself to another stranger at the table.

In a desperate attempt to dissuade Donna from sinking to her level of shame and depravity, Laura decides to take Donna on the equivalent of a joyride, the same violent educational trip Jeffrey Beaumont took in *Blue Velvet.* Donna manages to keep up until Laura strips her top off and the party takes a decidedly twisted turn. Before she can leave, however, her beer is spiked, and Donna ends up in a drunken stupor. Significantly, by the time she is stripped to the waist and thoroughly objectified, Donna lacks any moral responsibility for her actions. But for Laura, protecting Donna's implied virginity, her purity satisfies a vicarious need to preserve her own dignity, so she rescues her from her debauchery and delivers her from harm. The next morning, Donna claims not to remember the night before. Her moral amnesia exonerates her. Unable to recall or objectify images of her own passion, Donna asks Laura, "Why do you do it?" Before Laura replies, Leland, the beast in Lynch's hagiography, and the seed of destruction for Laura, interrupts the girls. The answer remains as ambiguous as Laura's impulse to excess.

Leland immediately imagines a pornographic fantasy involving the two girls. Later, driving with Laura in the car, he suffers a series of visions and flashbacks, vacillating between Leland—abject with self-loathing—and BOB—a bestial demon. The One-Armed Man (another bit, as it were, of disconnected business) accosts him in traffic, haranguing him like a crazed prophet. Leland finally pulls over at a mechanic's where his suspicions are confirmed: Laura suspects him. Her complicity, in the guise of fatalism, is as problematic as Leland's culpability. His will, after all, is BOB's possession. Leland's vulnerability, like original sin, stems from the same sort of momentary weakness Eliot moralistically describes as "the awful daring of a moment's surrender/Which an age of prudence can never retract." Laura's weakness stems from her abuse, her desire a form of self-destruction. She too is possessed. But the morality is clear: no matter if you are with the elect or the damned, your duty is to exercise moral righteousness.

This is Calvinism at its most severe: Leland and Laura, predestined to evil, are locked in an incestuous metaphysical *ménage à trois* involving a stranger Leland must share his daughter with in ritualistic sexual torture; but because they are aware of their sin, and the pain they cause others, they suffer in the knowledge of their absolute helplessness, futilely compelled to rectify Nietzsche's "weakness of fear" ("Notes" 74):

> Being moral means being highly accessible to fear.... it becomes clear that what is to be feared in the case of morality must inspire fear in the very highest degree. Therefore mores have been introduced everywhere as functions of a divine will.... Of anyone who denied the gods one expected anything: he was automatically the most fearsome human being, whom no community could suffer.... in such a person desire raged unlimited... [74–75].

Desire, or the absence of Nietzsche's "refinement of fear" (75), is Leland's sin, passed on to his daughter. Both are possessed by raw will, a demon beyond their control. Their resistance, expressed as guilt, underscores how their attempts to divorce themselves from nature and to assimilate culture as a correction for their animalism have failed. Their symbolic self-presentations—Leland's respectability, Laura's whorishness—are props of containment, costumes in which they play out their predetermined scripts.

Then Bobby kills a drug courier who attempts to double-cross him, and Laura becomes a passive partner in murder. But unlike Jeffrey in *Blue Velvet*, redeemed by his acute sense of restraint, Laura thrives on chaos. Even the angelic James is powerless to correct her fall. When she calls him, her knight in shining armor rides a Harley, not a white horse. He is a cool, fifties-style Lynchian normative value, an image of romantic earnestness: his counterculture pose is all image, not like Laura, who lives her serious drug habit, along with sadistic nymphomania. Laura, fatalistically complicit in her own demise, invites the incubus into her dreams, and he comes, vampiric, as her father. It is her recognition of BOB as her father's will, her awareness of her father's loss of self, his ontological weakness that condemns her utterly.

Laura is essentially irredeemable in this life, her fate sealed when the angel disappears from the painting in her bedroom. She tells James, "Your Laura disappeared." Her only chance for salvation lies in the Neo-Platonic, transcendental world Lynch explores in *Eraserhead*, that of spiritual purity and second chances. In a final act of depravation, Laura meets Jacques and his gang for an orgy of total self-abasement, only to be kidnapped by Leland/BOB and taken along with Ronette Pulaski to an abandoned railroad car for more brutal abuse. Significantly, Ronette sees angels, says, "I'm sorry," and, as if by divine intervention, her bonds drop away and she escapes. Laura, unrepentant, is slaughtered by Leland/BOB—killing her physical, corrupt self in a ritual sacrifice but releasing her to the avenging angel of justice, Agent Cooper, and to the white angel of mercy and forgiveness, hovering in a placid patio netherworld. Meanwhile the god-like dream-gnomes of evil are left in the Red Room impotently demanding that their human "garmonbozia (pain and sorrow)" be returned by BOB from the Manichaean battlefield of the spirits sent to Laura's hometown as if to warn the populace that its hokiness is no antidote to the terrors of temptation.

After *Wild at Heart* and *Twin Peaks: Fire Walk with Me*, Lynch, in *Lost Highway* (1997), returns to the sound if oxymoronic principles of allegorical realism that infused *Eraserhead* and *Blue Velvet* with aesthetic integrity and strength. As Gardner points out, "surreal fiction is superficially like allegory, but the meaning is much less imposed from without[;] ... the writer translates an entire sequence of psychological events, developing his story as the mind spins out dreams" (169). It is this linking of dreams to narrative, in the deepest moral sense, that creates the psychosexual dualism Lynch seems to have been striving to express in his other films but which had eluded him since *Eraserhead*.

Admittedly, Lynch's style of sermonizing is perverse. But so was Sade's. And certainly Lynch's prevailing concern with sex, guilt and moral privation aligns him with Sade, especially in *Lost Highway*. Roger Shattuck, for instance, in his reactionary polemic *Forbidden Knowledge*, rails against the "rehabilitation of Sade" (237), but he admits that Sade's "major works carry the reader fatefully toward such confrontations with inhumanity" (270) and that "Sade was always the teacher and evangelist" (282). The same could be said for Lynch. Carolyn J. Dean, in *A New History of French Literature*, writes that Sade explores "'the horrifying, inassimilable core of his experience, linking sexuality not to pleasure but to terror'" (qtd. in Shattuck 253–54). Again, the same conundrum applies to Lynch. Shattuck derides contemporary critical enthusiasm, especially that of Foucault, for Sade's "'madness of desire, the insane delight of love and death in the limitless presumption of appetite'" (qtd. in Shattuck 247); and it may be that same sort of Sadean evangelical zeal Lynch employs that caused many critics, and certainly the commercial market, to reject *Lost Highway*. (In New York, a few months after it was released, it played the midnight show at the Angelika, the equivalent of a book consigned to the remainders bin immediately after publication.) Dishing up his standard clichés, his trademark directorial tricks, the unmistakably Lynchian moments, the film is, nevertheless, a striking tour de force pointing to a new direction in Lynch's work. Paradoxically, *Lost Highway* may survive as Lynch's best film for the very reason it seems to have been rejected: he finally dispenses with the concerns that seem, in his other films, to hinder him, as if his need to conform to what a viewer might expect has otherwise kept him from creating narratives driven purely by the power of the images.

Not that the subject matter in the film is unique. As in his other "signature" films—*Eraserhead, Blue Velvet, Wild at Heart*—*Lost Highway* explores familiar taboos: the nature of evil, innocence, death, and redemption. But the nature of the narrative overrides other thematic considerations. The film forces the viewer to ask herself what she actually expects from a movie, any movie. The success of the film, in its best postmodern moments, results from its ability to breakup, attack, challenge and disrupt the linear narrative line while still "making sense"—not waking-life sense, necessarily, but moral sense—and it is this abandonment of plot-driven, situational ethics for a poetics of "pure" form, a concern for the deeper structures of meaning, that signals in *Lost Highway* a departure from the work that comes before it. The surface action is subjugated by Lynch's attempt to objectify a purely emotional state of being, employing asymmetrical framing, juxtaposed images, seemingly non sequitur narratives—in short, he creates a montage effect more similar in design to an anarchic film like Abigail Child's *Mayhem* (1987) than to the conventional models of fellow travelers like Eisenstein and Buñuel. The ethical framework, the moral drive, is no less intense, but the process, the shape of the investigation, takes on an ethical dimension of its own that situates the story outside of mere sermonizing.

The film opens with a familiar Lynchian two-lane blacktop shot from out of the front window of a speeding automobile, the passing-zone lines shifting side to side as the viewer is visually thrown down the recklessly unpredictable road. But by avoiding the potholes of *Wild at Heart,* Lynch veers sharply away from sentimentality. The saccharine turns to poison. This is Old Testament Lynch. A tight close-up frames the face of a worried man: Fred Madison, a sax player suffering acute bouts of insecurity in his relationship with his wife, Renee. Clearly he is desperate, ill with self-doubt, desire and fear. One morning Fred hears the simple, ominous message delivered through his intercom, "Dick Laurent is dead." Is it a threat? A fact? Another self-referential joke? What Lynch thinks will satisfy his critics? The mystery only adds to Fred's paranoia and self-doubt. He is acutely aware that he plays his sax better than he plays his wife. His music is controlled mania, and he envies how easily his horn sends him into a Dionysian ecstasy.

Like many of Lynch's women, Fred's wife Renee is both an object of desire and a source of insecurity. She is uninterested in his career, withdrawn and preoccupied. They whisper in the sterile sepulchre of their house, the rooms designed for space, not intimacy. Her desire seems to Fred to have degenerated into pity, their lovemaking merely perfunctory and unsatisfying. When he speaks to her, he is accusatory and suspicious. The package he receives—a video of the outside of their house—only adds to his paranoia. What the video depicts, a movement from the exterior in, works for Lynch the way intercutting television clips does in his earlier films. It is a reminder of the true subject of the film: accessing the recesses of perception, confronting the demons of desire, projecting primordial images from the unconscious. He utilizes the same effect in the radiator scenes in *Eraserhead*, and the burrowing camera shots in *Blue Velvet.* This first video only hints at things to come. Before actually entering their house, the tape cuts out. Lacking Fred's interiority, Renee decides it is from "a real estate agent."

Fred's performance anxiety stems from the way he views his wife. He looks at her the way other men do, thereby objectifying her while pretending to seek her subjective self and creating a vicious circle of marital strife: Fred's insecurity feeds Renee's disdain, as her contempt inflames his anxiety. When he plays a gig, she prefers to stay home and read (so she says). Desperate to reconnect his confidence to his passion, Fred loses himself in arpeggios of pure primal will and dissolution, unsullied by concepts (resonant of Nietzsche's description, after Schopenhauer, of music as a direct, unmediated conduit to the will). In bed, he mounts her to reclaim her, not to love her: she is too distracted for authentic intimacy, distant, controlling him through his desire—that A-bomb for Lynch of self-destructive forces. But at the very moment he wants to show strength, Renee disarms him, making love to him like a prostitute, allowing him to climax early, without her, then condescendingly patting his back, her affection reduced to pity. That night Fred dreams of a smoldering room where he finds himself in bed with Renee transmogrified into a demon.

Ostensibly, Fred awakes from his paranoiac dreams, but actually it is only the beginning of his nightmare. His suspicions are fueled one night when he spies Renee in the club with Andy, another of Lynch's typical lounge lizards. Then he and Renee receive another video, this time of the interior of his house: a bird's-eye shot of them in bed. They decide to call the police, hoping for answers. But the two detectives only reinforce Fred's insecurity. They question him about their other bedroom, and Fred tells them that it is his soundproof practice room. One detective then makes a pointed reference to his tenor sax—a play on the word sex, making explicit the implication that he can control his sax but not his woman. The police also ask about the home alarm system, and in an oblique reference to his sexual problems, Fred explains that the alarm "keeps going off—false alarms." Renee tells them Fred hates video cameras. He explains, "I like to remember things my own way. How I remember them[,] ... not necessarily the way they happened." His statement is prophetic, and becomes a motif for the rest of the film: how the present is construed from events in the past.

At Andy's party, Renee treats Fred like a gopher, sending him for drinks so she can flirt with Andy. But while ordering the drinks, he meets Mystery Man, a representative demon of the anxiety, self-doubt, impotence and fear that Fred is wrestling with, the kinetic Hyde released by irrepressible passions. Mystery Man also has magical doubling powers. He tells Fred, "We've met before" (in Fred's dream, of course). And when Fred asks, "How did you get into my house?" he answers, "You invited me." Lynch indicts Fred for the same crime of weakness committed by

Leland and Laura Palmer, for the same transgressions that doomed Henry in *Eraserhead* and nearly claimed Jeffrey in *Blue Velvet*. It seems that the demons of desire that plague so many of Lynch's characters cannot possess their subjects without an invitation, an opening created by a person's lack of willpower. This inability to resist temptation is the key to Lynch's hard-core Calvinism: not only does he portray this weakness as an innate character flaw, but it also separates the elect from the damned.

Frightened and angry about her behavior with Andy, Fred pulls Renee away from the party. Arriving home, they see lights mysteriously flash in their house. Inside, the phone rings but when Fred answers it, no one is on the line. As he watches his wife meticulously remove her makeup, he sees her isolated, in silhouette, and his desire begins to betray him. Fred recognizes his own malevolent potential—he has met his demon face-to-face—and his sexual anxiety builds, consuming him like a debilitating disease, until, to his wife still washing her face, he appears like an apparition. In a third video, Renee is a bloody corpse, supposedly a victim of Fred's murderous jealousy.

Fred is arrested and sentenced to death for Renee's murder. On death row he suffers from headaches and sleeplessness. Even with treatment Fred's symptoms continue, their severity unabated, culminating in a night of intense suffering. But the next day the guards discover that another, younger man, Pete Dayton, has replaced Fred in his cell. As no charges are pending against Pete, and since he has no idea what happened to Fred or how he ended up in Fred's cell, the police allow Pete to return home where he reunites with his biker-cum-yuppie parents, his old gang, and his girlfriend Sheila. Pete, like Jeffrey Beaumont, is a disaffected poser toying with the props of adulthood (his goatee and sideburns, his sulking in the backyard, his rowdy friends), a teen on the verge of making the difficult and painful transition from the relatively simple joys of adolescence to the complex and dangerous games of adulthood. Lynch illustrates Pete's predicament with a shot of him looking across his neighbor's fence at a puppy and a red plastic child's pool filled with toys—an image of childhood from which Pete is literally walled off.

Typical in Lynch, the primary urge that impels Pete from childhood to maturity—out of innocence into experience—is desire. The Pauline concept that desire must be overcome by will, reiterated throughout the history of Christian thinking, but especially articulated by St. Augustine and rarified by the radical elements of Calvinism, treats carnal desire as anathema to purity. This depiction of the human animal, however, confuses primal will with volition, and reverses the state of nature based on the myth of Man's Fall from Grace in Genesis. Lynch, of course, like his Puritan forefathers, is more concerned with the good old-fashioned reductive nature of sin and redemption, reward and punishment, than with intellectual subtleties. Both Fred and Pete suffer what Spinoza identifies as the source of human misery: passion rules us because we fail to comprehend the rational structure of reality. In a state of innocence, explanations are superfluous. In fact, it is the need for explanations that drive Fred and Pete into irrational acts, thus into their particular circles of hell.

Pete's parents are static, ineffectual, and in a sense regressive: their passion is passive. They have given up pursuing active pleasure and settled for sitting on the couch watching television. Sheila is submissive; she has sex with Pete to satisfy him, to fulfill her role as teen girlfriend, and is naïve enough to ask afterward, "You still care about me?" His friends are equally juvenile, wanting to know when they first meet him after his return home, "Are you contagious?" The police, as usual in Lynch's films, take on the monitoring role of a suspended conscience: two detectives tail Pete without intervening as he moves from his high school romance with Sheila into his treacherous affair with Alice, the implication being that Pete is operating on instinct, not logic, and this suspension of conscience leads to criminality.

At his job as a mechanic, with a sax riff identical to Fred's wailing in the background, Pete, like Fred, begins suffering from headaches, and gets relief only by turning off the music. Then Mr. Eddy, a psychotic hood, shows up and asks Pete to tune his Mercedes. He takes Pete for a ride that turns into yet another of Lynch's terrifying joyrides, and with a similar purpose: to demonstrate the seriousness of the consequences of action in the adult world. In a brutal display of manic road rage, Mr. Eddy proves exactly how dangerous and volatile he is, viciously retaliating after a minor tailgating incident by wrecking the offending driver's car and mercilessly pistol-whipping the driver. As in *Blue Velvet*, where the dyadic extremes situate Jeffrey between Detective Williams and Frank Booth as embodiments of, respectively, his superego and his id, in *Lost Highway* Pete finds himself in the same situation: caught between the law and Mr. Eddy, between his conscience and desire. In contrast to the police, who are impotent, Mr. Eddy is at least efficient, impulsively acting on his desire. By the time Pete meets Mr. Eddy's girlfriend, Alice, the blonde double of Fred's wife Renee, his choices are clear. He must check his passion with his fear of punishment, or submit to his desire—to act, like Mr. Eddy, to satisfy his most instinctual, primordial and selfish urges.

Alice is too sexually aggressive for Pete to resist, and she initiates a torrid affair that consumes him. Along with satisfaction, however, the affair also generates in Pete a paranoid fear that Mr. Eddy will find out about his illicit liaison with Alice. The intensity of their sexual encounters, heightened by fear of discovery, creates a familiar Lynchian matrix of pain and desire inextricably linking fear and guilt to sex and death. When it becomes evident that Mr. Eddy has discovered their affair and is planning his revenge, Alice concocts a way to finance their romance on the road by robbing a porn king (who turns out to be Andy). To help persuade a reluctant Pete to go along with her plan, Alice recalls in a flashback how Mr. Eddy sexually abused her. Driven more by his passion than Alice's confession, and having long ago abandoned any pretense to reason, Pete agrees to her scheme. But the instant he accepts, Alice, in a revealing turn, immediately shifts from being a sultry lover to a co-conspirator. All business, cool, calm and calculated, she gives Pete explicit directions, her sudden emotional reversal planting in Pete the first seeds of uncertainty. As his insecurity begins to erode his confidence, Pete finds himself suffering the same anxiety that ruined Fred, and it is this linking of their separate but identical losses of self-identity by doubt that sets the context for the reemergence of Fred in the story.

Pete's move from the childish toys in his neighbor's backyard to the sex toys of Alice and Andy estranges him from his routine world of family, friends and Sheila. When Sheila sees Pete for the last time—having discovered that he has been unfaithful—her visit stings like a pang of conscience. But Pete is too far divorced from his former self—his innocence and youth—and, knowing better, he breaks into Andy's house. The robbery is botched, Pete kills Andy, and with images of Alice performing in hard-core porn videos, Pete notices a photograph of Alice and Renee together. Suddenly, eerily, his doubts about Alice are realized. He sees her now for what she is, a materialistic opportunist, capable of anything—especially of seducing men into desperate acts of self-destruction. To clean his bloody nose, he goes in the bathroom where he sees more images of violently submissive women. When he returns to Alice, she puts a gun to his head and asks, "Don't you trust me, Pete?"

Suffering from the same demons that plagued Fred, Pete drives off, coincidentally, in a red Mustang identical to Fred's, searching for a "fence" Alice knows in the desert. The trip runs along the highway straight into the heart of darkness. Outside an abandoned shack, Pete and Alice engage in demonic sex. Pete asks, "Why me, Alice?" The only available answer, as always in Lynch-land, is that those with the most desire and

the least restraint are the most at risk, victims of themselves. Pete says, "I want you." Alice responds, "You'll never have me." Pete's final transgression, like Fred's, is his need for possession, to deny the subjective freedom of the Other, illustrating another of Lynch's self-reflexive, metacinematic comments—namely, how a film critic, for instance, through ratiocination tries to make a film hers, displacing the original imagistic text with the tropes of analysis.

At the moment Alice leaves him, Pete morphs back into Fred. The two men have reunited through their mutual need to possess—that is, to limit, to understand—the inexplicable. Their desire transcends its object. Paul S. MacDonald, in his introduction to *The Existentialist Reader*, addresses the distress caused by desire, and how it destroys both the self and the object. Discussing Kojève's lectures on Hegel, he writes:

> In contrast with knowledge that keeps him in passive quiet, desire disquiets him and moves him to action. The action taken to satisfy a desire negates or destroys the object as it was on its own (so to speak); the action of consumption transforms an object into something else [9].

In *Lost Highway*, Renee/Alice's subjectivity is too strong for Fred/Pete to negate. The transgression for which the men must suffer, which the women intuitively know, is that the men thought they could tame their women and still want them. MacDonald's summary of Kojève's understanding of Hegel is especially apt: "The self-conscious ego does not want to merely consume the other self-conscious being ... but to possess or assimilate the other's desiring power" (10). Caught without an object to contain their passion, the men are left with a transcendent need that nullifies the existing ego and reconstructs it (through one of Hegel's dialectical sleights-of-hand) as a thing composed essentially of a desire "that goes beyond the given reality [that Hegel describes as] 'a revealed nothingness, an unreal emptiness[,] ... the presence of an absence of a reality'" (10).

Desperate to resituate himself, clinging to whatever shreds of objective grounding he can knot together into a coherent cloak of reality, Fred finds the fence—who turns out to be Mystery Man—and Mr. Eddy, who is now Dick Laurent, a dealer in violent pornography. Fred asks, "Where's Alice?" Mystery Man replies, "Her name is Renee," and asks him, "What

Opposite: Femme fatale du jour: Alice (Patricia Arquette) in *Lost Highway* (1997). The blond flipside to Renee, Alice is Lynch's ideal Jezebel. Using sex to tempt an innocent into terror, she provokes a desire that transcends its object.

the fuck is your name?" He begins videotaping Fred—objectifying him the way Fred tried to objectify Alice/Renee—and the assault on his identity sends Fred tearing down the highway again. He ends up at the Lost Highway Hotel where he finds Mr. Eddy/Dick Laurent having sex with Alice/Renee. Fred kidnaps Mr. Eddy and brings him back to Mystery Man, who forces Mr. Eddy to confront his sin—pornography—before meting out his punishment. Pornography, a product of Augustine's displaced desire, unites all the doubled characters and condemns them equally. In an all-too-common Lynchian scenario of medieval justice, in which the punishment, no matter how barbaric, must fit the crime, Mr. Eddy, whose new line of films included snuff porn, finds himself on the wrong end of the camera before being murdered by Pete and Mystery Man. Meanwhile, the police find the bodies of Alice and Dick Laurent with Pete's fingerprints all over the crime scene. Fred returns to his house to deliver the opening message to himself—"Dick Laurent is dead"— before fleeing the police—that concrete image of his guilty conscience— wailing down the same blacktop that opened the film.

The parallels, the doubling, the mirrors and distortions seem an attempt by Lynch to capture the essence of sex, madness, guilt and desire. As Fred and Pete confront the events that lead to their own versions of desperation, anxiety, self-doubt and murder, the women, the stimuli, are essentially the same, just as the demons, the demiurges, are, too. The parallel stories are really one story in the development of a man's subconscious. In his depiction of the secret, dream-driven lives of his characters wrapped in a self-reflective narrative and framed by a snuff film of their own making, Lynch cannot avoid entering the weird, elusive, subconscious world beyond coherence and logical explanations.

According to Donald Lyons, in his *Film Comment* review, *Lost Highway* is "a painter's movie" (2). In fact, Lynch's style in this film echoes a description by the philosopher Jean-Francois Lyotard of a Barnett Newman painting: "Newman's *now* ... is a stranger to consciousness and cannot be constituted by it. Rather, it is what dismantles consciousness[;] ... it is what consciousness cannot formulate[,] ... what consciousness forgets in order to constitute itself" (244–45). As a spatial construct, *Lost Highway* resembles Lyotard's description of Newman's attempt to capture in paint the essence of aesthetic awareness: the "inexpressible does not reside in an over there, in another world, or another time, but in this: in that something happens. In the determination of pictorial art, the indeterminate, the 'it happens' is the paint, the picture. The paint, the picture as occurrence or event, is not expressible" (246). Lyons concurs. He writes that "the 'Twin Peaks' pilot stayed in touch with a possible narrative reality.... Here Lynch shuffles ontological levels" (4). *Lost Highway*, then, is finally more than a graphic rendering of emotional strata: it questions the context of experience, the certainty of sequence, the veracity of self.

The moralistic dualism Lynch employs in his earlier films—especially *Blue Velvet*, *Wild at Heart* and *Twin Peaks: Fire Walk with Me*, metamorphosed into an ontological schizophrenia in *Lost Highway*. But *Lost Highway* still suffers from a patina of pretense: like so many of Lynch's films, it becomes a pretext for the preening of canny critics working out their postmodernist theories of indeterminacy, suture, equivocal topologies and nonlinear narratives symbolizing cultural pathologies. In other words, the more circular, open and inexplicable Lynch's later films are, the easier it becomes for critics to fit them to their diverse agendas. Lynch definitely exploits the usual binary oppositions: nature and culture, dreams and the waking world, subconscious urges and conscious order. But even when he attempts to merge opposites in a weird Hegelian identity synthesis, as in *Lost Highway*, the overall structure of the film relies on his positivist moral dialectics: black and white, dark and light, right and wrong, good and evil. At this reductive level, the film, with all its imagistic permutations and narrative detours, hangs together as the dramatic portrait of a de-centered Lacanian subject anchored in and suffering from "linguistic legislation." Still, the doubling of Fred and Pete and the conflating of Renee and Alice work as a directorial contrivance, a convenient metaphorical device allowing Lynch to indulge in his pet perversities. Stephanie Zacharek, writing in *Salon*, sums up the problem succinctly:

> The big meanings are actually the most insignificant things about it. Aspiring to be the most artful and profound Lynch film yet, "Lost Highway" is really his most facile. ... Most of the bizarre happenings seem to have come from a recipe... [(3].

The film is "slippery" precisely because it lacks any normative value on which Lynch can ground his moral certainty, and its thematic nihilism leaks into the narrative structure. No innocent or even morally salvageable character—no Jeffrey Beaumont, Sailor or even Laura Palmer—emerges as either a recognizable victim worthy of genuine pity or a successful, socially integrated citizen of the community. The lack of empathy for the characters in *Lost Highway* is compounded by the hard determinism at the core of the film: the characters seem to lack sufficient free will to warrant identification; caught up in the machinations of forces beyond their control, they are driven to their mechanical destinies like manikins through a kinky carwash.

In *Mulholland Dr.* (2001), Lynch is more subtle, allowing the structure of the narrative to mirror the psychological motives of the central character by whose point of view the moral nexus of the action is framed. As a result, the doubling and conflating of characters are less arbitrary, more believable, justifiable, and integral. The dualism, however, is as stark, absolute and Manichaean as it is in any of his works; but it is also just as necessary as a shaping apparatus.

In the first segment, for instance, the jitterbugging teens mock their modest Eisenhower-era dress code and perceived naïveté with a barely containable, insouciant sexual energy. This incongruity sets up a subsequent conflict between the dream of wish fulfillment and the rough reality Diane tries to realize in her flashback. The Manichaean context differentiates *Mulholland Dr.* from its conspicuous model, *Sunset Boulevard* (1950). Wilder's film relied on an implausible beyond-the-grave voice-over to locate the viewer, setting up the flashback series of events that end with the narrator's body in the pool. Like *Mulholland Dr.*, *Sunset Boulevard* blends facts and fiction, dreams and reality, while excoriating the machinations of behind-the-scenes Hollywood. But unlike *Sunset Boulevard*, *Mulholland Dr.* allows no distinction between the dream story and the "true" story until the last third of the film.

The film opens with Betty, the heroine, embodying the perky optimism of the jitterbug contest, which she proudly wins, flanked by her beaming parents awash in the transcendental light of goodness, truth and beauty. But the next scene, a shot of the pillow on which Betty will dream her revisionist nightmare, undercuts the gaiety and naïveté of that other dream, the one of the wholesome girl from the country coming to Hollywood and against all odds making it as a star. The contrast between the goodness of Betty's self-image and the raunchy reality of her life centers the controlling dialectic on the small-breasted blond from the heartland—in this case, Deep River, Ontario—who comes under the spell of a voluptuous city-wise brunette. As Allen B. Ruch notes in his insightful essay "No hay banda," even the names reinforce the metaphor (4). Camilla, cast as the caring, trusting, vulnerable Rita in Diane's "revised" version of events, is in "real life" the lesbian vampire murderess from J. Sheridan Le Fanu's gothic novel *Camilla* (1871). Likewise, the revised Diane is the virgin goddess protector of women, but in reality she is an expendable bit-player, a sallow, vindictive loser in a world where winners take all.

The maddening witch of desire: Rita/Camilla (Laura Elena Harring) in *Mulholland Dr.* (2001). All image, she reflects an aggregate of wishes projected on her by Betty/Diane. One of Lynch's archetypal brunettes, she is sensual, mysterious and, because devoid of a conscience, ultimately destructive.

This black/evil and white/good material dualism is contained in a series of binary or doubling images invested with self-referential meaning that reflects and reiterates the psychological and narrative "truth" understood at the end of the story. Until the viewer realizes that the first part of the film—the Nancy Drew mystery of Rita's identity—is an inverted, mitigating reinvention of the seedy people responsible for her fatal humiliation, as well as a subconscious psychological defense strategy to ward off her despondency and eventual suicide, the only frame in which real-time narrative meaning can occur is provided by Lynch's overt moral dualism. The detectives investigating the initial car wreck announce this dualism as a shaping device when they stand together, Janus-like, among the debris—one facing forward, the other back. One says, simply, "Someone's missing," signifying the god of beginnings, of gates and doors, in this case opening a narrative that flows simultaneously back to a future and forward to a past.

The images of binary opposition continue after the car crash. Rita is a survivor among the dead, an individual lost in public, an intruder, an

The sacrificial ingénue: Diane (Naomi Watts) fantasizes that she is Betty, her alter ego, in a still from the trailer for *Mulholland Dr.* (2001). Her dreams of innocence and purity, linked to her overbearing awareness of Abrahamic justice, cannot save her from her need to be punished. A victim of her own morality, she possesses an acute sense of guilt that drives her to self-immolation.

outsider, a stranger to herself, anonymous to others, a fiction. Betty is authentic, a fresh face among the jaded, a white ingénue in a dark neighborhood, as secure in her past as she is in her present. In a significant shot, when she first meets Rita, Betty stands fully clothed watching a naked Rita in the shower. Betty is clearly defined; Rita's image is blurred. The graphic contrast between the blond, open, virginal Betty and the naked, mysterious, dark-haired Rita explains how Rita became Diane's idealized Camilla, the empty slate on which Diane can script her relationship. Rita needs Betty, responds to and reciprocates Betty's affection. The truth of their relationship, we learn in the end, is that Camilla is a callous, self-centered starlet who discards Diane as easily as a wad of used tissue paper. Diane is, to paraphrase Jim Morrison, just another lost angel in the city of night, an emotional wreck holed up in a Hollywood bungalow, tormented by guilt and self-loathing.

Diane's mental instability is echoed in the café scene. One man is telling another about a disturbing, recurring dream he has about a monster that lives behind the building. Their conversation seems like a session with an analyst, as the other man listens in a detached but clinically sympathetic manner. When they go outside, ostensibly to prove the man's dream has no basis in reality, the monster appears (in reality, merely a homeless man). The man's dream has become his reality. Forced to literally confront his demon, Schopenhauer's demi-urge, the man collapses. The episode is, of course, a projection from Diane's conscience: she too must confront her demon—having hired a hit man to kill Camilla—but her inability to live with her manifest evil impulse leads her to suicide. This conflating of dream and reality in the café scene is more than a reflection of Diane's psychological state. It is also a metacinematic comment on the film, illustrating the viewer's dilemma in trying to disentangle the narrative web of images that, on first viewing, seem arbitrary and digressive.

The amorphous conspiracy by which Diane justifies her lack of success in landing lead roles continues Lynch's pattern of using binary imagery to establish a self-referential system of meaning. The shady subterfuge of corporate moguls manipulating action from behind the scenes, overused to the point of distraction in *Wild at Heart, Twin Peaks* and *Lost Highway*, surfaces again in *Mulholland Dr.*, but at least this time these hidden devious forces have solid psychological grounding. They also enhance the dialectic between the naïve and the experienced, the insiders and outsiders, the philistines and the artists. The most relevant pairing in this series, however, may be that of the mobile and immobile, as Lynch often portrays "the boss" bound or restrained—in a wheelchair, for instance, or in a glass case. This opposition seems to signify the illusion of free will the players believe in, while their fates are actually determined by forces beyond their control. This becomes ontologically crucial for Diane: her killing Camilla is an honest attempt (from her point of view) to assert herself against the people pulling the strings of the other puppets.

The moral impetus in Diane's self-absolving fantasy is signified by her search for the "truth" of Rita's identity. Of course, the search leads to the corpse in the Sierra Bonita apartments, the image that prefigures her death. But it is her quest—as Diana, goddess of the hunt, of light— that forces her, like the man at the café, to confront herself. Still, she tries in her revenge fantasy to even the score with her nemeses, and in her wish-fulfilling revision she rejects the notion that it is her lack of necessary talent that prevents her from becoming a successful actor. She turns the director who betrays her into a cuckolded clown threatened with violence if he does not cast another actress in the lead role of his new film. Her audition for a B-movie—competing with "that other girl … the one with the black hair"—turns into a sultry tour de force that wows everybody involved. (To emphasize her allegiances, real or imagined, the agents at the audition dress in black to offset Betty's white sleeveless blouse.) But when she is overlooked for an important role—a victim, in her mind, of those malevolent industry forces working against her—the inescapable truth of her situation begins to realign her images, reshaping her fantasy from one of vengeful paybacks and self-rationalizations to one of remorse and self-retribution. Significantly, it is after her rejection for that career-making big break that she discovers the corpse at the Sierra Bonita apartments, and her carefully tailored revisionist drama begins to unravel. The distinct identities of Rita and Betty—even the "other" Camilla, a woman onto whom Diane has transferred the negative traits of her beloved real Camilla—collapse and merge just as her dream and reality conflate. In a last attempt to maintain the script of her desire, she imagines Rita passionately seducing her, but she can no longer sustain her self-deception, and instead her dream work begins to generate images that shift responsibility for her actions away from others and back onto herself, forcing her to acknowledge the facts of her existential crisis.

This crisis of conscience leads her to Club Silencio. After her fantasy of restorative lovemaking, Betty hears Rita saying in her sleep, "*Silencio. No hay banda.*" Betty wakes Rita and says, "It's okay." Rita responds, "No. It's not okay." This cryptic dialog refers to Diane's conscience. She is both acknowledging her guilt and the inefficacy of her dream to rectify her actions. In this context, their visit to Club Silencio represents an epiphany for Diane (as Betty). The venue at the club seems designed to expose the reality behind the illusion of the entertainment media. In other words, it is a place where the performance of the magician is not to fool the audience but to explain his tricks. The show is both a comment on moviemaking in general and Diane's attempt to disguise, dismiss or explain her reality in a dream. Rebekah del Rio's version of Roy Orbison's "Crying" sung in Spanish (prompted by Camilla's speaking Spanish at the dinner party where Diane learns the ugly truth of her situation) works like the "Candy Colored Clown" of *Blue Velvet*. Parallels to The Slow Club episodes are all too obvious, as the themes of both films are iterated in the lyrics of the songs. At Club Silencio, Betty's uncontrollable shaking in her seat mirrors her recognition of her crime, and "Crying" epitomizes her grief and despair. The blue box she discovers in her purse is a wake-up call, a reminder of her crime. (The hit man will leave a blue key on her coffee table after he kills Camilla.) When Betty and Rita return home, Betty disappears, and Rita opens the blue box. She tunnels through a passage, like the camera burrowing into Jeffrey's ear. Later, the same mysterious "cowboy" who threatened the director opens the door to her Sierra Bonita apartment and tells a sleeping Diane, "It's time to wake up."

Like the audience in Club Silencio, the viewer is now offered a glimpse behind the curtain to see the wizard at work, surfacing into real time with Diane as the facts of her fantasy are revealed. Diane did win a jitterbug contest in Ontario. After her aunt died and willed her some money, Diane decided to move to Los Angeles to try to make it in acting. She met Camilla on the set of "The Sylvia North Story," having lost the lead role to her, and she and Camilla began an affair that only underscored Diane's dependency and inadequacy. Soon, however, Camilla is dating the director of another film in which she has the lead and Diane only a small part. Camilla tries to break off her relationship with Diane, but because Diane is making it "difficult" Camilla invites Diane to a dinner party at her fiancé's house and humiliates her. Diane then hires a gunman to kill Camilla, but she cannot deal with the guilt and fear. In a psychotic frenzy, she is attacked by her superego-inducing parents and, to appease the monster of her id, she shoots herself dead.

In Hollywood, fragile people are easily ruined by the machinations of movie moguls, special interests, and fans, even by their own self-images. In this sense, Diane's death is symbolic of the loss of a stable self-presentation in the shifting celluloid semiotics of the Hollywood myth-making machine. Her innate goodness—expressed by her overwhelming guilt—is reinforced in the controlling dialectic: Diane is a decent person corrupted by the miscellaneous miscreants who populate the film industry. Compared to the others, whose sense of justice and respect is either less acute or non-existent—the real Camilla, the director, the cold-blooded killer—Diane is the character whose moral code remains exemplary and intact. Like Jeffrey Beaumont, her regret normalizes her urges. She is, therefore, in Lynch's eschatology, not beyond salvation. Lynch's punitive retribution is, as usual, severe, but the implication is that people as emotionally weak as Diane cannot handle the metaphysical responsibilities associated with self-determination. Her move into absolute freedom triggers an equally violent response from her moral conditioning. When she internalizes the subjective truth of being and, in Sartre's phrase, is condemned to freedom, it kills her.

Unlike his other road movies like *Wild at Heart*, which went nowhere, only doubling back on itself, and *Lost Highway*, which circled into an eternal Moebius strip, *The Straight Story* (1999) is a linear road trip into the artificial American heart, a paean to what critic Charles Taylor, writing in *Salon*, calls "middle American sturdiness." J. Hoberman, on the other hand, describes it in *The Village Voice* as "Disney material with a vengeance," acknowledging that "Lynch always was a closet conservative" (Rev. of "The Straight Story"). Whether a purposeful detour from his own deviant path or a cathartic flying of his true colors, Lynch's absurd realism in *The Straight Story* plays easily into the sensibility of an America in need of reassurance. Having temporarily exhausted—or, more precisely, exorcised—his demons, Lynch dispenses with layering and metaphysics and drives his story forward as ineluctably as Alvin Straight does his John Deere power mower. *The Straight Story* is just that: straight. Straight talking. Straight living. Straight shooting. And straight from the heart—the "Heartland," that is, the politically convenient idea of middle–America, that never-never land envisioned by Charlton Heston, Ronald Reagan and countless advertising agencies. No urban rot, complexity, sophistication, affectation, or inexplicable anomie clutter this landscape. Even Alvin's darkest secret—as a sniper he killed a fellow soldier—is mitigated by the fact that he was, after all, serving his country, and it was, after all, an honest mistake. The quirkiness has an acceptable context. The story is true.

But that is the problem. The film pretends to realism, except that Lynch's vision of America in *The Straight Story*, even more mythical than the Republican National Committee's version, does not exist. The straight and narrow, in reality, is crooked. Yet in Lynch's eyes, the heartland foregrounded throughout the film contains no tornadoes, droughts or floods, no minorities, migrants, cops or robbers, no violence, homelessness or drugs, no cynicism, no petty viciousness, no backbiting or bear-baiting. Only starlight and harmless lightning, benevolence, indulgence, kindness, honesty, openness: in short, simple people living simple lives populate the America between Laurens, Iowa, and Mt. Zion, Wisconsin. The question is, had Alvin been black, Mexican, Asian, Muslim—any variety of "Other"—would his experience have been the same?

But Alvin is privileged. He is a white veteran of World War II, one of Tom Brokaw's Greatest Generation, who—surprise!—does not abuse his mildly retarded daughter Rose but loves her, shares his life and home and passion for thunderstorms with her. And that is the "straight" story: Pat Boone doing *Easy Rider*, or *On the Road*, only not with Kerouac and Cassidy (or even Charles Kuralt, for that matter), but with George W. Bush at the wheel, doling out hokum. The effect, no matter how Lynch tries to distance himself from the material, for once allowing the characters to carry the action, is that Lynch is condescending. He approaches the story with what appears to be reverence, but he provides no foil for the absolute devotional dignity, decency and forthrightness of the town and the people Alvin meets on the road except his own sense of self-righteousness. And because Lynch stacks the moral deck, Alvin progressively seems more smarmy than likeable, less eccentric than cantankerous.

The film opens with a teasing allusion to *Blue Velvet*, but the point of view never burrows below the goofy surface. The complexities that haunted the subjective lives of the citizens of Lumberton stir no Schopenhauer angst and madness in Laurens. What you see is what you get in the Heartland. One of Lynch's Rubenesque women (viz. *Blue Velvet* and *Wild at Heart*) sunbathes in vain in the faint glow of a late summer afternoon. But there is nothing devious in her actions. All is surface, from the woman's geeky reflector to Alvin's falling down precisely when she cannot hear him. It is a scene that echoes Jeffrey's flushing Dorothy Vallens' toilet in *Blue Velvet* at the exact moment Sandy blows the car horn to warn him of Dorothy's arrival. But in *Blue Velvet*, the unheard warning builds tension, leading ultimately to Jeffrey's hiding in the closet, his observing Dorothy, and basically launching the plot. In *The Straight Story*, Alvin's fall out of earshot merely delays his being found on the floor, helpless but unhurt. Alvin's life is so regimented that his bar buddies go looking for him when he fails to show on time for one of their habitual meetings. These friends typify the goodwill of Alvin's fellow townspeople. Of course, Alvin, paragon of rugged American individualism, self-sufficiency and raw gumption, is the least enervated. His friend asks, "Are you stricken, Alvin?" Alvin responds, "I just need a little help getting up."

But Alvin's fall, if not a portentous sign, is an empirical warning. Even as a reified, iconographic embodiment of everything virtuous about small-town America, Alvin is old, as much a victim of the inevitable as any mortal prey to the natural ailments of age. Of course he doesn't trust doctors—not this archetype of common sense and folk wisdom—but he is also the epitome of a decent, upright, honest and trustworthy white American male who lives in a town that yearly loses more people than it gains, so having promised Rose that he will see a doctor, Alvin must keep his appointment—his word a sacred vow—making sure, however, in his own cantankerous way, to assert his no-nonsense philosophy by refusing to don the hospital gear. His pettiness masks his desperation for independence when he demands of the nurse, "Just bring me the doctor."

Starting with *The Alphabet* and *The Grandmother*, an undercurrent of anti-intellectualism channels through much of Lynch's work. In those shorts, the movement from the intuitive to the symbolic represented an interruption of the self. In *Dune*, the Sophists and the Pragmatists lose to the Dreamers. The Rationalists fail in *Twin Peaks*, and the Idealists ensure mediocrity in *Blue Velvet*. Voltaire, in Lynch's work, always loses to Rousseau. *The Straight Story* is no exception. Of course anti-intellectualism runs deep in the American psyche. To declare allegiance to a nostalgic "former" United States, a return to which would redeem the country, has proven to be a profitable political slogan throughout American history. As transparent and far-fetched as it seems, this romantic chimera of a virtuous past on which to model the future has never been far from mainstream thought (and has been revived with a vengeance in post–9/11 America). This sentiment is summed up bluntly by Bliss Perry in his curious 1912 study *The American Mind*: "No one can understand America with his brains" (84). Perry writes enthusiastically about the average American's optimism, her pioneering spirit, her "ideal passions of patriotism, of liberty, of loyalty to home" (75), values that, according to Perry, more than compensate for America's "catalogue of intellectual sins" (71). He instructs Americans to "turn frankly to our moral preoccupations, comforting ourselves … as we abandon … intellectual rivalry with Europe, in the reflection that it is the muddle-headed Anglo-Saxon … who is the dominant force in the modern world" (71). This sort of concrete nationalism and self-righteousness, inflamed by a culturally ingrained mistrust of intellectualism, Covici describes as "communal divine favoritism and protection" (3). The classic text on the American public's history of resentment towards academics is Richard Hofstadter's *Anti-intellectualism in American Life*. He describes "a kind of primitivism which has won extraordinarily wide credence in America" (47). He links primitivism with Christianity, but also to "a demand to recover the powers of 'Nature' … [and] the 'wisdom' of intuition" (48).

The exemplary primitive for Lynch is Alvin, whose intuition is sharper than the doctor's machines and science. The news, predictably, is bad: emphysema, bone degeneration, diabetes. We learn that, faced with his mortality, at least more acutely aware of his contingent self, beneath his tough guy pose Alvin is sensitive. Properly focused by his own mortality, he responds with Christ-like forgiveness and compassion to the news that his brother Lyle, to whom he hasn't spoken in years, has had a stroke. With a newfound fortitude, he resolves to "go back on the road," to visit Lyle and mend the rift between the brothers. The problem is, as Rose points out, that he can't drive a car, so in a spasm of ingenuity and gumption, Alvin decides to ride his power mower.

Rose, paradoxically, is a victim of the very do-gooders she insists her father see. Another idiot savant, she is Rousseau's ideal, smart but subservient, loyal but deferential, who treats Alvin like one of her children even as she dreams of the ones confiscated by the state. She allows Alvin his eccentricities, ignoring the madness of his plan. Alvin's friends, however, a stereotypical bunch of skeptical geezers, respond with the same incredulity as the viewer. To underscore their point, one teasingly asks, "What do you need that grabber for, Alvin?" Alvin, the pragmatic American as resilient as the Marlboro man, responds: "Grabbing."

The first of Alvin's ventures ends tragically. For a while, Alvin rides along at the pace of a riding lawnmower on a public highway, a trek filmed with an eye to the Hudson River School of landscape painters. Happy, free and productive people wave at him, more curious about his eccentricity than his existential mission. But a bad omen—his hat is blown off by a passing semi—foreshadows the inevitable: his mower, supposedly a classic, will conk out. He is forced into the communal world of, in this case, a bus full of goofy tourists snapping their throwaway cameras at the great American icon as he submits to mass-transit collectivism. Alvin is humiliated by having his mower, himself atop, towed back to town, but he has established his individual will, his independence, his patience, determination and, yes, his irrationality: he shotguns his old mower.

The most bizarre and truly unbelievable sequence occurs when Alvin visits an honest used-tractor dealer who sells him his own cream puff. Lynch wants us to like the salesman, but the impression verifies the worst: he shows favoritism to some customers over others, and thus categorically implicates a vast group of innocent salesmen. Alvin's hometown insider, the John Deere tractor salesman, sets him up with advantages an outsider (*der Auslander*) would never have. This time, when Alvin sets out on the John Deere, a semi tears by and—surprise!—his hat does not blow away.

His first encounter on the road is with an impudent runaway of about nineteen who calls Alvin's prized trailer "a hunk of junk." She triggers a solemn biographical recitation from Alvin, who refers to the girl's unwanted pregnancy as "your little problem." We learn that Alvin has had a full, hard, and, for him a morally complex life. His wife is dead. Their child mortality was fifty per cent. He doesn't like cheddar-heads.

But Alvin is not only wizened—he's shrewd too. He waits until the runaway reaches out, then double-barrels his sermon, a pro-life spiel that ignores the reality of her mental and physical abuse. In a nod to folksy, cynical, post–Reagan aesthetics, Alvin tells her that "a warm bed and a roof sounds a mite better than a hotdog on a stick." This cheap symbolism is outdone only by Alvin's discovery, in the morning, of a bundle of sticks shaped into an esoteric sign of affirmation. The girl will return home and accept responsibility for her actions. Alvin's gentle persuasion and Heartland values turn another wayward (read urban) teen around.

The film occupies a small social space, but shot from a romantic, spacious point of view it seems more operatic than it is. Alvin moves through episodes with equal alacrity, dispensing words of wisdom. He tells a couple of smart-aleck bicyclists that the worst part of getting old is "remembering when you was young." When he meets a serial deer slayer—the most classic Lynchian touch in the film—he can only stare in awed sympathy at a woman who must, because of her job, drive a highway on which she slaughters deer as part of her daily commute. Alvin and the woman exemplify two types: the hysterical stranger, the outsider, living against nature, and the instinctual naturalist, who laments the deer's death but skins and eats it anyway. To drive the point home, as it were, the woman tears off in her perennially wrecked car while Alvin mounts the horns of the deer on his trailer—a bit of crude posturing, given that the kill wasn't his—and, well fortified by this God-delivered meal, soldiers on.

Alvin almost crashes out negotiating a particularly steep incline, and the hairy, nearly tragic event underscores—for Alvin and the locals who witness his near miss with disaster—the foolishness of his odyssey. But by now his trip has become his *raison d'être*, and no amount of neighborliness can dissuade him from completing it "his own way." When a former John Deere salesman offers to drive him the rest of the way, Alvin politely turns him down. In one of the more sophomoric pronouncements, a neighbor rhetorically notes Alvin has "come a long way." Another cautions that there are "a lot of weird people everywhere now." Alvin tells her that he fought in Germany in World War II, so "Why should I be a'scared of an I-o-way cornfield?" The entire community shines with admiration and approval, alive in the knowledge that they are in the presence of a saint whose indomitable will and spirit will certainly prevail.

But Alvin's modesty seems more like moral arrogance than Messianic stoicism, his resolve just plain hardheaded obstinacy. Having borrowed a portable phone to call his adoring Rose for money to pay for repairs—refusing to enter the man's house out of a deep-seated respect, one assumes, for privacy, a right that Alvin would expect to be reciprocated (this while he is camped in the man's backyard)—he leaves money for the phone call—no moocher, Alvin—and advises the man against trying to change his mind. "You're a kind man," he says, "talking to a stubborn man." This tidbit of psychological insight is less an excuse than a declaration: Alvin knows the task before him, and no fool or mortal should attempt to impede his dogged righteousness with soft talk about the hazards of age or the pitfalls of the highway. Besides, Alvin has a secret, and has been living with regret most of his life. In his confession scene with another vet, he recounts the story of how as a sniper he shot one of his buddies by mistake. Alvin's life, it seems, has more dimension than most. He lives harder and suffers more than other people. But he is not one to wear his heart on his sleeve. He is a model of rectitude and reticence. While dickering over a repair bill inflated by two feuding brothers—the lawn mower repairmen—he not only discourses on honest work and fair prices but also uses his own dispute with Lyle—which he is, of course, at that moment out to resolve—to deliver "a hard swallow" sermon on brotherliness.

Back on the road, alone again in the rhapsodic splendor of amber waves of grain, he crosses the Mississippi and shares a night with a priest "in one of the oldest cemeteries in the Midwest." Alvin tells the priest about his conflict with Lyle, disparaging the pettiness of it, blaming the argument on liquor and ego. Wiser now, after his Great Awakening, he says he is ready "to make peace[,] ... to look up at the stars" and the priest actually says, "Amen to that."

The rest of the film plays out predictably. After a last-minute delay, his perseverance pays off. He finds his brother, and in an untypical (for Lynch) anticlimatic moment, discovers that his brother is reduced to using a walker, the one thing Alvin refused to do. So the surface image of the once estranged and now reunited brothers achieving a peace beyond words, a silent bonding, may be more enigmatic than Lynch intended: the closing shot implies that Alvin, who didn't have a debilitating stroke, and who refused the walker, and who has just ridden a lawn mower three hundred miles, has had the last laugh, and Lyle seethes with hatred and futility.

Of course some might find this reading of the final scene cynical, even malignant. But the film needs some trace of perversity to lift it from the morass of moral dogma the viewer must slog through to get to that last refreshingly ambiguous shot.

5

Television

Although Lynch dabbled in ephemeral productions like *American Chronicles* (1990), which Woods describes, predictably, as a "celebratory travelogue through the quirky side of the U.S.A." (132), and *On the Air* (1992), a goofy paean to his beloved fifties that ABC cancelled after three of seven scheduled episodes, in both endeavors he maintained his devotional patronage of Americana but had only a tangential involvement in the actual creative process. His signature television work consists basically of three significant pieces: *The Cowboy and the Frenchman* (1987), *Twin Peaks* (1990), and *Hotel Room* (1993).

For *The Cowboy and the Frenchman*, commissioned by *Le Figaro* magazine under the theme of "how I see the French," Lynch admits that "I didn't have any ideas" and nearly passed up on the project (*Short Films of David Lynch*). He should have gone with his first impulse. After hearing of Lynch's plans, the producer told him, "two clichés in one" (*Short Films of David Lynch*), but the clichés never transcend their context, and the result is silly, forgettable and irksome. Instead of an exposé of America's lack of curiosity for other languages and cultures, the film is a tribute to American jingoism and xenophobia. The point of view reflects less how Lynch sees the French as how the French see Americans, and the unintentional irony is that Lynch reinforces that condescending love affair the French have with Jerry Lewis while engaging in his own brand of good old-fashioned American-style gay-bashing.

In his reverence for the honest, good-natured, Reaganesque folk of the heartland, Lynch cannot resist undercutting his celebration of all their cute goofiness with a mean-spirited caricature, pitting a poetically

naïve, shifty, effeminate Frenchman—named Pierre, of course—against
a rowdy, rootin'-tootin' butch bunch of mythical Hollywood bunkhouse
boys appropriately named Slim, Dusty and Pete. Not content with reducing the complex cultural conflicts to the comical mutual mangling of our
respective languages—in a truly absurd scene, Slim tries to read out loud
in French a letter that Pierre has written to his fiancé—Lynch instead
goes for the cheap shot, the easy dig, couching his moral condemnation
of "other"—in this case, the French and gays—in a spoof that seems
designed to immunize him from accusations of bigotry.

     And while all of this bunkum might seem like harmless (if tasteless)
fun, the images and narrative reinforce rather than explode the pernicious
cultural stereotyping at the heart of the film and leave no ambiguity as
to where Lynch's sympathies lie: in this clash of clichés, he stacks American icons like a vintage wide-finned Studebaker coupe and Tex-Mex
rock 'n' roll against French trinkets like miniatures of the Eiffel tower,
rank cheese and cheap photos of Brigitte Bardot, so that, in the end, the
equilibrium the producer hinted at ("two clichés in one") is spoiled by
Lynch's fetishistic faith in America's iconographic hegemony—gay or
straight.

     But the jokes are too easy. In one early scene the cowboys cannot
figure out exactly what kind of critter they have captured. Slim shouts,
"This may be some kinda goll-danged alien spy!" Roped and terrified,
Pierre is nearly kissed by Pete. When the boys go through his valise,
pulling out bottles of Bordeaux wine, baguettes and, most threatening,
escargot, they find French fries, evidence that, indeed, the creature is a
Frenchman. A heavenly choir of angelic damsels sings about "tumbling
tumbleweeds," and the Franco-American allegiance is complete. Even
Broken Feather, an Indian scout who has been trailing Pierre (worried
that he was a "peyote nightmare"), settles old debts with Dusty and shares
a few beers with Slim, Pierre and the boys. The ensuing party—ostensibly a celebration of pluralism and cultural assimilation—unfolds through
a series of puerile Freudian images that culminate in an orgy of French
can-can dancers mixing with four buxom cowgirls cooking up some grub
and servicing the boys. Again, the imagery underscores French femininity and American machismo. The women are rounded up like steers
as everybody dances around an Elvis impersonator, and before the night
is out, the American girls are speaking French (that is, of course, "Voulez-
vous coucher avec moi ce soir?" from "Lady Marmalade"), Slim is decked
out in Pierre's beret, Pierre wears Slim's Stetson, Broken Arrow is rec-
onciled with both the Frenchman and the cowhands, and the film drips

with Rodney King–style mutual respect and cultural assimilation—except Slim is still panicked about snails.

The Cowboy and the Frenchman turns out to be more culturally astute than Lynch or his producers could have imagined, presaging the absurdity of patriotic hysteria during the 2003 war with Iraq, when xenophobia—especially involving Americans boycotting French products to protest France's moral objection to the invasion—became not only trendy but *de rigeur* for many red-blooded, flag-waving, pro-war Americans, culminating in the House of Representatives actually passing a resolution renaming French Fries Freedom Fries in the House cafeteria—reality in this case outflanking even Lynch's nutty take on Franco-American relations. Lynch's Reaganism was preternaturally prescient, fueling the new century's fashionable jingoism with the same sort of high-octane moralizing used by his fellow Manichaean, George W. Bush, to swell national pride during the conflict.

Twin Peaks is Lynch's take on the typical vampire tale (with owls instead of bats this time), and as such reflects more his Victorian fascination with forbidden sex and violence than any Romantic identification with monsters as sympathetic, misunderstood Byronic outsiders. The strict Calvinist moralizing that permeates the series indicates a dramatic return from the ethical ambiguity of *The Elephant Man* to Lynch's obsession with the nature of good and evil, redemption and damnation. The vampire genre also allows Lynch, as it did the Puritans, a perverse voyeuristic indulgence in vice while promoting a moral framework derived from his particular self-righteousness. In this sense, *Twin Peaks* reads like a raunchy Russ Myers/Wes Craven slasher/comedy laced with soap-opera sex and the moral certainty of an itinerant revivalist.

The two obvious models for the episodic *Twin Peaks* are *Batman* (1966) and *Dallas* (1978). In the original television series, Batman and Robin confront one of their archenemies in each episode and defend the city of Gotham against evil geniuses from its underworld, just as Cooper and Harry deal with the assorted criminals and madmen who populate Twin Peaks. The contrived acting, implausible situations and pretentious dialog in *Batman* and *Twin Peaks* signal both a camp homage to and a critique of contemporary society. Likewise, the endless entrepreneurial shenanigans and sexual intrigues of J.R. and the gang from Southfork, linking endless cycles of calamity with shifting allegiances among an ensemble cast, laid the groundwork for what became known by the 1980s as the prime-time soap, a format Lynch and Frost mock as much as they celebrate.

The theme of *Twin Peaks* is to preserve "a retrograde fifties-era vision of he American Way of Life[,] … the vision of a close-knit, family-oriented community of hard-working people who are decent, honest, open and forthright" (Pollard 298). It recurs throughout Lynch's work, but it was explored best, perhaps, in *Blue Velvet*, where burrowing below a "town's homespun surface" (Pollard 298) reveals an "incarnate evil beneath" (Pollard 298). The true prototype for this sort of puritanical exposé is the original prime-time soap *Peyton Place* (1964). Set in rural New England, *Peyton Place* chronicles the scandals of two generations, exposing the raw life of regular people and dismantling the balmy façade of small town rectitude. *Peyton Place* introduced all the ingredients exploited in *Twin Peaks*: a husband released from prison (Hank returns to Norma's cafe); miscarriages (Lucy is deciding whether to have Andy's baby); kinky family secrets (Ben's relationship with Donna and One Eyed Jack's, Leland's abuse of Laura); romantic triangles (among nearly all the characters, including James, Harry, Hank, Donna, Laura, Norma, Shelly, and Josie)—even wealthy kids romantically involved with people from the wrong side of the tracks (James's coupling with Laura, Donna and Evelyn)—all the trappings of the messy lives that make up soap-operatic "Peyton Place subplots" (Alexander 19).

But missing from *Peyton Place* is Lynch's black-and-white, absolutist moral code; in this Lynch and Frost share more with *Batman* and *Dallas* than with *Peyton Place*. *Peyton Place*, in its social realism, deals with the subtleties of human experience. Everyone is culpable; the demarcation between the moral and immoral, the acceptable and unacceptable, blurs in the adventures of Constance MacKenzie and her daughter Allison. In *Batman*, the villains are literally two-dimensional pop-ups animated for television but hardly human in their cartoon psychology and megalomaniacal predictability. *Dallas*, though more realistic, for the most part dispensed with ethical subtlety too: the bad were predictable predators, the good willing—if guileless—victims. As a pastiche, *Twin Peaks* employs the prime-time soap opera elements pioneered in *Peyton Place* but drops the campy morality in lieu of Lynch's sincere perorations against the evils of contemporary society. In the prototypes, the villains were loveable. J.R., more class bully than crazed sadist, had a smidgen of redeeming qualities. The Joker was more interesting than Batman. And the convoluted plot lines of the original *Peyton Place* afforded even the dastardly characters an inkling of human frailty so that no one was singularly bad. In *Twin Peaks*, no such moral subtlety interferes with the strictly Manichaean split separating the good from the bad.

Like its predecessors, *Twin Peaks* utilizes a stable of writers and directors whose scripts are stylistically and episodically consistent with a pre-established concept or pilot, a necessary assembly method given its episodic structure, but one that creates as many problems as opportunities. Unlike the 120-minute movie format that demands a tight integration of image and theme, the story in a sprawling, open-ended framework of an on-going television serial can become diffuse, individual episodes eclectic, the general pacing erratic and inconsistent. And though *Twin Peaks* takes its theme straight from *Blue Velvet*—the mysterious violent subtext beneath the surface of a seemingly benign small town—the structure resembles *Wild at Heart*, where a series of tenuously connected events are strung together on a simple line of action. Designed for the serial format, and trying to accommodate the various styles of associated writers and directors working within the soap-opera genre, *Twin Peaks* still suffers the same aesthetic problems as *Wild at Heart*: too many random events with no causal connection to the resolution, weak linearity in the general story line, too much improvisation, a lack of integrity between the characters' motives and actions, and basically a lot of unfinished business.

An outline of the story reinforces Lynch's hard-core Manichaeism. In the supernatural world are two forces: "the white lodge" and "the black lodge." The white lodge is a place of peace, analogous to heaven, home to benevolent creatures like The Friendly Giant. The black lodge, on the other hand, is a place of power, populated by evil spirits like BOB. Those whose souls affiliate with the white lodge live in harmony with nature and identify with water (especially as coffee). People like the reformed Ben, who opposes over-development and works for environmental causes, represent their interests. Those affiliated with the black lodge, however, are associated with fire (and a sulfurous smell like burning oil); thus the ominous mantra: "Fire walk with me." Their interests reflect consumption and commercial exploitation. Given this context for Lynch's metaphysics, an event like the mill fire illustrates a confluence of dueling primary forces, the lack of sufficient water to douse the fire indicating a spiritual deficiency that threatens the "innocent" citizens of the community. This cosmic logic also infuses the multivalent resonance in the title. The name *Twin Peaks* reflects the doubling that anchors the symbolism and moral standing of the characters in the oppositional alignment of forces emanating from either the white lodge or the black lodge. The name of the town, of course, carries a range of signifiers, including a sophomoric sexual allusion, a pun on the word "peak" as "peek" suggesting two

ways of seeing the world, the dual natures of many of the characters
(Leland/BOB, Laura/Maddy, Gerard/Mike, Agent Dennis/Denise Bry-
son), and a self-reflexive reference to the doubling imagery itself. The
double-entendre of the title also carries over into the geographic layout
of the town. Situated between two mountains and next to a waterfall,
its landscape is unmistakably feminine (think of Dali's landscapes, or
Courbet's *The Origin of the Universe*); and, like the women of Twin Peaks,
the nature surrounding the community can be as destructive as it is nur-
turing.

    Drawn into this mix of Mayberry and mayhem, representatives of
the white lodge ("the gifted") and the black lodge ("the damned") con-
verge to battle for the souls of the townsfolk ("the innocents") who are
unaware of the epic Zoroastrian struggle being fought around them.
F.B.I. Special Agent Dale Cooper, assigned to help investigate the murder of Laura Palmer, is one of the gifted. Major Garland Briggs, once
part of a classified military operation called Project Blue Book designed
to probe extrasensory phenomena in the area, joins Cooper in battling
their archenemy Windom Earle, a former colleague of both Cooper and
Briggs and one of the damned seeking power through the black lodge.
BOB, the incarnation of evil, is the face of the force from the black lodge,
capable of possessing people who, through intense feelings of fear, allow
him to enter their spirit. The wanted poster for BOB then becomes a
phenomenological joke: to ask, "Have you seen this man?" is to ask, with
Calvin, if you are gifted or damned. Leland Palmer, who murders his
daughter and niece, is BOB's current host and therefore the resident
manifestation of evil in the community. The One-Armed Man, as Mike,
is a refugee from BOB's influence and has joined forces with Cooper,
Briggs and Sheriff Truman.

    This good/bad dyadic structure controlling the supernatural world
defines the moral positions of the other members of the community too,
framing them in distinct categories: either good or bad, with the salvageable characters shifting between the two poles in a sort of moral purgatory. Good characters include the staff at the Twin Peaks Sheriff's Station—
Harry S. Truman, Hawk Hill, Lucy Moran and Andy Brennan—as well
as Pete Martel, Audrey Horne, Maddy Ferguson, Annie Blackburne,
Donna Hayward, James Hurley, Ed Hurley and Norma Jennings. These
characters all share an innate sense of fairness, a genuine willingness to
help others, and a general appreciation for common decency. They are
hardworking, sensitive and respectful, their sexuality tender and grounded
in affection. The bad characters include Leo Johnson, Hank Jennings,

Catherine Martell, the gang at One Eyed Jack's—Blackie, Jacques and Bernard Renault—Thomas Eckhardt, Josie Packard and Jerry Horne. They are selfish, duplicitous, and driven by materialism and spite. Their sexual exploits satisfy only their lust and feed their sense of power. Manipulative, insensitive, and greedy, they finance themselves at the expense of others, usually by trafficking in illegal narcotics. The salvageable characters, those with a strong enough sense of guilt and self-awareness to qualify them as capable of reform, include Shelly Johnson, Bobby Briggs, and Ben Horne.

Shelly, for instance, after so much abuse from Leo, gains a sense of self-confidence and a better self-image, giving up her scamming with Bobby and even entering the Miss Twin Peaks competition. Bobby discovers a renewed respect, love and appreciation for his father, and intimates that he has given up his old bad habits and is finally serious about his relationship with Shelly. Before his murder by Dr. Hayward, Ben Horne, shamed by his daughter, shifts from an exploitative commercial developer to a champion of industrial ethics and staunch tree-hugging environmentalism. In Lynch's eschatology, these salvageable characters represent the possibility of salvation, but they are a pronounced minority in the overall population of the series, and indicative of Lynch's intractable moralistic stance regarding sin, depravity, eternal punishment, and the slim chances people have for redemption. Leo Johnson, for instance, has a last-minute change of heart, releasing Briggs so he can help Shelly, but for Lynch his atonement is incomplete and Leo must suffer the medieval torture of the damned (bound and holding with his teeth a string attached to a jar full of tarantulas above his head). Curiously, Leland Palmer should be included in the salvageable category, if only because of the self-torment he suffers from being able to recognize his sin—his hair turns gray from the trauma—but, as BOB's victim, he is powerless to rectify or explain the awful cause of his actions. This is Lynch at his most unrelenting and absolute in applying his extreme nonconsequentialist morality: it is the act not the intention that determines the spiritual condition of man. Causal determinism does not preclude personal responsibility, so even though people's actions may be predetermined, as Calvin held, the perpetrators are nevertheless responsible for what they do. In his corresponding view of moral responsibility, Lynch holds Leland responsible for letting BOB enter his spirit in the first place, when as a child he wanted to "play with fire."

Within these absolutist moral parameters, Lynch unfolds his ghost story, but underpinning the search for Laura's killer is another moralistic subtext relating to the War on Drugs. The bad people in Twin Peaks use and/or deal illegal drugs. It is the source of violence and misery for anyone associated with Leo or Jacques or any of their minions. Closely linked with illegal drug use is prostitution. One Eyed Jack's is the nefarious nexus of sin, a place where satisfying cravings of the senses pollutes the pure vessel of the soul. This equating of the pleasures of the senses with impurity dates back to the Pre-Socratics—especially in the teachings of Pythagoras—but it is especially evident in Plato's work (*Phaedo* et al.), is reiterated in St. Augustine's *Confessions*, and is revived with a vengeance in the American evangelical movement that Lynch's theology most resembles. But aside from its philosophical pedigree, Lynch's moral reductivism also reflects the zeitgeist of the Reagan/Bush years, when right-wing social reformers made their careers blaming recreational drug use by middle class sensualists for fueling civic disillusionment, personal anomie and the general breakdown of what they called "traditional American values." According to these virtuecrats, illegal drug use was responsible for every social ailment from teen pregnancy and gang violence to Bill Clinton being elected president.

Drugs and sex are the focus of the same neoconservatives driving the social reformist movement in America, especially in the second Bush administration, and unfortunately Lynch plays right into their hands, even interjecting himself into the politics of abortion rights and negative gay stereotyping, coming down squarely in the conservatives' camp. In episode 21, for instance, not directed by Lynch but reflective of his moral authoritarianism, Dr. Hayward tells the story of Little Nicky. His mother "was a poor immigrant chamber maid at the Great Northern[.]... [He was] conceived during an assault in a back alley by a man who fled across the border. She had a dream ... of a better life for herself and her child[:] ... she decided to carry that child." She died "before Nicky drew his first breath" and was buried in Potter's Field. A "young childless couple" adopted him but were killed in a car wreck and Nicky "was alone again, as he is today." That she "kept her child" is the key, even though he was a result of a vicious rape, this being consistent with the view of antiabortion extremists who believe that life is sacred from conception so abortion should be banned in all cases. At the end of this tear-jerking speech, Lucy swats a mosquito and smears a telling bloodstain on the wall, a reiterative image of violence, birth, death, and abortion that undercuts any ironic intent in the scene and underscores the sincerity of the speech. (Incidentally, episode 21 also contains Cooper's confession to having committed adultery, the implication being that he has brought his sin to Twin Peaks and the citizens are caught up in his struggle for purification.) Similarly, episode 22 finds Leo under the control of Windom Earle. Leo awakens in Earle's cabin to find Earle playing a huge phallic flute placed strategically between Leo's legs. Earle strokes the flute lasciviously and describes it as "truly an instrument of pleasure" before beating Leo and shocking him with an electric dog-training collar, the crazed Earle—and homosexuality—thus equated with not only immorality but inherent evil as well. (In an earlier bit of gay bashing, Sheriff Truman warns Albert—in one of their many urban/rural standoffs—"You'll be looking for your teeth up on queer street.") Although Lynch is not credited specifically with writing or directing these episodes, as creator he certainly had control over the material; and the blatant gay baiting and anti-drug propagandizing in *Twin Peaks* was established as early as *Dune* and *Blue Velvet*. The homophobia continues through *Wild at Heart*, and Lynch's Reaganesque crusade against countercultural values that grew out of the sixties' antiwar movement permeates *Fire Walk with Me*.

Besides the series pilot, Lynch is credited with writing episodes 1, 2, and 8, and directing episodes 2, 8, 9, 14 and 29. The pilot dictates the spine of the narrative, but it is through his directing that Lynch most seriously, and egregiously, imposes his sensibility on the series. Because of its episodic structure and the creative ensemble that produced it, and given the individual styles of its various writers and directors, *Twin Peaks* cannot be read as a scene-by-scene Lynchian construct. What is certain, however, is that the overall style of each component derives from the directorial devices Lynch employs in *Blue Velvet*: the weird close-ups, the camp sentimentality delivered without irony, the lingering shots that transform ordinary objects into portents of disaster and the mundane into the bizarre. But in the context of Lynch's overarching moralizing, the five episodes Lynch directed out of the original 29 released for the American market provide convincing evidence of his quirky Puritanism.

Episode 2 opens with a typical Lynchian juxtaposition. With Johnny in his Native American regalia and Jerry fetishizing sandwiches, Ben Horne and his family dine formally in one of their vast private rooms at The Great Northern Hotel. In a less salubrious part of town, James Hurley, Donna Hayward and her parents share a more modest moment of family (ir)reverence. Instead of playing the rebellious teen, or withdrawing into insanity, Donna offers to "clean up." But after acknowledging that she will be ready for her father's early morning wake-up call for church, she makes out with James, only flirting with, not succumbing to, Laura's serious bad-girl habits. Her father is a respected doctor in the community, her mother a woman of indomitable spirit who, confined to a wheelchair, still manages to retain her independence. But Donna envies the appeal generated by Laura's subversive (edgy) reputation, and she and James convince themselves that their romantic relationship is the right thing because they respect Laura even after finding out she was a dangerously kinky drug-crazed sex fiend. While James and Donna dramatize their budding sexuality, Ben and Jerry Horne check out "the new girl" at One Eyed Jack's. Ben wins her in a coin toss, an awkward ingénue brimming with only half-reluctant possibilities.

This pairing of innocence and experience, purity and corruption, creates a neat moral dialectic, a doubling of oppositional images, an interplay between dreams and the waking world, that shapes Lynch's moral vision. Donna, for instance, out with her parents, decides to greet Audrey, out alone, in the soda shop. Audrey, the vamp, is the cautious (if curious) virgin. Donna, the church-going do-gooder, is craving sex with James. What they talk about contrasts Audrey's intuitive take on things with Donna's rationality, but even their methods of thinking are reversed by Audrey's skill at working with her father psychologically and Donna's abandoning reason for passion in her relationship with James. Cooper, too, counterintuitively relies on dreams in his investigation, while Sheriff Harry Truman, the quintessential country cop, prefers inductive detective work and good old-fashioned vigilantism to spooky paranormal high jinks.

In a comic and desperate attempt to extricate himself from this logical trap, Cooper tries to synthesize the dialectic between himself and the sheriff. Combining Freudian dream analysis, Tibetan spiritualism, Dadaist psychology, analytical philosophy and Aristotelian logic, Cooper throws rocks at a glass jar on a stump, calculating the culpability of the suspects by the proximity of the rocks to the jar. The scene provides an easy way to review the action and characters, but beyond its function in the narrative drive, it reinforces Lynch's value system, the glue that holds this episode (and the other 28) together. Leo beats Shelly because, after all, she chose to marry him. Ed Hurley has dirty hands because, in love with Norma but living with Nadine, he has a bad conscience. Leland Palmer cuts himself on Laura's photograph because, of course, he has blood on his hands, and blood connects him to Laura.

In episodes 8 and 9, Lynch continues to pursue his pet themes: masking, doubling, illicit sex coupled with violence and an unmitigated sentimentality. Cooper has been shot (by Josie Packard), and the scene in which the old room service waiter from the Great Northern finds

Cooper on the floor plays out in Lynch's typical mannerist style. The incongruity between what has happened to Cooper and the old waiter's response—he is oblivious to the seriousness of the problem—creates a frustrating bit of Kafkaesque deadpan humor. The waiter, who morphs into The Friendly Giant, is studiously disconnected, his actions completely appropriate to the situation at hand. Bleeding and fast losing consciousness, but resigned to the inability of the waiter to respond logically to the situation, Cooper signs the bill and asks, "Does this include gratuity?" It is the only viable question, given Cooper's stoic philosophy and the waiter's senility.

The next scene has Ben visiting his daughter (a.k.a. Prudence), another of the new girls at One Eyed Jack's. In a classic touch of dramatic irony, Audrey hides from her father behind a kitten mask. It is a moment of discovery for her, as her father is exposed as the lecherous owner of the brothel. (Only a *deus ex machina*—brother Jerry telling Ben that they have a "situation"—saves her.) But the set-up is a moral trap for Ben: he cannot know that the young girl is his daughter, but his lust is enough to warrant Lynch's moral condemnation. The fact that the object of his desire is his daughter only amplifies the inexcusable sin of an adult man hungering after a teenage woman, as Lynch uses the overt taboo of incest to underscore Ben's transgression. A highly sexed virgin equally intrigued and repelled by the action at Blackie's, Audrey highlights her own moral ambiguity in a striking pose, just when her father leaves her: she holds the mask below her face half-shrouded in black lace. It is a tableau of moral ambidexterity, an image of the dueling forces of nature and convention defining the existential dilemma plaguing Twin Peaks.

Meanwhile, the dark side of life, at least as represented by Laura Palmer, is becoming more alluring as Donna continues her affectations, appropriating Laura's bad-girl image by wearing seductive sunglasses and learning to smoke. Donna plays the sultry role of a gangster's moll when she visits James in jail, coming on to him like Kathleen Turner in *Body Heat* (1981), prowling outside James's cage, biting his knuckle and telling him to "get out fast." But she is only acting within the safe world of her social theatre. She can always slip back into the security of her familiar self, surrounded by her loving family and loyal friends. Like the Betty/Diane double in *Mulholland Dr.*, Donna plays Nancy Drew mystery games in which the discoveries are harmless and you can always close the book when things get scary. Laura, by contrast, was living her nightmares. But Lynch treats Donna's role-playing as if it were a potential

first step—a gateway—into vice and depravation. Accordingly, he plants
reality checks for Donna, as when Harold Smith hangs himself, cautionary reminders that you can get burned if you play with fire. So, like
Oedipus, Donna strives blindly for truths that are ultimately more
destructive than enlightening.

Lynch's moral mouthpiece in the series is, of course, Cooper, and
the Special Agent's brush with death allows Lynch to pile on the hokum.
As Cooper lies wounded, he has a chance to review "things you regret
or might miss." At the top of his list is to "treat people with more care
and respect," a notion as unoriginal and idealistic as the Golden Rule,
Kant's categorical imperative, or the oath in *The Boy Scout Handbook*.
Also, besides "cracking the Lindbergh kidnapping case," Cooper "would
like very much to make love to a beautiful woman who I had genuine
affection for." It is that last relative clause (couched in a quaint solecism)
that puts Lynch's hokey nostalgia in perspective: Agent Cooper's overriding virtue is his corny morality. He has control over his emotions,
knows how "to keep the fear from your mind," yet he displays enough
empathy to make friends, to sense the stirring of desire—in his case, natural healthy urges—but even then, his passion is balanced by an icy logic.
His ultimate love interest, Annie, is, after all, fresh from a convent.

Cooper, stoically back on the job only a few hours after surgery,
leaves nothing to chance, explaining how a wood tick killed by the bul-
let had caused him to lift his bulletproof vest, exposing him to the shot.
Cooper's involvement with the irrational is aesthetic, data to be analyzed
and explored for meaning. Gerard, as Mike, tells Cooper that the answer
will be found in his heart, not in his head, but Cooper's mental wiring
is more aligned with Major Briggs and Windom Earle than, say, Maddy
or Leland or Laura. Cooper and Briggs are the dynamic duo of logical
positivism. For them, signals from the woods demand investigation, doc-
umentation, and explication. In contrast, Maddy complains, while talking to Laura's photograph, that all she did was come to Twin Peaks for
the funeral, and "it feels like I fell into a dream." The truth is, Maddy,
like Laura, lives her dreams. She sees blood on the rug, watches BOB
come over the sofa after her, foresees her own murder in all its horror
and gore. Her dream experience is beyond analysis. It is not an alternative but a parallel world. It is not until Cooper enters the Red Room for
the last time that he comes to understand how real dreams can be. He
cannot crack the case because he does not understand the reality of
Leland's nightmare. Leland's hair turning white indicates that he is aware
of his crimes, and his hell is living with the knowledge, suffering from

the fact that he is both guilty and innocent but nevertheless responsible, in Lynch's world, for abusing and finally murdering his daughter and Maddy. Because Leland's reality is so far removed from Cooper's understanding, no matter how much Cooper dabbles in what Sheriff Truman calls "mumbo jumbo[,] … the dreams, the visions, dwarfs, giants, Tibet and the rest of the hocus pocus," the Special Agent cannot logically solve or explain the immediate mystery in Twin Peaks of who killed Laura Palmer.

Two vital images contain the doubling that represents a moral dilemma in *Twin Peaks*. First, the One-Armed Man (Gerard/Mike) is a physical representation of the psychic split between the rational and irrational, the orderly and the chaotic, the dream world and waking life—those dyadic oppositions in Lynch's Manichaean vision framing the motivational drives of the characters. Over the course of several episodes, Gerard emerges as a traveling shoe salesman who happens to have a sort of split personality or schizophrenia that he treats with Haloperidol, a drug that seems to prevent BOB from entering his spirit. His condition, like Leland's, is more metaphorically than clinically accurate; nevertheless, without his medicine Gerard, who is, according to Hawk, "clean, no record, no warrants," reverts to Mike, one of BOB's vehicles and a mass murderer. Gerard claims he lost his arm in a car accident. Back then he was selling pharmaceuticals, not shoes. But while Sheriff Truman is inquiring about footgear for the department, Gerard sees BOB's wanted poster and nearly faints. It is significant that, when the sheriff asks if he needs anything, Gerard answers, "Water," as if to drench the fire of BOB's wrath. Later, and significantly, in a bathroom, BOB re-inhabits his "vehicle" and a different Gerard—Mike, in fact, as BOB's possession—exits the stall. In police custody, he is denied the Haloperidol. Cooper's supervisor warns, "If we give him the drug, Coop, you'll never see the other side." Mike claims to be "an inhabiting spirit." Gerard "is host to" a kind of parasite. Mike used to walk with fire, on killing sprees with BOB. But then, Mike says, he "saw the face of God" and now Mike visits only to try to stop BOB. Where BOB comes from "cannot be revealed," but he "feeds off fear" and "the pleasures are his children."

The other image is Laura's necklace, the one Sarah Palmer saw in her vision. She tells Sheriff Truman it was broken in two, but she is unaware that James and Donna buried one half of it the night after Laura was murdered. When confronted by Cooper and Sheriff Truman in the hospital where he is recuperating from a beating, Dr. Jacoby confesses to following Donna and James and taking the necklace "as a keepsake."

Jacoby sees the necklace as an image too. "It was her," he says. "The necklace. A divided heart. She was living a double life. Two people." Jacoby admits that she did not commit suicide, but "allowed herself to be killed." Laura is anointed town saint and scapegoat, victim and perp, the broken necklace an iconic representation of her beatification. Like her classical and mythological counterparts, Laura Palmer is the key enigmatic figure driving the action. She is also a metaphor for the community and by extension for Lynch's view of the human condition in general. Just as the people of Twin Peaks are not as simple and morally righteous as they seem, denying their secret shadow selves or hiding them from others in various guises, Laura was not what she appeared to be. On the surface, she presented a sensitive, caring daughter from a respectable, prominent family who worked with the handicapped and the local Meals on Wheels program; but she was also a lost soul into masochistic sex and hard drugs. An archetypal femme fatale, she is a nymph of desire and destruction, responsible not only for her own violent demise but for setting in motion the chain of events that leads to the various epiphanies, discoveries, reversals, revelations, deaths and transmogrifications that culminate in the Miss Twin Peaks debacle and Cooper's ultimate possession by BOB.

Episode 8 continues to develop various subplots snaking though the series. Shelly and Pete are hospitalized for smoke inhalation after Leo sets the mill on fire. Nadine and Leo are both comatose, Nadine having tried to kill herself, Leo shot by Hank Jennings. The conflict heats up between the cynical, emotionless professional Albert and the sensitive, upright Andy and Sheriff Truman. Josie visits Seattle to indulge in what Pete naïvely calls "A secret vice—shopping." Ben and Jerry are connected with Leo, Josie, Hank and the arson attempt at the mill. Blackie confronts Audrey (who traipses around the room in her negligee and heels, the epitome of innocent sexuality), explaining that "the owner was disappointed in your performance last night," an ironic comment on Ben's hypocrisy. Donna borrows the station wagon from the aptly named Double R diner to begin her investigation of the Meals on Wheels program. Cooper reviews the clues The Friendly Giant gave him in a vision, Audrey prays her "Special Agent" will find the note she left him and rescue her, while Ronette replays Laura's murder in violent stroboscopic images.

Two scenes in particular help shape the moral perspective Lynch uses to order the disparate plot lines, no small task given the web of intrigue crisscrossing the community. One involves Major Briggs and his son

Bobby when they run into one another at the Double R. Lynch's sympathy is consistently with Briggs. He speaks in what appear to be empty pat phrases, with less emotional engagement than a rhetorician reviewing a technical manual, emotionally estranged from any hint of sentiment, but in fact what he says reflects a strong will, a good heart, and a genuine concern for decency and truth. He is a uniformed patriot, a man of achievement and character that represents all that is righteous and blessed in America. In contrast, Bobby, the handsome high school quarterback, is a slacker, a scammer and small-time drug dealer with no plans, no ambition, and no respect for authority. He cannot see through his father's detached language to the man behind the words; of course, his articulation is usually restricted to blank looks and empty gestures. He slouches, smokes, and shrugs a lot, animated only by his adulterous sex with Shelly or criminal dealings with Leo.

When his father spots him at the lunch counter, the two exchange a tentative "Son?" "Dad?" that establishes the crux of the problem with life in Twin Peaks: the inability of people to engage each other, to experience true human interaction in what Habermas calls an "'ideal speech situation'" (qtd. in West 76), where individuals can express themselves "free from relations of power and dominance" (76), opening a more transparent subjectivity and allowing for honest communication. After another attempt at superficial banter—"How was school?" "Fine. How was work?" "Good."—Briggs acknowledges that there are things about his work that make family life difficult. When Bobby asks him, for instance, what he actually does for a living, the major replies, "That's classified." But Briggs, like a patient, caring father, seems intent on drawing Bobby out of his nihilism, noting that the huckleberries are "particularly delicious today." Then he relates a vision he had, which, in his textbook fashion, he distinguishes from a mere dream. He says he saw Bobby "living a life of deep harmony and joy" and when they embraced it was "warm and loving ... nothing withheld." Briggs realizes, "We were in this moment one." This is, of course, the overriding desire of every person seeking self-integration in a balanced life that unites father and son, age and youth, the super-rational and the poetic. Operating within the iconographic thematic structure of Twin Peaks, Briggs' vision works to restore the two halves of Laura's necklace and resolve the duplicitous doubling—the Manichaean struggle—threatening the soul of the community. His speech overwhelms Bobby, and exposes him as a sensitive son capable of deep feeling. Truly moved by his father's opening up to him, Bobby appreciates their intimate moment. This sets him off, in his authenticity, from

Hank, working behind the counter, who mocks the major with a perfunctory and exaggerated salute. Significantly, that is the moment when
Bobby recognizes Hank as the man who shot Leo.

The other key scene takes place at the Haywards' as they gather
with their daughters Harriet, Gersten and Donna, along with Maddy and
Leland and Sarah Palmer, for a special tribute to Laura. The *mise-en-
scène* is goofy and sentimental, but hauntingly touching too, the strange-
ness heightened by Lynch's juxtaposing the innocent reaction of the
youngest daughters—who respond with music and poetry—with the serious grieving of the adults who seem more focused on the horror and
reality of Laura's murder. Strangely, Leland is emotionally aligned with
the children, while his wife identifies with the other adults, Maddy,
Donna and her parents. This emotional misalignment indicates Leland's
attempt at denial, his inability to face the harsh truth of his actions. He
prefers the children's approach, as their anesthetic rendering of tragedy
into art plays closer to the safety of the madness into which Leland is
ineluctably retreating.

The tension is established immediately by the staginess of what
should be a solemn occasion. The youngest daughter welcomes the guests
to "The Hayward Supper Club" as if they were gathered for a recital.
She brags that she has been chosen to play the fairy princess in her school
play and that she had the highest scores in math and English, just like
her sisters before her, thankful that she doesn't "have to worry about being
ashamed anymore." In all its innocent charm, the moment must be torture to Sarah Palmer, having to witness the successes of these beautiful,
privileged overachievers while her lovely, promising but seriously conflicted only child has just been butchered in a sordid sex-and-drugs murder ritual.

The poem Harriet reads is filled with the same terrible beauty. It is
an account of hope and horror, as well as a catalog of correlative images
interspersed throughout the series: "It was Laura and I saw her glowing
in the dark woods. I saw her smiling. We were crying and I saw her
laughing. In our sadness, I saw her dancing. It was Laura living in my
dreams. It was Laura … the glow was life … her smile was to say it was
alright to cry … the woods was our sadness … the dance was her calling … it was Laura, and she came to kiss me goodbye." Sarah, of course,
is on the verge of breaking down with grief, while the others sit in respectful silence. Gersten begins playing Mendelssohn, and the mood is maintained through dinner. Dr. Hayward finally asks Leland about his hair
having turned white overnight, and Leland tells him that seeing it made

him realize that he has "turned a corner somehow." Then he suddenly says he feels like singing and, prompting Gersten, stands from the table and tears into "Get Happy," exasperating his wife and embarrassing the others. But the pace of the song increases until Leland is not singing so much as ranting, desperate and mad, before he collapses. Just as he did at Laura's funeral, when he fell sobbing onto her casket, causing it to be lowered and raised in an ugly parody of sex, Leland manages to ruin the dinner, reducing a moment of high drama to low comedy.

In episode 9, Lynch dutifully advances the quickly multiplying plot lines. Cooper continues to graft parapsychology to inductive reasoning, trying to intuit the killer's identity while explaining his fascination with Tibet. Albert, in his Sergeant Joe Friday mode, sticks to the empirical facts surrounding the strangulation death of Jacques Renault. Ronette panics when she sees the poster of BOB; Cooper learns that Windom Earle has escaped from a mental asylum; Donna begins investigating Harold Smith, who supposedly has Laura's secret diary; and Major Briggs translates a message from the Log Lady's log and delivers it to Cooper. Andy, convinced he is sterile, wonders who could be the father of Lucy's baby. Audrey figures out how the prostitute-recruiting scheme operates in Horne's department store, learns that her father owns One Eyed Jack's, and begins to suspect that her father slept with Laura. Meanwhile, Donna grows jealous of James and Maddy's relationship, Ben reports Audrey missing, Bobby convinces Shelly to keep Leo home instead of testifying against him and sending him to jail so they can pocket the insurance money, and Maddy (clearly one of the damned) sees BOB, foreshadowing her murder.

More interesting than the endless plot permutations is Lynch's return to his dramatic reversing, described above in the scene with Leland at the Haywards', where he transforms the transcendent into the ridiculous, and, likewise, the inane into the sublime. The scene in which James sings to Maddy and Donna in the Hayward's living room typifies Lynch's aesthetics, and his moral message is no less explicit than his subversive use of cliché: the corrupt are seriously comical, the innocent comically serious. Lynch understands the nature of a cliché: its truth precedes it, therefore its meaning is over-determined, but this preconditioning to the point of meaninglessness leaves it ripe for reinvestment, the opportunity to reinvigorate it with significance. The setup is the same Lynch uses elsewhere (for the same purpose, and usually with similar results): Dorothy Vallens' show at the Slow Club, Ben's miming Roy Orbison's "In Dreams," Sailor's Elvis impersonations, some of the sequences from *Lost*

Highway, Rebekah del Rio's performance of Orbison's "Crying" at the Club Silencio.

The music in *Twin Peaks* (with a nod, again, to *Scorpio Rising*) evokes a complexity of emotions, which, more importantly, contain moral subtleties that highlight the general theme of the series: the symbiotic connection between innocence and guilt. The difference between the music of Donna and James, for instance—in the living room at the Haywards' and at the roadhouse bar—and that of Leland—his penchant for show tunes—expresses more than a gap of generational tastes in styles: the moody, emotionally-laden songs by Julee Cruise suggest a moral context of innocence, a purity of desire, an intensity of restraint. In contrast, Leland's silly, pathetic rendering of "Get Happy" masks a guilty conscience, so the lyrics become a rant of madness, not an expression of the breezy optimism they are meant to convey. It is no coincidence that the two sequences both take place at the Haywards', Leland's in episode 8, James's in episode 9. By setting the sequences in the same location, Lynch reinforces the contrast between the conflicted adult, whose deceit and murderous criminality corrupt the lyrics, and James, whose sincerity and innocence invest the lyrics with more significance than their literal meaning can convey. Whereas James is serious about what could be construed as a shallow teenage crush, the mawkish stirrings of puppy love, Leland strives to be flippant about heinous acts of violence and the suffering of the damned. Leland's singing, in a sense, is an act of contrition, a symptom of his conscience and his own recognition of the severity of his sins.

James, of course, is conflicted too. His repetition of the line "just you and I" is delivered to Laura, whom he sees in Maddy, and to Donna as well, who, now that Laura is dead, has become the object of his desire. The unreality of the props—the goofy microphones, the girls singing back-up, the absurd ambiance of teens partying in the living room while the parents stay upstairs—intensifies the emotional complexity of their situation: in Maddy, James sees his true Laura, the good Laura, unblemished by her sordid indulgence in raunchy sex, drugs and violence. But in his yearning, he causes Donna first to panic in jealousy, then to explode in a possessive bout of sexuality, kissing James passionately as if to reclaim him, all of which isolates Maddy and leaves her vulnerable to BOB, whom she sees in a vision immediately after being abandoned by James and Donna. Her terrified screaming unites the trio again in an intense emotional bond that restores the harmony they shared earlier in the music before Maddy's flirting and Donna's insecurity ruined the moment.

So for Lynch, music can provoke and heal. In both scenes—Leland's frenetically launching into "Get Happy" and James's crooning "just you and I" at Donna and Maddy—the music illustrates another layer of doubling and reflects the overall design of conflicting motifs in *Twin Peaks*, inherent in the portrait of Laura Palmer: nothing is necessarily what it appears to be; what seems innocuous often turns insidious; where innocence corrupts, corruption purifies.

This effect is achieved again in episode 14, which opens and closes with music sequences, the last one culminating in Maddy's murder while most of the other principal characters are watching the band at the roadhouse bar. At this point, the series is half-finished. Some plot lines have been resolved; others are still being introduced. Harold Smith hangs himself. Maddy tells Leland and Sarah that she is going home to Missoula. Shelly and Bobby continue to mock Leo, but discover that the insurance money amounts to only $42 a week. Audrey confronts her father about One Eyed Jack's, and after he confesses he slept with Laura, she turns him in to Cooper, who is already suspicious because of a reference to Ben in Laura's secret diary. Catherine, disguised as Tojamura, reveals herself to Pete.

The episode begins with Laura's mother, wracked by grief, dragging herself down the stairs of her house while on the phonograph a record plays Louis Armstrong singing "What a Wonderful World." The obvious contrast between the lyrics of the song—a reverential celebration of the beauty of nature and the preciousness of life—and the reality of Sarah Palmer's isolation and despair increases the tension as Lynch pans the living room, using low shots of the furniture seen from Sarah's point of view, until she has a sudden, enigmatic vision of a white horse. As long as the music plays, the promised threat of violence remains in abeyance. Not until the record finishes, the stylus repetitively tracking in the final groove—opening what Olson identifies as an "interdimensional conduit" (46)—does BOB emerge in Leland's image to terrorize Maddy.

Concurrently, at the roadhouse, acting on a tip from the Log Lady— "There are owls," her log told her, "in the roadhouse"—The Log Lady, Sheriff Truman and Cooper stake out the club. Bobby is there, listening to the band. James and Donna sit together in a booth, Donna anguishing over her indirect involvement in Harold Smith's suicide, James fretting about his conflicted feelings for Laura, Donna and Maddy. Julee Cruise dreamily sings, "I want you right back inside my heart," Donna, at the moment of their reconciliation miming the song to James. On the surface, the music is catchy and simple, but complex too, eerily elliptical, mirroring the feelings of Donna and James as they renew their romantic connection in the shadow of Harold Smith's suicide and Laura's murder. But intercut with this sensual scene, Leland, at home, finds BOB in his mirror. Possessed, dancing madly without music, he murders Maddy during the most violent scene in the series. At the bar, The Friendly Giant suddenly appears to Cooper and announces, "It's happening again." After Leland/BOB viciously finishes off Maddy—slamming her into a glass picture frame and shouting "You're going home to Missoula," then jabbing another letter clue under her fingernail, The Friendly Giant disappears and the music at the bar resumes, this time a different song, no less haunting but moodier, again reflecting the mixed feelings of apprehension, sadness and dread everyone in the bar senses. Donna begins to cry. James stares away, distant. Bobby seems distressed. Finally, the old waiter from The Great Northern walks over to Cooper and apologizes. "I'm so sorry," he says, ostensibly referring to his earlier bumbling incompetence after he found Cooper lying shot on the floor of his room, but more presciently the old waiter embodies the grief of the town that once again must face the murder of one of its children. The action in the series has come full circle, and Lynch, as he did in the previous scenes, cleverly manipulates the musical interlude at the club to contrast the horribly simple animal violence of Maddy's death with the intense emotional complexity of the characters left to deal with it.

By episode 29, the last in the series, many of the plot lines are hopelessly convoluted. While some are all too easily resolved, others merely peter out. The action opens after Annie, having won the Miss Twin Peaks competition, has been kidnapped by Windom Earle. Andy and Lucy are a couple again, as are Ed and Nadine. Bobby and Shelly plan to get married. Exonerated from suspicion in Laura's murder, Ben confronts Dr. Hayward about his relationship with Donna's mother. "I wanted to do good," he says, "to be good," but in a fit of anger Hayward kills him. Cooper enters the Red Room again, looking for Annie. He finds Windom Earle, who tells him, "Give me your soul, I'll let Annie go." But he kidnapped the wrong girl, because Annie has faith, not fear, which limits Windom's power over her and opens the door for BOB to intervene. "He can't ask for your soul," BOB tells Cooper. "I'll take his." Cooper engages several doppelgängers in the Red Room, then he returns to Twin Peaks possessed by BOB. "I need to brush my teeth," he says, indicating his corruption, before smashing his head into BOB's reflection in the mirror. The nihilistic ending returns Lynch to his Zoroastrian roots: evil cannot be eliminated as a material force in the world and everyone is vulnerable to its pernicious influence.

Twin Peaks, like Lumberton, is a town like any other in America, only different, having been touched by the finger of Lynch. His ability to turn the mundane into the extraordinary, as Hawthorne, Melville and Poe did before him, transforms the idyllic into a nightmare landscape where moral lessons are burned into certain initiates chosen for instruction. Most of the themes in *Twin Peaks*, however, had been exhausted in *Blue Velvet*, as were the techniques he brought from the film to the series. Of all the devices he imported from the earlier film, the one original is the Red Room, but the effects first introduced in episode 2 are not improved upon in 29, and as a result that last sequence feels flat, convenient and perfunctory. This fault may be due to the design of the series, as the visit to the Red Room seems to have offered the easiest way to conclude the show while also leaving it open-ended. Nevertheless, these two scenes, along with the music sequences in 8, 9 and 14, are exclusively Lynch's, and seem integral to his moral vision. Even so, the action in the Red Room seems superfluous, doing little to advance the story, and the plot elements gained during Cooper's "visits" add little either to his character or the overall moral framework dramatized more effectively in other sequences.

Cooper's faith in restraint and his desire "to look at the world through love" at "what lies beyond the darkness" are themes Lynch played out in *Blue Velvet*, so in *Twin Peaks* they seem rehashed. But one theme still ripe for investigation that Lynch carries over from *Blue Velvet* (and that he continued in *Lost Highway*), exploited by all the directors throughout the series, is a focus on heightening sexual tension by fear of discovery. The model is, of course, the affair between Jeffrey Beaumont and Dorothy Vallens. The intensity of their encounters in her apartment increases the clearer it becomes just how violent Frank Booth can be and what he is capable of. But the very covert nature of their affair, and the serious danger involved in the possibility of their being discovered by Frank, also intensifies the sexual energy during their meetings. At first, Jeffrey is tentative, but the more he learns about Frank, the bolder Jeffrey becomes. The more brazen his visits, and the more he puts himself at risk, the more satisfying the sex. The entire sequence is designed to reflect the normal pacing of a usual sexual liaison: the initial engagement, exploratory foreplay, all of which builds to a final climax. Jeffrey's last visit does culminate in his satisfying both himself and Dorothy, but when he leaves her apartment he meets Frank, who takes him on that savage, bizarre postcoital joyride. After his discovery by Frank, the source of his fear and tension and therefore the key to his pleasure, Jeffrey needs no more visits because now that he has been found out, the sport in his game exposed, subsequent visits would be redundant; so Jeffrey's affair with Dorothy is finished, the possibilities exhausted. For Lynch, in his moral context, Jeffrey's punishing encounter with Frank (the joyride), after crossing the line with Dorothy (by beating her), is the moment when Jeffrey experiences true remorse and clearly understands the need for restraint, qualifying the ironic twist to the Golden Rule that Dorothy lives by: Do unto others what they want done to them. Jeffrey draws back from facilitating the self-destructive impulses of Dorothy and achieves what, in Lynch's view, amounts to moral superiority.

In *Twin Peaks*, this duplicity, fear of discovery and pairing of moral equals is best expressed by Ben's encounter with Audrey at One Eyed Jack's, where discovery would have forced Ben to confront his hypocrisy and moral depravity, but because the discovery is delayed, the tension of the situation is increased for the viewer (and Audrey). The scariest relationship, however, is between Bobby and Shelly. Leo, like Frank Booth, is psychopathically dangerous. When Bobby visits Shelly at her house, the threat of Leo's discovering them creates a palpable anxiety that drives their furtive lovemaking with a death-wish defiance. Both Bobby and Shelly, however, are salvageable characters, and their pairing reinforces Lynch's moral schema: they are bound by their moral equivalence, and their complementary pairing at Leo's expense restores balance and harmony to the natural order of things.

Though not nearly as frightening as the situation Bobby and Shelly are in, or as reprehensible as Ben's unwittingly incestuous intrigue with Audrey, James too, after dallying with Maddy and Evelyn, settles with his moral equivalent, Donna. His flirting with Maddy is transgressive because he is really trying to recreate what he had with Laura, so he is doubly guilty: cheating on Donna and using Maddy as a surrogate to vicariously resurrect Laura. The edginess of his brief episodes with Maddy is relatively tame, but his fear of discovery lends a moral impetus to his frustration and drives him into the arms of Evelyn, a truly treacherous femme fatale. The fear of discovery with Evelyn comes from both her husband and her other scheming lover, though for James this romantic duplicity creates more of a moral dilemma than excitement as he tries to disentangle himself from Evelyn. Ever the Boy Scout, he explains that sleeping with her is wrong because she's married. "It's wrong," he says, and assures her, "You're good," to which Evelyn replies, "No I'm not."

The affair between Ed and Norma follows a similar pattern. They both married their partners out of misplaced compassion and found themselves mismatched. Their pairing expresses a moral equivalence that "corrects" the earlier mistakes. The threat of exposure from Nadine is, of course, fairly innocuous. In fact, in her amnesiac condition her knowledge of and participation in the liaison parodies the more dangerous elements of discovery in the other affairs. Once Nadine reverts to being a teenager, she not only encourages Ed and Norma, but also at one point joins them in bed to tell them about her new love interest, Mike. Ed and Norma's pairing turns threatening only after Hank is paroled, but the effect is again more comical than dramatic when Hank catches them *in flagrante* and Nadine arrives to beat the thug senseless. But even with its parodic effects applied here, the pattern, as with James, Donna and Evelyn, and with Bobby, Shelly and Leo, demonstrates a balanced moral alignment threatened by a decadent third party.

The pairing of Catherine and Ben is successful as long as both are scheming (against each other as well as others) but ends as soon as Ben is "reformed." When Donna's mother's relationship with Ben is finally exposed, discovered by Donna's eavesdropping through the spy hole in the hidden chamber of The Great Northern, the discovery is fatal, as Dr. Hayward would rather kill Ben than hear him admit that he is Donna's biological father. Equally fatal is Sheriff Truman's relationship with Josie. It collapses once her past is exposed and she is revealed to be a murderous courtesan who dies inexplicably (as if from self-loathing) when Cooper and Truman come to arrest her.

Just as BOB sows evil in the community, Cooper seems to have brought in his own brand of contamination: righteousness. As Jacques Renault explains, Twin Peaks was a "simple" town until Cooper arrived. "Maybe you brought the nightmare with you," he tells him. When Cooper asks Josie why she shot him, she answers, "Because you came here." Cooper idolizes Annie, saying, "I'd love to see the world through your eyes"; then he sees the scars on her wrists. Like Harold Smith, she had tried to withdraw, first into suicide, then into a convent, having understood all too well what Ben confesses: "Sometimes the urge to do bad is nearly overpowering." Of course, Ben is saved when he converts from cynicism to sincerity (and as a reformed sinner, he is a much less interesting character), but his turning good gets him killed. Even Andy (Barney Fife to Cooper's Andy Griffith) is culpable, evident in a startling flash of an image juxtaposing the wanted poster of BOB with Andy's face in the glass door beside it. Nothing in the series is more economically illustrative of the main issue in the story, the struggle of innocence in the face of evil played out within the innate duality of nature.

Major Briggs addresses this dualism as he speaks in prophetic terms of "powerful forces of evil" and a "great darkness." He warns that some people, like Windom Earle, "cultivate evil for the sake of evil." Cooper tries to comfort Sarah by explaining, "There are things dark and heinous in the world. Things too horrible to tell our children." She should feel relieved, however, because Leland "fell victim ... when he was innocent and trusting." Leland's flaw was showing fear in the face of evil, and that opened the door for BOB. But Cooper insists that in the end Leland's death was not in vain because he recognized his sin and, in a sense, was capable of repentance. "Before he died," Cooper tells Sarah, "he confronted the horror of what he had done to Laura, and agonized over the pain he had caused you. Leland died in peace." In keeping with this strict Christian moralizing, he finishes his benediction by assuring Sarah that Laura "welcomed him" and "forgave him." Perhaps James sums up the plight of the citizens of Twin Peaks best when, referring to Laura, he tells Evelyn, "I thought I knew her but I didn't. I guess nobody did."

The moral context of Lynch's earliest work resurfaces in *Hotel Room*. This Home Box Office series features a pair of episodes written by Barry Gifford that seem more like the one-act plays of Harold Pinter than television or movie scripts. And even though Lynch's overly mannered directing style is readily apparent, he cannot match Pinter's ability to wrench mysterious significance from seemingly innocuous statements and elliptical action. The two pieces, "Tricks" and "Blackout," pretend to explore the twilight zone between the objective and subjective worlds of the people who find themselves at the Rail Road Hotel, room 603. The idea of a hotel room as a metaphor for the transience of life and relationships is in itself a bit hackneyed, but according to the voice-over narrator, this room is different because the temporary residents are "brushing up against the secret names of truth." Too often, however, the action flounders in absurdity, and the effects that once seemed fresh in *Eraserhead* and *Blue Velvet* now seem stale and repetitive.

In "Tricks," Moe Boca enters the hotel room with Darlene, a prostitute. Lou, another man who seems to have known Moe for some time, soon joins them. Lou prompts Darlene to demonstrate one of her cheerleading routines, engages her in sex, then tells a story about his ex-wife Felicia. But Moe claims Felicia was *his* wife, not Lou's, and that she was a cheerleader from Iowa too, just like Darlene, and that they had a son named Arthur. Alarmed at the mounting violence between the two men, Darlene manages to get out of the room. Lou, before leaving, switches wallets (and presumably identities) with Moe. Later the police show up and arrest Moe for the murder of Felicia.

The central metaphor personifies the split psyche of a man caught between desire and regret. The freewheeling, dangerously libidinous Lou offsets the guilt-ridden, conscience-plagued Moe. Images of the shadow self—BOB, Frank Booth, Baron Harkonnen: personifications of raw id, portrayed as villains—abound in Lynch's work, and in "Tricks" Lou joins the pantheon. He represents the irrational self, exuberant and demanding satisfaction with no regard for consequences. Moe, on the other hand, is paralyzed by his rationality. His shout at the end of the film—"I don't understand!"—illustrates both a rationalist's desperate frustration at his inability to comprehend his own motives, as well as a tongue-in-cheek response from Lynch to many of his critics who complain that his films— especially the Gifford/Lynch collaborations—are too oblique and, like *Wild at Heart*, hermeneutically unsound. Moe's shout becomes metalinguistic and self-referential, summing up his existential predicament while commenting on the actual dramatic action. Understanding—that process by which experience is reduced to concept (what Schopenhauer calls reification)—is ultimately an exercise in corruption. As in *The Alphabet*, the poetic, primary, instinctual sense of the world is ruined by its transformation into conscious, logical, cause-and-effect sequences that bring order to experience. Moe is divorced from his essential self, and he is literally arrested for it.

When Darlene, for instance, offers Moe marijuana, he says, "Let me think about it." This indecision is typical of Moe's need to rationalize his actions and further illustrates how divorced he is from Lou's spontaneity. The effect of pot, supposedly, is to ease access into the imaginative subconscious, to transcend the thinking self, and so Moe's declining to smoke neatly illustrates his dilemma. Darlene states flatly: "You think too much." In a feeble attempt to overcome his reticence, to move from reason to passion, from the rational to the impulsive, Moe kneels at her feet, embraces her legs, but can only mumble, "The white knight is about to undertake a dangerous journey through the dark forest." The elevated language, the lyrical allusions to vainglorious honor, duty, and sex as a threatening experience further underscore Moe's problem. His superego is hyperactive. His passion is forced, artificial, as if he solicited the prostitute to test his spontaneity, and in the crux he fails miserably.

Darlene, a typical Lynchian woman, represents Lynch's moral dialectic in all its simplicity. A big-hearted girl from the heartland (Lynch's

beloved Iowa, home of Alvin Straight), a cheerleader, an image of wholesome innocence (a.k.a. Laura Palmer et al.), Darlene made the mistake
of following an actor-boyfriend to New York (Lynch's first city of fear)
where she was abandoned and now, apparently, is trapped in a life of drugs
and prostitution. She is also, like other Lynch women, the vehicle that
drives men to confront their universal fears.

The timing of Lou's arrival is crucial. He knocks as soon as Darlene begins to undress, enters the room just as Moe is about to "embark"
on his sexual "journey," and displaces Moe, emerging as his double, the
intrusive, irrepressibly raw violent id of Moe's subconscious—Schopenhauer's primal will. Lou is dangerous, dirty, destructive, but ready for
action. The embodiment of Moe's desire, lust incarnate, he steps in to
perform when Moe hesitates. Unlike Moe, Lou is unencumbered by fear,
regret, or any need to rationalize his behavior. He immediately homes
in on Darlene, concerned only that Moe has paid her. Moe feebly utters
the principal phrase of his (and Lynch's) diametric moral dilemma: "This
is not right." After Lou and Darlene have sex, Moe is reduced to Darlene's errand boy—she asks him to "hand me my things"—as he could
never be her lover. After all, as he confesses to Lou, his idea of being
lucky as a kid was receiving good tips while delivering Chinese food, and
he seems mystified as to why one of his sultry female customers would
initiate a sexual encounter with him. Unfortunately for Moe, as the con-
science-bearing side of his self he must ultimately be held accountable
for Lou's actions, including, it seems, responsibility for whatever has
happened to Felicia and Arthur, Moe/Lou's wife and child.

The psychic dualism of Schopenhauer and Freud informs "Blackout" too. The surface action resembles a Freudian psychoanalytic session, in which repressed episodes are brought up from the subconscious
to the conscious and rendered impotent, psychically, by acknowledg-
ment. The bellboy basically announces this dramatic ploy when he says,
ostensibly referring to the blackout but alluding to the young couple,
"There are many people who take advantage of a situation like this."
Sure enough, their stay in the hotel turns out to be what Sartre calls in
Nausea a privileged situation. At certain times people find themselves in
circumstances where, if they choose to take advantage of it, they can
realize what Sartre calls a perfect moment, a rare opportunity to glimpse
the truth of existence, usually involving a relationship with a partner. And
that is exactly what happens in "Blackout."

As usual in Lynch, the woman represents the mysterious, poetic,
illogical force in the world that her man must dutifully demystify, explain

and control. Whereas Danny is a stereotypically literal-minded Okie naïf who thinks "Tulsa's a big city" and confuses "the city of lights" with "the great white way," his wife is a visionary who thinks visiting New York "feels like being inside a Christmas tree." When one of the "Chinese fellows" from the takeaway tells Danny to "be careful," the context implies a Heideggerian care for both the self and each other. The couple, who admit that "fooling around is what we've always been best at," must move to a deeper commitment and understanding of each other.

Lynch again relies on his predictably Romantic notion of the city as a threatening, corrosive site that forces the good people from the Heartland to reassess their priorities. Danny and Diane are in New York to visit a doctor who they hope may be able to help Diane with her mental instability, a condition caused by the traumatic accidental death of their two-year-old child, Dan-Bug. Significantly, the boy drowned while the couple was self-absorbed, carelessly making love, leaving the boy to frolic unsupervised around the lake. This linking of irresponsible sex with death is typically Lynchian. The woman's guilt for, presumably, enjoying a selfish moment of sexual dalliance has caused her to retreat into a poetic perspective, safe from the brutal world of causation and responsibility. Her primary elements are confused: the water of life has become a "sea of red," as if her mythical wires got crossed. For Diane, the healthy sexual imagery of fish and water has become mixed up with death (more imagery from Eliot's *The Waste Land*). In her view, she is so fatally flawed that she is almost ready to believe what one of her friends tells her: "Some people don't deserve to have kids." Danny's mission is to rescue her, to bring her back into the light of logic, but for the time being he is both symbolically and literally in the dark. Of course, Danny needs her cooperation. She must come to terms with the tragedy, understand death as the farce it is, and confront the situation, or as Danny puts it, "quit pretending."

But her instinct is to stay in denial. She doesn't want to tell the doctor about Dan-Bug. She wants to "forget" about him. She confesses that the dark is "kinda beautiful" and that she "could get used to it." The more Danny tries to understand and explain her condition, the more she retreats into her intuition. She thinks the dark is "kinda beautiful," because there, in the subconscious, sex, death and guilt—even gender, according to Freud—are undifferentiated. But just as she is about to sink into despondency, the phone jars her back from the depths of despair. Purgatory is temporary. Her abrupt resurfacing again recalls Eliot's line, "human voices wake us, and we drown" (Eliot, "Prufrock" 7).

Diane, in her own dark Dionysian world, speaks in poetical terms that preclude any rigid sense of reality, thus creating a more fluid perspective by which she can mitigate the pain of her perceived failure as a parent. She describes a "sea of red" instead of the Red Sea, conflating Danny's service in the navy with her son's drowning in Lake Osage (phonetically "Oh, sage," connoting a font of wisdom). The problem is that logic can organize events but not necessarily explain them, and even explanations cannot account for the heavy subjective burden of experience. In Diane's world, fish talk to her and the telephone delivers a "message." Although Danny tries to locate her in a recognizable context, suggesting, for instance, that maybe the doctor "has a name" for her illness, she has retreated too far into her instinctual self, where "A fish by any other name is still a fish."

The fish, which works to restore her innocence, is countered by Danny's story of being in a car stuck in a frozen rut and using a "stiff dead dog" to get out. He is slightly embarrassed when he tells the story to some others, but one man dismisses his uneasiness: "That's what the dead dog's body's been there for." The couple must adopt this attitude, to use death as a truth to get beyond remorse and thereby reconstitute their relationship, to build on the strength of their possibilities for the future, not on what has happened in the past. The stories they tell—about Diane's friend Rinky-Dink crushed by a car because of a "woman's miscalculation" and Danny's friend Famine killed by a freak snakebite—underscore the burlesque nature of death and the tragic absurdity of life which they must come to terms with.

Like the dead dog Danny used to drive his car out of a rut, the couple must use the death of their son to come to a deeper understanding of each other. It seems that, ever since the boy drowned, they have been avoiding the issue. As Danny puts it, referring to a phone call he receives in the dark but which lyrically summarizes his situation with his wife and her difficulties communicating with him, "I could hear someone talking, but the connection was bad, full of static." He later admits, just before the lights come on, "I'm glad that we could talk about it." This talking it out, no matter how painful and necessary the journey, assures Diane's return to the land of logic.

In Lynch's moral system, Diane's escape from madness lies in the couple's sudden opportunity, during the blackout in room 603, to reevaluate their relationship, to recognize the difference between "fooling around" and the serious business of devoting themselves to a transcendental, Platonic, universal love through which they may find salvation.

Only when Danny kisses her without physical passion, in a gesture of pure care and concern for the spirit of the self and others (Heidegger's *Sorge*) do the lights come on in the room. Unconditional love recalls them out of dread and back into humanity.

Afterword
The Avenging Angels of Reason

Most moviegoers do not think of David Lynch as a cinevangelist.

Part of Lynch's status as a director and cult celebrity comes from his perceived iconoclastic approach to cinema. Lynch began his career as an artist and came to film in art school, working with animation and collage intercut with highly stylized snippets of filmed sequences. Not at first formally schooled in contemporary film studies, he could, early on, be considered an outsider. (He did end up at the American Film Academy, but by then he had three films in the can.)

Most critics focus on Lynch's use of pastiche, his self-referential constructions and his experiments with nonlinear narrative. Working through pastiche implies more film knowledge than might be expected from an outsider, but Lynch's approach is intuitive and eclectic. He is never showing off the way Godard and other film-school bullies do. This same naïveté salvages his self-referential films: as an artist he seems intensely aware that language cannot transcend itself, so his tendency to recycle motifs from his earlier films as well as other iconographic Hollywood images betrays insecurity, but his is a lack of faith in his filmmaking, not in his overall vision.

What is most at play in a Lynch film, it seems, is the concatenations by industrious, even (un)canny critics. Too often, because of his playful style, Lynch provokes idiosyncratic readings that offer more subjective elaboration than elucidation. Such approaches are fine when offering plausible readings (if there can be any such thing, according to many of Lynch's commentators). But even if point of view can be separated from method, how Lynch is read depends more on the attitude of the viewer/critic than on any methodological approach she employs. Still, his "play" needs a "ground," and not even the inventive critic can escape Lynch's severe moral code. It is the one thing that unifies his work: an Old Testament railing against innocence and corruption, thundered with the seriously straight face of Charlton Heston playing a vengeful Uncle Sam.

Populism is another reason for Lynch's prestige. During the late seventies literary studies were hot. Critics at Yale—including Miller and de Man—were gaining cult status. Graduate assistants were inundated with recycled Nietzsche and Heidegger, ground through Foucault and Derrida. This privileging of criticism over the original text ("there is no original text") infected the new "film appreciation courses" springing up around the country, and with the advent of the VCR—making archival films available to a wide audience—a whole new class of film connoisseurs began to talk about closed systems of self-referential codes, univocal signs, shifting sets of indeterminate signifiers and indeterminate contexts, formalism, feminism, Marxism, Lacanian psychology, Saussurean linguistics, Derridean deconstruction and cinematographic semiotics. Meaning was unfixed, and explication became perspective.

Especially in the fluid medium of film.

Lynch, like his literary forbearers, attempts to re-situate the individual as the American Manichaean hero whose vision of justice and self is preserved only by his own initiative and perseverance. The typical Lynch character is trapped in an insidious dialectic: he craves and resists cultural assimilation. His transcendence, purchased at his own expense, is qualified only by his need to integrate into a social network. This illusion of maintaining his freedom while at the same time entering the collective as a type—the individual, as it were, declaring himself as he is reified, finally, into a national character—creates the dramatic tension at the heart of Lynch's best work.

But too often his films are less a critique of this paradoxical existential struggle than they are wistful, nostalgic wish-fulfilling fantasies. Lynch tends to simplify his allegories, as if to compensate for the psychic damage the complexity of the contemporary world has wreaked upon the idealized American spirit he strives to resurrect. In his Edelstein interview in *The Village Voice*, when asked if *Blue Velvet* were a "nostalgic vision" (20), Lynch explained, "Yeah, because it deals with a sort of innocence ... from the '50s[,] ... an innocent time for me" (20). He even managed, in a typical Lynchian twist, to garner positive reviews from both the *Village Voice* and the *National Review*. But no matter how much Lynch flirts with stock Romantic virtues of sincerity, nostalgia and a fascination with the grotesque, the true Romantic sensibility aspired to authenticity, something Lynch can only simulate.

And even at his most sentimental, when his material becomes a parody of itself, Lynch casts the cultural, spiritual and political crisis of his world in a decidedly moral context. He documents the struggle between forces of light and darkness at play in the world, vying for souls torn between damnation and redemption. As Lynch says: "Films should have power. The power of good and the power of darkness" (Lynch 150). Isabella Rossellini admits that Lynch is "quite a religious person[;] … that's the core of his film-making" (126). For Lynch, "there's light and varying degrees of darkness" (139), and when he tells Rodley that "[t]he world we live in is a world of opposites … [and] to reconcile those two opposing things is the trick" (23), he is referring more to Mather's *Wonders of the Invisible World* (1692) than to Coleridge's *Biographia Literaria* (1817).

"What is going on in Lumberton," he asks Rodley, "if not a Holy War…?" (109).

Bibliography

Abrams, M.H. "The Deconstruction Angel." *Contemporary Literary Criticism.* Eds. Robert Con David and Ronald Schleifer. New York: Longman, 1989. 553–564.

Alexander, John. *The Films of David Lynch.* London: Charles Letts, 1993.

Bell, Daniel. "The National Style and the Radical Right." Qtd. in *A Partisan Century.* Ed. Edith Kurzweil. New York: Columbia UP, 1996. 220–232.

Blackham, H.J. "Søren Kierkegaard." *Six Existentialist Thinkers.* New York: Macmillan, 1959.

Carroll, Michael. "Agent Cooper's Errand in the Wilderness: *Twin Peaks* and American Mythology." *Literature Film Quarterly* 21.4 (1993): 287–294.

Caughie, John. Panel discussion on "Off-centre Authorship." Twelfth Screen Studies Conference. Gilmorehill Centre, Glasgow University. 29 June 2002.

Carruth, Hayden. "Introduction." *Nausea.* By Jean-Paul Sartre. New York: New Directions, 1964.

Chion, Michel. *David Lynch.* Trans. Robert Julian. London: British Film Institute, 1995.

Cocteau, Jean. *Two Screenplays.* Trans. Carol Martin-Sperry. New York: Orion, 1968.

Covici, Pascal. *Humor and Revelation in American Literature: The Puritan Connection.* Columbia: U of Missouri, 1997.

Dieckmann, Katherine. "Stupid People Tricks." *The Village Voice Film Special* 30 June 1987: 11+.

Edelstein, David. "Kitsch 'N' Tell." *The Village Voice Film Special* 30 June 1987: 17+.

Eliot, T.S. "The Love Song of J. Alfred Prufrock." *The Complete Poems and Plays, 1909–1950.* New York: Harcourt Brace Jovanovich, 1980. 3–7.

_____. *The Waste Land. The Complete Poems and Plays, 1909–1950.* New York: Harcourt Brace Jovanovich, 1980. 37–55.

Fieser, James, and Norman Lillegard, eds. "Søren Kierkegaard (From *Either/Or*, vol. 1 and 2)." *A Historical Introduction to Philosophy*. New York: Oxford UP, 2002. 555–584.

Foerster, Norman, et al., eds. *American Poetry and Prose*. 5th ed. Boston: Houghton Mifflin, 1970.

Foucault, Michel. *Madness and Civilization: A History of Insanity in the Age of Reason*. Trans. Richard Howard. New York: Random House, 1988.

Gardner, John. *The Art of Fiction*. New York: Knopf, 1984.

Garrow, David J. "Visions of Vice and Virtue Rule a Nation's Heart." *The New York Times* 9 April 2003, natl. ed.: E7.

Gifford, Barry. *Wild at Heart*. New York: Grove, 1990.

Habermas, Jurgen. "Modernity—An Incomplete Project." Qtd. in *Postmodernism*. Ed. Thomas Docherty. New York: Columbia UP, 1993. 98–109.

Hampton, Howard. "David Lynch's Secret History of the United States." *Film Comment* May-June 1993: 38–41, 47–49.

Hoberman, J. "What's Stranger Than Paradise?" *The Village Voice Film Special* 30 June 1987: 3+.

_____. Rev. of "The Straight Story." *The Village Voice* 15 Oct. 1999 <http:www.geocites.som/Hollyqood/2093/straightstory/revvilvoice.html>.

_____. *Vulgar Modernism*. Philadelphia: Temple UP, 1991.

Hofstadter, Richard. *Anti-intellectualism in American Life*. New York: Knopf, 1966.

Hughes, David. *The Complete David Lynch*. London: Virgin, 2001.

Hurley, Jennifer A. "A Historical Overview of American Romanticism." *American Romanticism*. Ed. Jennifer A. Hurley. San Diego: Greenhaven, 2000. 13–25.

Johnson, Jeff. "Gendermandering: Stereotyping and Gender Role Reversal in the Major Plays of William Inge." *American Drama* 7.2 (1998): 33–50.

James, Caryn. "Today's Yellow Brick Road Leads Straight to Hell." *The New York Times* 14 Dec. 1990: 1+.

Kael, Pauline. "Out There and in Here." *The New Yorker* 22 Sept. 1986: 99+.

Kaleta, Kenneth C. *David Lynch*. New York: Twayne, 1995.

Kaufmann, Walter. *Existentialism from Dostoevsky to Sartre*. New York: Meridian, 1989. 11–51.

Kazin, Alfred. "The Self as Power: America When Young." *An American Procession*. New York: Knopf, 1984. 23–127.

Kierkegaard, Søren. "Dread and Freedom." Trans. Walter Lowrie. *Existentialism from Dostoevsky to Sartre*. Ed. Walter Kaufmann. New York: Meridian, 1989. 101–105.

_____. "Truth Is Subjectivity." Trans. Walter Lowrie. *Existentialism from Dostoevsky to Sartre*. Ed. Walter Kaufmann. New York: Meridian, 1989. 110–120.

_____. "The Concept of Irony." *The Essential Kierkegaard*. Eds. Howard V. Hong and Edna H. Hong. Princeton: Princeton UP, 2000. 20–36.

Kimball, Samuel. "'Into the light, Leland, into the light': Emerson, Oedipus, and the Blindness of Male Desire in David Lynch's *Twin Peaks*." *Genders* 16 (1993): 17–34.

Le Blanc, Michelle, and Colin Odell. *The Pocketbook Essential David Lynch.* North Pomfret, VT: Trafalgar Square, 2000.

Lacan, Jacques. "The Mirror Stage as Formative of the Function of the I as Revealed in Psychoanalytic Experience." Trans. Alan Sheridan. *Contemporary Critical Theory.* Ed. Dan Latimer. Orlando: Harcourt Brace Jovanovich, 1989. 502–509.

Lawrence, D.H. "Herman Melville's 'Moby Dick.'" *Studies in Classic American Literature.* New York: Viking, 1971. 145–161.

Lynch, David. *Lynch on Lynch.* Ed. Chris Rodley. Boston: Faber and Faber, 1997.

Lyons, Donald. "La-La Limbo." *Film Comment.* Jan.-Feb. 1997: 2–4.

Lyotard, Jean-François. "The Sublime and the Avant-Garde." Qtd. in *Postmodernism.* Ed. Thomas Docherty. New York: Columbia UP, 1993. 244–256.

MacDonald, Paul S. "Introduction: Background and Themes." *The Existentialist Reader.* Ed. P.S. MacDonald. New York: Routledge, 2000. 1–46.

Madden, David, ed. "Introduction." *American Dreams, American Nightmares.* Carbondale: Southern Illinois UP, 1972. xv–xlii.

Mather, Cotton. "The Wonders of the Invisible World." Qtd. in *The Norton Anthology of American Literature.* Vol. 2. 3rd ed. Eds. Nina Baym et al. New York: W.W. Norton, 1989.

Matthiessen, F.O. "Symbolism in Moby Dick." *American Romanticism.* Ed. Jennifer A. Hurley. San Diego: Greenhaven, 2000. 149–154.

Mulvey, Laura. "Visual Pleasure and Narrative Cinema." *Film Theory and Criticism.* Ed. Gerald Mast et. al. New York: Oxford UP, 1992. 746–757.

Nietzsche, Friedrich. *The Birth of Tragedy.* Trans. Walter Kaufmann. *The Basic Writings of Nietzsche.* Ed. Walter Kaufmann. New York: Modern Library, 1968. 29–144.

_____. "On Truth and Lie in an Extra-Moral Sense." Trans. Walter Kaufmann. In *The Portable Nietzsche.* Ed. Walter Kaufmann. New York: Penguin, 1982. 42–47.

_____. "Notes (1880–81)." Trans. Walter Kaufmann. *The Portable Nietzsche.* Ed. Walter Kaufmann. New York: Penguin, 1982. 73–75.

Nochimson, Martha P. *The Passion of David Lynch: Wild at Heart in Hollywood.* Austin: U of Texas, 1997.

Olson, Greg. "Heaven Knows, Mr. Lynch: Beatitudes from the Deacon of Distress." *Film Comment* May-June 1993: 43–46.

Palmer, Donald. "Kierkegaard." *Looking at Philosophy.* Mountain View, CA: Mayfield, 2001.

Perry, Bliss. *The American Mind.* Port Washington, NY: Kennikat, 1968.

Pollard, Scott. "Cooper, Details, and the Patriotic Mission of *Twin Peaks.*" *Literature Film Quarterly* 21.4 (1993): 296–304.

Ruch, Allen B. "No hay banda." *The Modern World.* <http://www.themodern world.com/Mulholland_drive.html>.

Russell, Bertrand. *A History of Western Philosophy.* New York: Simon and Schuster, 1972.

Sartre, Jean Paul. *Essays in Existentialism.* Ed. Wade Baskin. Secaucus, N.J.: Citadel, 1999.

_____. *Huis Clos, piéce en un acte*. Paris: Gallimard, 1945.

_____. "Self-Deception." *Existentialism from Dostoevsky to Sartre*. Ed. Walter Kaufmann. New York: Meridian, 1989. 299–328.

Schopenhauer, Arthur. *The World as Will and Representation*. Trans. E.F.J. Payne. Vol. 1. New York: Dover, 1969.

Schwartz, Tony. "On the Werewolf Circuit." *Newsweek* 11 Sept. 1978: 95–97.

Scruton, Roger. "Continental Philosophy from Fichte to Sartre." *The Oxford History of Western Philosophy*. Ed. Anthony Kenny. New York: Oxford UP, 2000. 207–253.

Shattuck, Roger. *Forbidden Knowledge*. New York: St. Martin's, 1996.

Short, Robert. "Dada and Surrealism." *Modernism*. Eds. Malcolm Bradbury and James McFarlane. London: Penguin, 1987. 292–308.

The Short Films of David Lynch. Dir. David Lynch. Absurda, 2001.

Spivak, Gayatri Chakravorty. "Feminism and Critical Theory." *Contemporary Critical Theory*. Ed. Dan Latimer. Orlando: Harcourt Brace Jovanovich, 1989. 634–658.

Staebler, Warren. "American Romanticism Challenged the Values of America." *American Romanticism*. Ed. Jennifer A. Hurley. San Diego: Greenhaven Press, 2000. 52–58.

Stafford, John. *The Literary Criticism of "Young America": A Study in the Relationship of Politics and Literature 1837–1850*. New York: Russell and Russell, 1967.

Taylor, Charles. "The Straight Story: Forget the G-Rating—This Road Movie Is as Weird as It Gets." *Salon* 15 Oct. 1999. http://www.salon.com/ent/movies/review/1999/10/15/straight/index.html>.

Tompkins, Jane. "Masterpiece Theatre: The Politics of Hawthorne's Literary Reputation." Qtd. in *Falling into Theory*. Ed. David H. Richter. Boston: Bedford, 1994.

West, David. *An Introduction to Continental Philosophy*. Cambridge, MA: Blackwell, 1996.

Wilde, Oscar. "The Preface" to *The Picture of Dorian Gray: Oscar Wilde's Plays, Prose Writings, and Poems*. London: Dent, 1967. 67–254.

Williams, Linda. "When the Woman Looks." *Film Theory and Criticism*. Ed. Gerald Mast et al. New York: Oxford UP, 1992. 561–577.

Woods, Paul A. *Weirdsville USA: The Obsessive Universe of David Lynch*. London: Pleaus, 2000.

Zacharek, Stephanie. "Highway to Heck." *Salon* 28 Feb. 1997. <http://www.salon.com/feb97/highway970228.html>.

Index

Kierkegaard, Søren 26–27, 48, 65, 71, 72, 92, 93, 103, 104, 106, 112
Kimball, Susan 23–4
King, Rodney 147
Kojève, Alex Andre 129
Kuralt, Charles 139

Lacan, Jacques/Lacanian 51, 52, 131, 176
Lawrence, D.H. 13, 31
LeBlanc, Michelle 42–43
Lee, Sheryl 102
LeFanu, J. Sheridan 132
Leibniz, Gottfried Wilhelm 4
Lewis, Mark 10
Lillegard, Norman 49
Lost Highway 8, 12, 43, 94, 121–132, 135, 138, 161–162, 165
Lynch, Jennifer 21, 43
Lyons, Donald 15, 130
Lyotard, Jean-Francois 130

MacDonald, Paul S. 129
MacLachlan, Kyle 3, 4
Madden, David 15
Magritte, Rene 31
Malick, Terrence 102
Man Ray 31
Manichaean 2, 9, 11, 15–16, 18, 23–25, 28–29, 36–37, 42, 43, 46, 59, 71, 80, 81, 87, 98, 103, 121, 132, 147, 148, 149, 157, 159, 176
Manz, Linda 6, 8
Mather, Cotton 9, 12, 13, 14, 16, 29, 58, 177
Matthiessen, F.O. 19
Méliès, Georges 31
Melville, Herman 18–19, 31, 101, 165
Milius, John 11
Miller, Henry 14
Miller, J. Hillis 40, 176
Morone, James 18
Mulholland Dr. 8, 12, 94, 105, 117, 118, 132–38, 155
Mulvey, Laura 52, 89
Myers, Russ 147

Nicholson, Jack 8
Nietzsche, Friedrich 3, 4, 15, 48, 50, 52, 77, 83, 120, 124, 176
Nochimson, Martha 2, 35–37, 39, 48

O'Connor, Flannery 13, 19, 36
Odell, Colin 42–43
Olson, Greg 27–28
On the Air 145
Orbison, Roy 96, 97, 98, 136, 161, 162

Palmer, Donald 113
Perry, Bliss 140
Peyton Place 148
Pinter, Harold 168
Plato/Platonic 17, 56, 152, 172
Poe, Edgar Allan 13, 19, 21, 30, 46, 165
Pollard, Scott 19, 28, 148
Powell, Michael 10
Preminger, Otto 25–26
Premonitions Following an Evil Deed (Lumiere et Compagnie) 58–59, 60
Protestants 12, 14, 18
Puritan/Puritanism 2, 3, 9–10, 15, 16, 18, 58, 60, 126, 147, 153
Pynchon, Thomas 14
Pythagoras 152

Reagan, Ronald/Reaganesque 6, 9, 10, 24, 27, 37, 39, 92, 114, 116, 138, 142, 145, 146, 152, 153
Resnais, Alain 5
Richter, Hans 31
Riefenstahl, Leni 83
Rockwell, Norman 1
Rodley, Chris 40, 42, 43, 80, 177
Romanticism 18–21, 31, 44, 46, 48, 171
Rossellini, Isabella 3, 7, 177
Roth, Philip 14
Rousseau, Jean-Jacques 46, 140
Route 66 102
Ruch, Allen B. 132
Russell, Bertrand 12, 114

Sartre, Jean-Paul 26, 48, 90, 138, 170
Schlafly, Phyllis 11
Schopenhauer, Artur 3, 60–61, 84, 124, 135, 139, 169, 170
Schwartz, Tony 5
Scorpio Rising 82, 162
Shattuck, Roger 122
Sheen, Martin 102
Short, Robert 41
Six Figures Getting Sick 20, 29, 35, 38, 42, 47, 48, 49, 52, 53, 59, 94
Socrates 48